D1095687

3 9345 01183364 1

NOUS·SOMMES·PRETS

The Governments of
COMMUNIST EAST EUROPE

The Governments of COMMUNIST EAST EUROPE

The Governments of COMMUNIST EAST EUROPE

H. Gordon Skilling UNIVERSITY OF TORONTO

THOMAS Y. CROWELL COMPANY
New York Established 1834

CROWELL COMPARATIVE GOVERNMENT SERIES

Library of Congress Catalog Card Number: 66-14616

SERIES DESIGN BY JUDITH WORACEK BARRY

MANUFACTURED IN THE UNITED STATES OF AMERICA.

TO SALLY

EDITOR'S FOREWORD

In our time the study of comparative government constitutes one of many fields or specialities in political science. But it is worth recalling that the most distinguished political scientists of the ancient world would have had difficulty recognizing the present-day distinction between the study of comparative government and study in other subject areas of the discipline. Think of Plato, for example, whose works abound in references to the political systems of his own and earlier days. Or consider Aristotle, whose *Politics* and related writings were based on an examination of more than one hundred constitutions. Twenty centuries after Aristotle the comparative emphasis continued strong in the work of Montesquieu and Rousseau, among others. In the nineteenth century the comparative tradition entered upon a period of decline, but there are signs that the merits of comparative political analysis are once more gaining recognition. At many colleges and universities, the introductory course in political science is no longer focused exclusively on American government. The comparative approach—in politics, in law, in administration—is becoming increasingly important in the political science curriculum.

This book, one of a series, is designed to reflect that approach without, however, marking a sharp departure from the substance and method of most comparative government courses. Thus most of the books in the series deal with one national government. Several volumes, however, deal with more than one government, and the approach of the entire series is distinctly comparative in at least two senses. In the first place, almost all of the books include material descriptive of other political systems, especially that of the United States. In addition, the books follow a common outline, so far as possible, that is designed to promote comparative treatment. Of course, there is nothing to keep the instructor or student from treating a particular governmental system in isolation, if he chooses to do so. On the other hand, his lectures on political institutions and functions can be as comparative as he wishes.

A further advantage of this series is that each volume has been written by a distinguished scholar and authority in the field; each author is personally and professionally familiar with the political system he treats. Finally, the separate books make it possible for the instructor to design his course in accordance with his own interest or the interests of his students. One book may be substituted for another or any book put aside for one semester without affecting the others. The books, in short, unlike most one-volume texts, give the instructor maximum freedom in organizing his course. This freedom will be virtually unlimited as the forthcoming titles in this series complete a survey of representative governments of the world.

But to return to Aristotle once again, it remains true that the best judges of the feast are not the cooks but the guests. I have tried to indicate why, in my view, the recipe for the series is a good one. Let all those who teach comparative government, and all those who take courses in that field, proceed to judge the books for themselves.

ARNOLD A. ROGOW

PREFACE

THE GOVERNMENTS OF COMMUNIST EAST EUROPE has been long in preparation and has many and varied roots. My interest in Eastern Europe was kindled in the mid-1930's when I first visited many of the countries of the region. Subsequently, research for a doctoral dissertation on the rise of Czech nationalism took me to Prague where I was at the time of the Munich crisis of 1938 and the first months of Nazi occupation. When, after the war, communism came to Eastern Europe, my studies shifted to the history of the Czechoslovak communist movement and its impact on the politics of the country. Somewhat later, the growing diversity among communist states stimulated my interest in the relations of communism and national tradition and led me to make a comparative analysis of the several communist systems. In 1961 and 1962, I visited all of the communist countries of Eastern Europe except Albania, seeking to make some sense of the riddle of national communism.

This book therefore owes much to the people of Eastern Europe whom I have met over the past thirty years, and to Western specialists who have concerned themselves with this neglected region. In particular, I am indebted to the late Professor R. W. Seton-Watson of the School of Slavonic and East European Studies at the University of London, who contributed greatly, before 1914 and between the wars, to Western knowledge of Eastern Europe, and to Professor John N. Hazard of the Russian Institute, Columbia University, who has devoted so much of his time and attention to the comparative study of communism. I also must acknowledge my indebtedness to many other scholars, too numerous to mention, both in Eastern Europe and elsewhere, whose research on the countries of this area has been a source of information and insight to me in my own efforts to understand this fascinating part of the world. Beyond words is my obligation to my wife, who first joined me in Prague in 1937 for our marriage in the Old Town Hall, and was with me during most of my later residence and travel in Czechoslovakia and elsewhere. Most of all, readers will be in her debt for her contribution to whatever lucidity of style this book may possess in contrast to the original manuscript. Finally, I would like to record my gratitude to Maria Mikhailovna Sosula, whose secretarial skill, knowledge of languages, and uncanny ability to read the unreadable aided so much in the preparation of this volume.

H.G.S.

January, 1966
Toronto, Canada

CONTENTS

PART TWO
THE PATTERN OF POWER

PART THREE
THE HOLDERS OF POWER

Maps

PART ONE
COMMUNISM COMES TO EASTERN EUROPE

1: Roots of Postwar Triumph

At the end of World War II, communism spread rapidly from its original home base in the Soviet Union into the adjacent region of Eastern Europe, engulfing in its westward sweep over one hundred million people, and eleven once distinct states, from the Baltic Sea to the Aegean. Of this new domain of communism, the most easterly belt was incorporated directly into the USSR itself and does not form part of the subject matter of this book. These territories, which included Estonia, Lithuania, and Latvia, as well as eastern and southern Finland, eastern Poland, and eastern Rumania, might be regarded from a Russian point of view as "regained territory," as they once were part of the Tsarist empire and had been briefly recovered by Soviet Russia prior to the German invasion in 1941. In addition, the end of the war witnessed the acquisition by the USSR of lands never previously Russian, such as a part of East Prussia, including the port of Königsberg (renamed Kaliningrad), part of Czechoslovakia (Sub-Carpathian Ruthenia, renamed the Carpathian Ukraine), as well as a section of Rumania (northern Bukovina), only briefly in Soviet possession in 1940. As a result of these gains, the borders of the USSR were shifted substantially westward as compared with 1938, and the extent of Eastern Europe outside the USSR correspondingly narrowed. Polish territorial acquisitions to the west and the formation of a separate communist East Germany, on the other hand, extended the western margins of this region.

Our attention in this volume is focused on the eight communist states that have emerged outside the bounds of the USSR, namely Albania, Bulgaria, Czechoslovakia, Hungary, Poland, Rumania, Yugoslavia, and the "half-state" of East Germany.[1] It is at once apparent that communism is not co-extensive with the entire expanse of Eastern Europe at the present time. As we

[1] A fuller treatment of East Germany is given in Arnold J. Heidenheimer, *The Governments of Germany* (2d ed.; New York, 1966), which is also a volume in the Crowell Comparative Government Series.

shall show in greater detail in the subsequent chapter, the region of Eastern Europe has always been vaguely defined, with its boundaries shifting throughout history and its political structure varying from age to age. Whatever its previous incarnations, Eastern Europe, after 1919, had become a zone of small, independent states, occupying roughly the territory between the Baltic and the Aegean to north and south, and between Germany, Italy, and the Soviet Union to west and east. Of the fourteen states that had existed in this region prior to the outbreak of war in 1939, three were absorbed directly into the USSR (Lithuania, Latvia, and Estonia). Four others, Finland, Austria, Greece, and Turkey (in Europe), maintained their independence and escaped communist rule. The seven others, named above, together with the newly-created East German state, became communist, either in the final year of the war or in the two or three years immediately following. These were the so-called "satellites," or, as they were termed officially, the "people's democracies," of Eastern Europe. Ostensibly and formally independent, their status has in fact varied from more or less complete subordination to the Soviet Union to the substantial freedom of action they presently enjoy. Although the eight are ruled by communist parties, their "communism," while bearing striking resemblance to the Soviet model, has often manifested significant differences of form and content.

Although geographic proximity to the USSR is often regarded as the decisive factor in the establishment of communist power in Eastern Europe, this alone is not a sufficient explanation. For reasons that cannot be explored here, neither Finland, on the very borders of the USSR and an enemy state in World War II, nor Austria, one zone of which was occupied by the Soviet army at the end of the war, nor Greece, where civil war between communist and noncommunist forces raged from 1947 to 1949, came under communist rule. Turkey, located on the edge of Soviet power, successfully maintained its neutrality during the war and its independence afterward. Even in the case of the eight states that ultimately became communist, the process of taking power was not as simple and as uniform as is commonly supposed, and was nowhere entirely foreordained by geography. Particularly in the case of remote Albania, location could hardly be regarded as a decisive, or even influential, factor. Elsewhere, geographic nearness to the Soviet Union no doubt facilitated the establishment of communist power, but other crucial elements were requisite for complete triumph.

It is usually assumed that the presence of Soviet military forces on the territory of certain states during the closing years of the war, and especially their continuance after 1945, was the critical factor explaining the victory of communism.[2] There can be no denial of the intimate relationship between Soviet military presence and communist rule in most of the eight states, in particular in the defeated enemy states, Bulgaria, Hungary, Rumania, and East Germany, and in the states liberated predominantly by Soviet forces, Czechoslovakia and Poland. Turkey, Finland, and Greece were able to escape the fate of these peoples, either as a result of armed neutrality, successful belligerent action against the Soviet Union, or the ability to win a domestic civil war against communist forces. In the case of Austria, special circumstances, including a joint occupation shared by the Western powers, made it possible for her to regain independence and remain noncommunist, and to effect the withdrawal of Soviet forces from their eastern zone of occupation. The victory of communism in Albania and Yugoslavia, on the other hand, was clearly the result of other factors, inasmuch as a Soviet military presence was either non-existent, in the former state, or a peripheral factor, in the latter. Moreover, in the case of Czechoslovakia, the withdrawal of all Soviet troops occurred two years before the consolidation of full communist power in 1948.

The presence of Soviet armed forces, although exerting a substantial influence on the course of events, was not always, then, the decisive factor in the communist seizure of power, and in any case has itself to be explained. That there should have been Soviet troops in certain areas of Eastern Europe was due, in part, perhaps in large part, to the fortunes of war, including the ability of the Soviet Union to recover from the devastating German assault and to move back into the zone lying between liberated Russia and the main enemy, and the incapacity of Western forces to do more than penetrate to the margins of Eastern Europe. It was also due, however, to political factors, in particular to deliberate decisions by the Soviet and Western governments.[3] For the Soviet Union, the policy of pursuing the retreating German armies was no doubt motivated partially by

[2] R. V. Burks, "Eastern Europe," in Cyril E. Black and Thomas P. Thornton (eds.), *Communism and Revolution: The Strategic Uses of Political Violence* (Princeton, 1964).

[3] A detailed, although highly opinionated, study of prewar and wartime diplomacy is John A. Lukacs, *The Great Powers and Eastern Europe* (New York, 1953).

purely military considerations, including the desire to defeat completely these forces and safeguard itself against future attack, and partially by the calculation that military advance would greatly enhance Soviet influence on the political constellation of Europe as a whole, or, at the very least, Eastern Europe. Western governments, apart from their military inability to act decisively in most of the area, lacked appreciation of the political significance of military power and were disinclined to subordinate wartime strategy to postwar considerations. As a consequence, they decided not to intervene in southeastern Europe, the only area in which Western forces might conceivably have played an independent role. At the Yalta and Teheran conferences, agreements were reached with the USSR on combined operations against Germany, defining the respective zones of action and assigning to the Soviet forces exclusive responsibility in almost all parts of Eastern Europe. Marginal efforts by the West to take limited actions beyond the lines of demarcation, such as the offer of air assistance to the revolt in Warsaw or to the Slovak uprising, or of military aid to Prague in the closing hours of the war, were frustrated by the unwillingness of the Soviet Union to permit such measures in what it regarded as its exclusive military domain. Ironically, Western airborne assistance to communist partisan activity in Yugoslavia and Albania promoted rather than prevented the victory of communism in these two countries. The nominal share of the Western Allies in the postwar occupation of the enemy states of Bulgaria, Rumania, and Hungary did not seriously affect the final outcome, as the main responsibility was left to the Soviet military. Only in Germany and Austria, and in the city of Trieste, did the presence of Western armies constitute a power factor counterbalancing Soviet strength and contributing to the maintenance, as noncommunist entities, of a part of Germany and of Berlin; at first a part, and ultimately the whole, of Austria; and the city of Trieste. Western occupation of Greece and aid to noncommunist elements in the civil war during and after hostilities, and the absence of Soviet power, brought about a similar result.

The predominant position of the USSR in Eastern Europe was the result, then, of a combination of military and political factors. Indeed, Soviet preeminence reflected, not only the fortunes and the diplomacy of war, but also the prewar diplomatic constellation in Europe. The eastern realm of the continent, always a source of controversy between the great powers, and after 1919 consisting of small and relatively weak states, had become more than ever a vacuum of power. Because of the temporary and somewhat unnatural impotence of both Germany and Russia, Eastern Europe was strongly influenced for two decades by more remote states, notably France, with certain countries such as Czechoslovakia, Poland, Rumania, and Yugoslavia treated as privileged beneficiaries, and others as the less-favored ones. Seeds of discord, sown in the peace settlement and in postwar diplomacy, grew to maturity with the restoration of the strength of Germany and Soviet Russia in the thirties. As these contradictions exploded in 1938 and 1939, the policy of Britain and France, dominated by appeasement, proved incapable and unwilling to dam the flooding of German power throughout the area, thus undermining the very status quo that they had themselves created. The Munich agreement of 1938, providing for the dismemberment of Czechoslovakia and the subsequent German occupation of the rump, was a stark symbol of the decline of Western influence. Even when the Western powers at last took a stand, they were unable to save Poland from destruction. Italy had also joined in the hunt, seizing Albania in 1939. Soviet Russia, which had for a time seemed a guardian of the status quo and had firmly resisted the Munich treaty, turned from collective security to appeasement, and advanced her own borders and influence in the zone between the Baltic and the Black seas, seizing first the eastern reaches of Poland and parts of Finland, then the three Baltic states, and finally portions of Rumania. When, in the spring of 1940, German and Italian invasion of the Balkans completed the tragedy, the long night of foreign occupation had set in.

When the USSR was later involved in the war and recovered her military strength after initial disaster, it was inevitable that she would enjoy the lion's share of diplomatic and political influence in Eastern Europe. Having made the major contribution to the defeat of the widely hated Germany, she had added further to the esteem already gained by her original prewar stand in the face of German aggression. There was fear of the Soviet Union, too, and intense hostility, but there were no available counterweights in the new political balance. Germany and Italy were shatteringly defeated and reduced to utter political impotence. France, herself defeated in the first months of war, had not sufficiently recovered to dream of exerting an influence comparable to that after 1919. Great Britain had absented herself in large part from the interplay of forces, even during the prewar period of Western ascendancy, and, except in Greece, was unable, in her weakened position, to play a more forceful role. The United States, having taken almost no part in the diplomatic affairs of Eastern Europe in the interwar years, sought to develop a more positive and effective policy, but was hampered by the actual military balance of power, by the necessities of the wartime alliance and of military strategy, and by her reluctance to jeopardize postwar relations with the USSR. When the United States and the West sought to modify the full effects of Soviet paramountcy in Eastern Europe, as in the diplomatic measures designed to implement the Yalta agreement concerning the treatment of liberated Europe, they were foredoomed to failure because of Soviet Russia's determination to utilize her position of advantage to enhance the status of the communists and weaken the noncommunist forces in the new states. Increasingly, therefore, in those countries where full communist control was not established from the moment of liberation, the equilibrium of forces at home, mirroring the diplomatic balance, shifted in favor of the communists.

Diplomacy and strategy are not conducted in a vacuum of domestic politics. The rise of communism in Eastern Europe was greatly influenced by the political and economic conditions as well as the historical and cultural experiences of each of the states concerned. To what extent, the question must be posed, was communism forced on entirely unwilling peoples, and to what extent did it represent a spontaneous outgrowth of economic and social discontents and of political and historical inclinations? How far were Soviet military presence and diplomatic paramountcy aided by positive attitudes toward communism and the Soviet Union, or by the absence of viable and attractive political and social alternatives? Was the prewar experience of these peoples such as to encourage a hopeful response to communist offers and to discourage a return to a political and social order reminiscent of that era? How strong were the communist movement and its leaders, and how determined were they to force through at all costs a total revolution of the Soviet type? Were there significant differences in these respects between one people and another? Answers to these questions are complex and presuppose a knowledge of the interwar experience of these nations, their economic and social setting, their ethnic and religious composition, their cultural and historical patterns and traditions, and their political experiences. An examination of these factors, attempted briefly in the following chapters, will give some clues as to the ripeness or unripeness of each of these countries for communism, the reasons for the course followed at home and abroad prior to and during World War II, and the causes of their diverse evolution after the war.

We may assume that a greater degree of unity of action among the small states of Eastern Europe would have rendered much more difficult the rise of Soviet power and the victory of communism, and might even have averted the coming of war in the first place, thereby warding off the expansion of communism. If there had been a single large federal state, such as Austria-Hungary, or an entity embracing even a greater part of the area, or several such federal unions, would not the outcome of interwar diplomacy and of postwar politics have been markedly different? Why has there been such disunity in Eastern Europe, not only between the wars, but throughout its history? Why has the region not been able to organize itself politically into a stable system capable of resisting the coming of communism, or indeed other pressures from outside prior to 1939? Why was it impossible to coordinate the diplomacies of the several states toward common ends? Again we are driven back to an examination of the enduring historical features and patterns of Eastern Europe—its geographic disunity, its ethnic diversity, its economic differentiation, its religious and cultural complexity, and its distinctive traditions—if we are to clarify our understanding, not only of the rise of communism, but of the increasingly distinctive experience of each country in the years after the death of Stalin.

2: The Lands and Peoples

Communist East Europe is a fairly compact land mass, lying athwart the European continent between its massive Russian "heartland" and its peninsular extensions to west, north, and south, and stretching from the Baltic to the Adriatic and Black seas. At present it extends approximately 1,000 miles from north to south, and from 400 to 800 miles from east to west. Other noncommunist states often classified as Eastern Europe lie on the periphery, Finland to the north, and Greece and Turkey to the south, with Austria thrusting a wedge into the middle. Historically a zone of economic and social backwardness, of intense national conflict, and of political weakness, Eastern Europe has long been a focus of conflict, both between its own peoples and states, and among the great powers pursuing their own interests in the area. The concentration of a large portion of the region under communism has in some ways enhanced its power, but has not by any means eliminated the tensions for which it has long been notorious.

At present, the eight states constituting communist East Europe vary considerably in territory and population, but none is able to claim the rank of a great power. Three—Poland, Rumania, and Yugoslavia—may be classified together as comparatively large in relation to the others; four—Bulgaria, Czechoslovakia, East Germany, and Hungary—as of middle rank; and one—Albania—as small, indeed, tiny.

In spite of a certain territorial contiguity, Eastern Europe does not constitute a geographic unit, with fixed and definite boundaries and common physical features. Insofar as Europe as a whole may be divided at all geographically, the several regions run across Eastern Europe, cutting it into markedly distinct zones. Indeed, the term "Eastern Europe," like analogous terms, such as "Western" or "Central Europe," has been used to describe a complex of geographical, historical, cultural, and political factors that mark this area off from other parts of the continent. It is employed currently to refer to the tier of small states that lie between West Germany and the Soviet Union, and hence retrospectively to the areas now occupied by these states. Even in this primarily political meaning, the concept of Eastern Europe has not had, and indeed by the nature of things cannot have, a permanent and fixed connotation. Although for over fifty years it has been a zone of small states, prior to 1914 it was mainly a realm of great empires that between them controlled

COMMUNIST EAST EUROPE: AREAS AND POPULATION

Country	Area (sq. km.)[1]	POPULATION (MIDYEAR ESTIMATES, IN THOUSANDS)			
		1948[1]	*1953*[2]	*1958*[3]	*1963*[3]
Albania	28,748	1,175	1,250*	1,507	1,762
Bulgaria	110,669	7,100*	7,450*	7,728	8,078
Czechoslovakia	127,869	12,339	—	13,474	13,951†
East Germany (including East Berlin, except for 1953)	108,299	—	18,318*	17,355	17,158
Hungary	93,030	9,165	9,600	9,882	10,088
Poland	312,520	23,970	—	28,770	30,691
Rumania	237,500	16,000*	16,500*	18,056‡	18,813‡
Yugoslavia	255,804	—	17,288	18,018	19,065†

* Unofficial estimates.
† Provisional estimates.
‡ Estimates of questionable reliability.

[1] *Statistical Yearbook, 1949–50* (New York: Statistical Office of the United Nations, Department of Economic and Social Affairs, 1950), Table 1, pp. 24–25.
[2] *Statistical Yearbook, 1954* (1954), Table 1, pp. 29–31.
[3] *Statistical Yearbook, 1964* (1965), Table 2, pp. 37–38.

the bulk of the area. Moreover, its eastern and western boundaries have constantly shifted from age to age, depending largely on the strength of Russia and Germany, and of Italy and Turkey, at a given time. Constantinople, for instance, was once a significant capital of Eastern Europe, its influence extending far into the Balkan peninsula; now it is a secondary city of a primarily Asiatic country having limited relations with the area. In the same way, Trieste, now a lesser Italian port on the Adriatic, was for centuries controlled by Vienna and was the main entrepôt for much of the trade of Eastern Europe. Even Berlin, erstwhile capital of the German Empire, has been transformed by circumstances into a divided city, its eastern sector the capital of a small artificially formed state, which entirely surrounds its western sectors.

GEOGRAPHIC ZONES

Although the political aspects of the Eastern European tradition will be discussed more fully in the next chapter, it has been necessary to refer to them here to indicate the transient and

ever-changing character of Eastern Europe as a concept of political geography. In a stricter geographic sense, Eastern Europe falls into three sharply distinguishable physical regions, each with its own configuration and resources, largely cut off from each other, but open to easy outside penetration. To the north lies the North European plain, extending from the Atlantic to the Urals, deep in Russia. Here stands Poland, astride the Vistula and its tributaries, with "natural" frontiers to the north in the Baltic Sea, and to the south in the Carpathian and the Sudeten Mountains, which have sometimes isolated her historically from the affairs of Eastern Europe beyond the sea or the mountain chains. To east and west, however, the plain stretches with almost no natural obstacles other than the Pripet marshes in the east, leaving Poland open to pressure and invasion from either direction, and causing her territorial extent to vary greatly from age to age.

Dominating the second region of Eastern Europe is the mighty Danube, flowing from its source in southwest Germany, constantly gathering in the waters of East European rivers such as the Morava, the Drava, the Tisza, the Sava, and the second (Balkan) Morava, and emptying finally through its great delta estuary into the Black Sea. Ringed on all sides by mountains, by the Alps and the Bohemian Forest to the west; the Carpathian Crescent, including the Transylvanian Alps, to north and east; and the Dinaric and Balkan Mountains to the south, its plain has for centuries provided a route for migrating peoples, for invading armies, and for trade. Vienna, once "the Queen of the Danube," derived wealth and power from its favorable central location at the juncture of corridors leading to western Europe, Poland, and the Adriatic, and dominated far-flung reaches of the entire basin. On this great plain, to the north of the river, lies Czechoslovakia, snugly enclosed but not too safely protected by its mountain frontiers (the Bohemian Forest, the Ore and Sudeten Mountains, and the Carpathians), its southern border on the Danube for about 100 miles only. Hungary is located almost in the center of the Danubian plain, with the Danube and the Tisza cutting through its territory. She was once mistress of Croatia between the Sava and Drava, and of Transylvania within the Carpathian triangle, and even possessed a port, Fiume, on the Adriatic. Since 1919 she has been reduced to a compact flat land almost entirely within the Danubian plain. Rumania, whose southern border runs along the Danube for 600 miles, embraces not only the old provinces of Wallachia in the Danubian plain; Moldavia, between the Prut River and the Carpathians; and the smaller Dobruja, south of the Danube delta; but also the great arc-shaped land of Transylvania, won from Hungary in 1919 and regained, after temporary partition, in 1945.

Finally, the rugged and mountainous Balkan peninsula, roughly extending south of the Sava and the Danube to the seas around, is somewhat a world of its own, a third distinct environment for the remaining three communist states. Bulgaria, cut by two parallel east-west mountain ranges, the Balkans and the Rhodopes, neither a serious barrier, comprises two fertile plains, that of the Danube, serving as its boundary for 290 miles, and that of the Maritsa, leading down to Istanbul and the Straits. Cut off from the Aegean by Greek and Turkish territory, Bulgaria has, like Rumania, the advantage of a long Black Sea littoral. Yugoslavia exhibits the greatest geographical diversity, including the productive plains of the Danube and its tributaries to the north, the historically separate and rocky coast of Dalmatia on the west, and between them, isolating each from the other, the extremely rugged Dinaric Mountains, on which Bosnia-Herzegovina and Montenegro are located. Alpine Slovenia, enjoying relative ease of access to Austria and the Adriatic, forms another distinct zone. Belgrade, the capital, standing at the juncture of Sava and Danube, looks down the conjoint plains of the Morava and Vardar rivers, a corridor that has exposed throughout history parts of what is now Yugoslavia to repeated incursions by Turks, as well as by Bulgarians. Little Albania, perched on the lower Dinaric Mountains, is almost entirely cut off from the interior, including its closest neighbors, Yugoslavia and Greece, and its Adriatic coastline, because of a poorly developed economy, hardly modifies its remoteness and isolation.

NATIONALITY MOSAIC

At least a dozen nationalities, each numbering at least a million, have for centuries formed a mosaic of ethnic diversity as striking as the geographic multiformity of these varied zones, and the distribution of peoples has been greatly influenced by the physical configuration described above. Their ancestors came mainly from Asia during the "wandering of the peoples," and their descendants have remained in roughly their present locations for more than a thousand years. Most of them trace their origin to the Slavs who once lived in the upper Dnieper valley, but even these have developed differences of language and of culture after centuries of separation. Although speaking languages that are in varying degrees related to each other, and at times entertaining vague ideas of Slavic community or even of pan-Slav union, these "Slavic," or "Slavonic," nations have not escaped intense national rivalry, and have seldom been able to tranlsate their cultural kinship into a meaningful political association, except in the narrower

relations of Czechs and Slovaks, or Serbs, Croats, and Slovenes. Even within such special groups, hostility has often been serious, and hardly less deep than the traditional mutual hatreds of other Slavs, such as Russian and Pole, or Bulgarian and Serb.

Of the western Slavs, Poles and Czechs have had relatively few historic associations and yet more than one period of bitter conflict. Even the Czechs and Slovaks, very closely related linguistically, lived apart for more than a thousand years and attained a unity, somewhat uneasy and troubled, only in the past half-century. Of the eastern Slavs, apart from the Russians, two others, Ukrainians and Byelorussians, have at certain historical periods been subjected to Polish rule, but at present are almost entirely within Soviet territory and hence not part of our subject.

The southern Slavs have manifested a similar counterpoint of conflict and cooperation in their historical relations. Those who inhabit the so-called "South Slav" (Yugoslav) state had for centuries lived separately, the Serbs under the Turks and then independently; the Croats, under Austria and Hungary; and the Slovenes, under Austria; until they were united in 1919 in modern Yugoslavia. Serbs and Croats, speaking one language but using different scripts, Cyrillic and Latin, have historically experienced many conflicts with each other, as have the Croatians of the Danubian plain, and their Croatian kinsmen living on the coast of Dalmatia and in the Bosnian mountains. Still another "South Slav" people, the Bulgarians, are actually descended from non-Slav Asiatic invaders who took over the Slavic language of their subjects. In spite of occasional vain efforts at unity with their neighbors in Yugoslavia, the Bulgarians have often been at odds with them, and have never been incorporated in this reunion of South Slavs. An even more anomalous position is occupied by the Macedonians, in the valleys of the Vardar and of the Struma. Regarded by the Bulgarians as a branch of their nation, who spoke a local dialect, they were long treated by the Serbians, too, as a subject people. They are now considered in Yugoslavia as a separate nationality, with their own language, and enjoy a special autonomous position.

The non-Slav nations of Eastern Europe—Magyars, Rumanians and Albanians—are sharply marked off, at least in their own consciousness, and objectively in their different cultures, from their Slav neighbors, but have no linguistic and few cultural ties in common. The Magyars, occupying a central position between western, eastern, and southern Slavs, and dividing them from each other, speak a tongue that is altogether outside the Indo-European group to which almost all the languages of Europe belong, and is linked remotely only with Finnish and Estonian. The Szeklers, who speak Magyar and live in large numbers in Transylvania, have often had strained relations with their Rumanian cohabitants. The Rumanians, descended from the natives of the Roman province of Dacia, and preserving a Romance language from those remote times, often show pride in their "western" origin and hostility toward their Magyar and Slavonic neighbors. Finally, the Albanians, or Shiptars, living in their mountain fastness in Albania and southern Yugoslavia, speak an Indo-European tongue, but one unlike any other in Europe, and without Slav or other connections.

Until World War II, another ethnic fact of overwhelming importance was the German nation in Eastern Europe. As a result of migrations and settlements commencing in the thirteenth century, people of German speech lived in compact masses, or interspersed with non-Germans, in what they liked to call "the German East." Some of them, in East Prussia, Silesia, Pomerania, and Posen, in Bohemia and Moravia, and in Austria, were contiguous with the main body of Germans; others were scattered throughout Eastern Europe, in cities such as Prague or Budapest, and in ethnically mixed rural areas such as Transylvania or the Banat, north of the Danube at Belgrade. As long as Austria-Hungary existed and Poland was partitioned, the Germans occupied a position of power among the Slavic and other peoples of Central and Eastern Europe. Later, under Hitler, they served as a springboard and a pretext for German eastward expansion. However, the final boomerang effect of Nazi occupation was the expulsion or withdrawal of most Germans from the entire area, so that what had been a decisive element for centuries ceased to exist at all. Indeed, Poland, as we have seen, pushed eastward at the expense of Germandom, recovering lands of which some were authentically Polish in population. Others, such as Danzig (Gdansk), Stettin (Szczeczin), or Breslau (Wroclaw), had not been occupied or controlled by Poles for centuries. The expulsion of Germans from Bohemia and Moravia, and from other parts of Eastern Europe, brought to an end other ancient settlements. The historic Slav-German duel thus ended in a resounding Slav victory.

RELIGIOUS AFFILIATIONS

Superimposed on ethnic diversity was religious differentiation, sometimes reinforcing the conflict of nation and nation, less often blurring nationality differences. Through Eastern Europe runs the line between Roman Catholicism and Eastern Orthodoxy, with the Poles, Czechs, Slovaks, Slovenes, Croats, Austrians, Germans, and Hungarians mainly on the Catholic side, and the Ukrainians, Rumanians, Bulgarians, Serbs, and Macedonians on the Orthodox side. The break of the two great branches of Christianity in 1054 intensified the national conflict of Pole with

Ukrainian and Russian, and of Serb with Croat and Slovene. It did not, however, bring close together the countries of Orthodoxy, each of which developed in the late nineteenth century an autocephalous Church, using its own language and only loosely subordinated to Constantinople. Nor for that matter has Catholic Eastern Europe been linked significantly by the common faith, and it was further divided by the rise of Protestantism, especially in Hungary, and to a lesser degree among Czechs, Slovaks, Poles, and Germans. Some Catholics, notably among western Ukrainians (sometimes known as Ruthenians) and Rumanians, used the Byzantine rite and the Church Slavonic language of Eastern Orthodoxy, but continued to owe allegiance to Rome. The Balkan situation was further complicated by long historical domination by Moslem Turks, who had on the whole preserved intact the Orthodox and other religious communities of their peoples; after their rule had ended, important Mohammedan residues were left in the form of small Turkish minorities; some Moslem Slavs, among Bosnians, Macedonians, and Bulgarians; the largely Moslem Albanians; and perhaps more significantly, the strong influence of Turkish and Moslem ways among Albanians, Bulgarians, Rumanians, and Serbs.

The Jews, like the Germans, once a factor of great significance, have in the main disappeared from the scene as a result of World War II and German occupation. Emigrating long ago from Western Europe to escape persecution in Germany and Spain, the Jews had lived for centuries among the peoples of Eastern Europe, sometimes segregated in ghettos, but often assimilating with one or other nation. Forming a religious and cultural entity rather than an ethnic one, Jews had become Germans, or Poles, or Czechs, learning one or more languages as well as their own Yiddish, Spaniol, and Hebrew. Anti-Semitism varied considerably from people to people and reached its high point between the wars among Austrians, Hungarians, Rumanians, and Poles. Numbering over six million in 1939, the Jews became the target of Nazi attack, and of persecution by most of the local governments; their ranks were decimated by liquidations and forced exile and some postwar emigration to Israel.

ECONOMIC UNDERDEVELOPMENT

Almost all Eastern Europeans shared in common a backwardness of economic development that condemned most of them, whatever their nationality or location, to a life of hard work and poverty. Even in the interwar years, the continent was divided distinctly into what has been called "the two Europes, the farming and the industrial."[4] A line drawn between, say, Riga and Trieste bisected Europe, the population to the east overwhelmingly occupied in agriculture, and that to the west, by majority, in industry, transport, trade, and services. Czechoslovakia, with only 33 per cent of her population in agriculture, was unique in an area where the proportion was normally over 60 per cent, in the Balkans even above 75 per cent. Only western Poland, western Czechoslovakia, eastern Germany, and, of course, cities such as Vienna, Budapest, Zagreb, and Belgrade, were predominantly industrial and commercial. The rest of the area was dependent on agriculture, and on an agriculture notorious for its lack of capital investment, technological backwardness, low productivity, rural overpopulation, and the predominance of very large and very small land holdings. With this went the social ills usually associated with economic underdevelopment, namely high population growth; very low income; inadequate food, clothing, and housing; high infant mortality; a low life expectancy; a high rate of illiteracy; and poor educational standards.[5] Not richly endowed with the resources needed for economic development, these countries lacked above all the political conditions necessary to enable them to imitate Western Europe's advance and to secure the benefits of modernization. Political independence stimulated some agricultural reforms and some degree of industrial development, but did not, with the notable exception of Czechoslovakia, produce the balanced economy characteristic of a modern society.[6] Even there, Slovakia continued to be much more a part of the underdeveloped east than of the developed west.

Right down to 1939, Eastern Europe remained what it had always been, "a great sea of peasantry," with islands of urban life in cities and towns and in certain favored areas on the western border. The common plight of the peasantry did not, in view of ethnic and political separateness, produce a unity of action, or even of outlook. Moreover, differences in social class added another element of heterogeneity and source of conflict.[7] In the countryside, wide variations of wealth and status existed between

[4] See Dudley Kirk, *Europe's Population in the Interwar Years* (Geneva: League of Nations, 1946), p. 190.

[5] For these matters, apart from Kirk, see also Wilbert E. Moore, *Economic Demography of Eastern and Southern Europe* (Geneva: League of Nations, 1945).

[6] See *Agrarian Problems from the Baltic to the Aegean* (London, 1944).

[7] See Hugh Seton-Watson, *Eastern Europe Between the Wars, 1918–1941* (Cambridge, 1945), chaps. 4 and 5.

large landed proprietors, their agricultural workers, and smallholding peasants, a gulf that continued even after 1919 in Hungary and Poland. Elsewhere, in countries where a landed aristocracy had not existed, wealthier peasants merged with the commercial and industrial bourgeoisie and a growing bureaucracy to form a new ruling class, little interested in alleviating the lot of the agricultural population. The development of industry and commerce, where it occurred, created two new and sharply opposed classes: a middle class of businessmen and an industrial working class often not far removed from a peasant background, and not enjoying a significantly higher standard of living. Before 1914, class conflicts were often reinforced by nationality differences, with Polish or Magyar landowners facing Ruthenian or Slovak peasants, and German industrialists facing Czech or Polish workers. A rising small bourgeoisie, such as the Czech, found itself at odds with the established German or Jewish bourgeoisie of Vienna and Prague. Indeed, the Jewish middle class, occupied mainly in industry, trade, and the professions, was frequently the object of the envy and hostility of its non-Jewish competitors or customers. Social factors thus contributed to the rising tide of nationalism and racialism. The workers tried to bridge the gulf of nationality, organizing their parties and trade unions at first on an international basis, but succumbed more and more to the disintegrating effects of national hatreds. After the formation of independent states in 1919, the social democratic parties became strongly conscious of their national identity and were often ready to associate themselves with their class rivals in political action. The ruling classes, a land-owning aristocracy or the commercial, industrial, and bureaucratic bourgeoisie, saw in the new national states the means of advancing their own interests at the expense of the masses at home and of their rivals in other countries. Economic nationalism was the order of the day.[8]

[8] Frederick Hertz, *The Economic Problem of the Danubian States: A Study in Economic Nationalism* (London, 1947).

3: Diversity of Political Tradition

The extraordinary geographic, ethnic, and religious heterogeneity of Eastern Europe and its persistent economic and social backwardness have permanently conditioned its political life, and have combined, through most of recorded history, to prevent the emergence of a stable and viable political structure embracing the whole, or even the greater part, of the region, and to invite its penetration and subjugation by outside states possessing greater power. Unlike Western Europe, where great states largely homogeneous in nationality have long existed, Eastern Europe has exhibited a kaleidoscopic changeability in its political organization and its international boundaries that has earned it, with some justice, the name of "shatter zone." The successive patterns have left deep imprints on the historical consciousness and the political attitudes of the peoples of Eastern Europe and still further differentiated them from each other.

ROME AND BYZANTIUM

Even the legacy of Rome was a divided one in the European east. At its peak, the empire had embraced under its authority the whole of the Balkan peninsula and the Danubian basin, including for a time, in Dacia, much of present day Rumania. This great effort at universal political dominion, however, contained within itself the seeds of its own breakup, especially in the differences between its western, primarily Roman, and its eastern, Greek or Hellenic, realms. When in A.D. 395 the formal division of the empire into two parts occurred, their capitals, Rome and Byzantium (later Constantinople), emerged as two great centers of power, from each of which radiated a distinct brand of Christian civilization, one Latin, the other Greek. This basic cultural differentiation was reinforced during the next 700 years by the gradual division of the Church into two distinct wings, one in the west, using the Latin language and rite, the other in the east, using the Byzantine rite and Greek or other languages, such as Old Slavonic or Rumanian. Long before the final breach in 1054, the peoples of Eastern Europe were receiving the Christian faith from two different sources—some, such as the Slovenes, the Croats, and Hungarians, from Rome; some, such as the Bulgarians and Rumanians, from Constantinople; and others, such as Serbs and Albanians, from both. The Czechs, who had been converted in A.D. 863 by Cyril and Method, the famed missionaries from the Eastern Church, ultimately accepted their Christianity from Rome. The Poles, who, like the Czechs, had never been under the political authority of the Roman Empire, were also converted by Rome in the tenth century.

It is difficult to overrate the profound and continuing effects of this ancient separation of Eastern Europe into two vast spheres, one Catholic and Roman, and the other Orthodox and Byzantine. The stamps of Rome and of Constantinople were indelibly imprinted on the peoples involved, even though each nation adapted its particular tradition to its own special circumstances. For some the Roman legacy was paramount. For others, including the Russians and the Balkan peoples, "Byzantium was what Rome had been to the Western and Germanic world," writes a distinguished scholar, "that is to say the great educator, the great initiator, the bringer both of religion and civilization," and "supplied them with all the elements of their future greatness," including their faith, their conceptions of government and law, their artistic and intellectual culture, even their alphabet and literary language.[1] To this very day, these ancient facts exert their imponderable but undeniable influence. That Bulgarians and Poles, for instance, speak languages called Slavic pales into insignificance beside the fact that they stand on opposite sides of the historic gulf of cultural tradition between Rome and Byzantium.

The succession to these two foci of power was also vastly different. After the collapse of Rome, the Byzantine Empire continued in the east, mainly in the Balkans, its territorial extent ever-varying, but its centralized authority maintained, for another thousand years, until the invasion of the Ottoman Turks and their capture of Constantinople in 1453. In the west, the glory of Rome was replaced by a series of barbarian kingdoms and restored in A.D. 800 in a pale image of its former self, in the Carolingian Empire, and a century and a half later in the so-called Holy Roman Empire of the German Nation, which endured until 1801. This loose federation of German princes had its center of gravity in northwest and central Europe, but included Bohemia, Moravia, and the Austrian lands, and hence, of the peoples of Eastern Europe, the Czechs, Slovenes, and Austrians, as well as some Poles. Even more significant for the future was the breach within the Catholic Church occasioned by the Reformation and the attendant rise of Protestantism. Although no nation of Eastern Europe became by majority Protestant, some, notably the Germans,

[1] Charles Diehl, in the *Cambridge Medieval History*, Vol. IV, chap. XXIV, p. 776.

Hungarians, Czechs, Slovaks, and Poles, had substantial Protestant minorities destined to exert considerable influence on their lives. Byzantine Europe, on the other hand, which had not experienced the Renaissance, was uninfluenced by the Reformation and remained united in its Orthodoxy, although increasingly divided along national lines, as each nation sought an autonomous position for its own church. Another contrast was that between the profound conflicts of Church and State in Western Catholic Europe, and their close union, through the subordination of the former to the latter, in Eastern Orthodox Europe.

HEIRS TO ROME AND BYZANTIUM

More significant for our study were the ultimate political successors to Rome and to Byzantium, namely the empires of the Ottoman Turks and the Russians in the east, and the realms of Brandenburg-Prussia and the Habsburg dynasty in the west. Once again, the nations of this region were to live for centuries under different authorities, and thus to be subject to varied political traditions that further compounded the diversity and complexity of Eastern Europe.

For the Balkan peoples, the overwhelming fact of modern history has been the power and expansion of Ottoman Turkey, which after the capture of Constantinople (renamed Istanbul) had advanced northward, encompassing in its domain all of Europe up to the Danube and Sava, and even beyond, in Wallachia and Moldavia. Only the Dalmatian coast, north of Albania, almost entirely escaped Turkish rule. At its maximum in the seventeenth century, the Ottoman Empire thrust forward even further, to include the larger part of Hungary, Transylvania, Bukovina, and the Banat, and to lay siege, in 1683, to Vienna. The tide receded, but Turkey remained the predominant influence in the Balkans proper for about four centuries—for Serbs, Rumanians, and Bosnians until 1878, for Bulgarians, Macedonians, and Albanians until almost 1914. For these nations of Eastern Europe, then, in varying degrees, the paramount political experience was the despotism of the Turkish state, with its established church in the Moslem Caliphate. This was relieved somewhat by the fact that the Orthodox peoples enjoyed a degree of religious and cultural autonomy in the so-called "millets," for the non-Moslem peoples, under the Orthodox patriarchate in Istanbul.

Another successor to Byzantium in the east, in the cultural, if not in the strictly geographic, sense, was the Russian Empire that grew up around Moscow, sometimes thought of by its rulers as "The Third Rome." Orthodox and Slav, this Muscovite realm succeeded the earlier kingdom of Kiev, which had received its Christianity from Constantinople in the tenth century. Although at first challenged by the Polish (later Polish-Lithuanian) kingdom, which at times incorporated lands that were Ukrainian and Byelo-Russian in population, and included even Moscow from 1610 to 1612, the restored Russia of the Romanov dynasty after the seventeenth century steadily expanded westward, to encompass the Baltic states, Finland, the Byelo-Russian and Ukrainian territories once dominated by Poland, and after 1830 large areas of ethnic Poland centered on Warsaw. For almost a century, the greatness of earlier Polish kingdoms remained only a memory and an inspiration for the future. The decisive political fact for most Poles was the Russian system of unconcealed despotism, scarcely modified down to its fall in 1917. The Poles occasionally enjoyed a limited degree of autonomy and at times participated actively in the politics of the Russian Empire, but on two occasions rose in abortive revolt against Moscow.

For many other Poles, the political setting of their lives was the hardly less absolutist system of the Prussian Empire. As in the east, so, too, in the west, the Poles had memories of earlier greatness, when their kingdom had stretched far into the German domain up to the very city of Berlin. With the formation of Brandenburg-Prussia under the Hohenzollerns in the fifteenth and sixteenth centuries, however, the tide turned. Already including East Prussia, the new kingdom pushed eastward after 1740 to incorporate West Prussia and Silesia, with a significant Polish population, and after the partitions of Poland at the end of the century, Posen (Poznan) and other predominantly Polish territories. The ensuing national struggle was reinforced by religious factors, with Catholic Pole facing Protestant German, as in the east he faced Orthodox Russian and Ukrainian. In some respects, the fate of the Poles under Prussia was worse than that of the Russian Poles, as they never possessed local autonomy and had little or no opportunity for active participation in Prussian politics generally.

Within the Holy Roman Empire, long before its demise, there were but two realities of power—namely Brandenburg-Prussia and the realm of the Habsburg dynasty. The latter, a vast conglomerate of territories, had comprised, from 1526, the dynasty's original "Austrian lands," largely German in language, but including Slovenes and Italians in the south; and two other great complexes, the lands of the Bohemian and of the Hungarian crowns, linked in personal union under the Habsburgs. The Bohemian crown lands were largely Czech, but contained a substantial German minority; the Hungarian, with a Magyar plurality, included a medley of other nationalities—Rumanians, Serbs, Slovaks, Ruthenians, and others. After the freeing of Turkish-controlled areas, the Hungarian territories included not only Transylvania and the Banat, but also the Kingdom of Croatia-Slavonia, with its Croatian majority. To these possessions the Habsburgs added at various times Galicia, with its Polish majority; Bukovina, with its mixed Ruthenian, German, and Rumanian population; the Banat (Serbian, Magyar, Croatian); Dalmatia (Croatian); Istria (Croatian and Italian); and Bosnia and Herzegovina (Serb and Croatian). This patchwork of territories and nationalities was woven together into one of the great powers of Europe, controlling for several centuries most of the Danubian basin, and spilling over the Carpathians to Galicia, and beyond the Dinaric Mountains to the Adriatic. Hence it dominated the central core of what we have termed Eastern Europe.

The Habsburg monarchy was a unique and long-lasting effort to organize a large part of Eastern Europe in a single political entity, but it suffered from grave internal weaknesses that in the end proved fatal. The so-called "Dual System," established by a compromise between Austrian Germans and Magyars in 1867, placed these nations in the dominant position and deprived the other nationalities in varying degrees of a just share of political power. Hungary, only 48 per cent of whose population was Magyar, was governed centrally from Budapest, and although Croatia enjoyed a token autonomy, the Slovak, Rumanian, Ruthenian, and other minorities were almost without participation in the political system. In the Austrian half, governed centrally from Vienna, the Germans, who amounted to only 35 per cent of the total population, held the reins of government mainly in their hands. Only the Kingdom of Galicia had a substantial degree of autonomy, thus giving the Polish majority control of its own affairs, and permitting them to subjugate the Ruthenian minority. Unlike their compatriots under Russian and Prussian rule, the Austrian Poles thus enjoyed a substantial degree of local freedom and took a considerable part in the central government in Vienna. Czechs and Slovenes had a much more modest share in the process of governing Austria, the former enjoying a limited home rule. Both Austria and Hungary, and the Empire as a whole, were governed under political systems that involved a high degree of royal and imperial power behind a deceptive and highly unrepresentative parliamentary facade. None of the peoples of the Monarchy, whether rulers or ruled, had therefore known anything but a stunted form of democracy, although greater by far than that of the subjects of Turkey, and somewhat greater than those of Russia and Prussia.

DIVERSITY OF RULE

The political experience of the peoples of Eastern Europe prior to 1914 was varied in the extreme. Some had lived within a largely Moslem and Turkish world; others in a Russian and Orthodox world; others in a Germanic world, Protestant in Prussia, Catholic in Austria; and still others within a Magyar one, itself strongly influenced by German Austria. A few, mainly the Croats on the Dalmatian coast, had for centuries been in an Italian (Venetian) milieu before their incorporation in Austria after the Napoleonic wars. In more than one case, nations such as Poles and Rumanians, or closely related nationalities, such as Czechs and Slovaks, or Serbs, Croats, and Slovenes, had long been divided and subject to contrasting influences.

Almost without exception, the systems under which the nations of Eastern Europe had existed were not democratic in a genuine sense, although there were differences in the form and the degree of autocracy and in the extent to which constitutional forms masked the reality of power. The four great empires were absolute monarchies, modified, as time went on, with the exception of the Ottoman, by limited degrees of popular representation, by some parliamentary influence on public policy, and by some freedom of political activity. To varying extent, the subject peoples reacted negatively to the dominant traditions to which they were subject, but were also subtly and often unconsciously affected by them. All were able at least to form their own parties and to undertake some political activity, however limited in scope. The nations under the Habsburgs in Austria, such as the Czechs and Slovenes, enjoyed something closer to constitutional democracy, especially after the introduction of universal suffrage in 1907, than any of the other peoples of Eastern Europe. Hungarian constitutionalism had endured for many centuries, but in a form that excluded the subject peoples and the exploited classes from any share of power. The Poles, under constitutions formulated in 1791, and later, in 1807 and 1815, had experienced democratic constitutionalism for a few years. Nations freed from Ottoman rule in the late nineteenth century, such as Serbs, Bulgarians, and

Rumanians, had established political systems based on newly drafted constitutions, but apart from the Bulgarian Tirnovo constitution of 1879, these were not distinguished by democratic features and were in any case not fully applied in practice.

The constellations described provided new fuel for the fires of future conflict, in particular the differentiation between ruling and ruled nations, or, as they were sometimes called, the "historic nations" and "nations without history."[2] The former monopolized not only political power but wealth and status; the latter were the hewers of wood and drawers of water. The ruling nations possessed a fully developed class structure, with an aristocracy, a business class, political, bureaucratic, and military personnel, and professional people. These nations often had their main base outside the area proper, as in the case of the Prussians, the Russians, and the Turks, but some, such as the Austrian Germans, the Magyars, and the Poles, were indigenous to the region. The "nations without history" lacked the middle and upper classes of a developed social hierarchy, and were made up mainly of peasants and, increasingly, of industrial workers, with sometimes a rising middle class of small businessmen and professional people. They included the Ruthenians, the Rumanians, the Serbs, Croats, and Slovenes, the Czechs and Slovaks, the Bulgarians and Macedonians, and the Albanians. Economic and social relations were not stagnant, however, but in a process of dynamic development, so that the slow but steady advance of the backward nations and their aspirations for its continuance and acceleration generated intense antagonism.

NATIONAL INDEPENDENCE

Space does not permit more than a mention of the familiar story of national self-determination, as the nations of Eastern Europe more and more rejected political domination and cultural assimilation and demanded broadened national rights, and often autonomy, or political independence. The struggle of each people was directed against its own historic enemies, sometimes the Prussian, Russian, or Turk, sometimes the Austrian German, Magyar, or Pole. Almost all had memories of ancient statehood, often ending in tragedy, such as the partition of Poland, the defeat of the Serbs at Kossovo in 1389, the Hungarians at Mohacs in 1526, or

[2] Rudolf Springer, pseudo. (Karl Renner), *Grundlagen und Entwicklungsziele der Oest.-ungarischen Monarchie* (Vienna, 1906). See also O. Jászi, *The Dissolution of the Habsburg Monarchy* (Chicago, 1929).

the Czechs at Bilá Hora in 1620. Some continued to seek their ends through "organic cooperation" with their rulers, but usually the goal became independence, to be attained through revolution, abetted by the diplomatic or military intervention of outside powers. The fragmentation of the great empires began in the early nineteenth century in the Balkans, not because of the strength of the local nationalities, but rather because of the weakness of the Ottoman Empire, and produced an independent Serbia, Rumania, and Bulgaria. The ultimate climax was reached in 1919, when national struggles, diplomatic pressures, and the fortunes of war combined to bring about independence for almost all the nations of the area.

World War I and the ensuing peace changed the face of Eastern Europe. Now, fourteen small nation-states existed in a region where, a century before, there had not been a single independent nation. The great empires that had held sway were gone —Austria demolished, Turkey, Prussia, and Russia expelled. Only one outside power, Italy, profited from the collapse to extend her possessions in Eastern Europe, securing Trieste, Fiume, much of Istria, and parts of Dalmatia. Although this transformation represented in a sense the triumph of the nationality principle, it did not eliminate, but rather aggravated, the national conflict. The historic reversal of roles between rulers and ruled—for instance, in the case of German and Czech or Magyar and Rumanian—was bound to produce bitterness and hatred. Moreover, the ultimate territorial settlement reflected not merely national, but also diplomatic and military, considerations, so that Poles, Czechs, Rumanians, and Yugoslavs emerged as victors and Magyars, Bulgarians, and Austrian Germans as losers, all on a grand scale. Even apart from the play of power factors, the geographical intermingling of peoples could not but create points of future friction over boundaries, disputed zones, national minorities, and regional autonomy.

Independence brought with it the problems of founding new political systems and evolving fresh political traditions in vastly changed circumstances. The winners had the difficult task of fusing together into single entities regions with diverse backgrounds. Poland, for instance, had to unite her former separated brethren from Austria, Prussia, and Russia, together with very large German, Ukrainian, and White Russian minorities, within her far-flung territory. Czechoslovakia had to merge Czechs from Austria and Slovaks from Hungary, along with Ruthenians, also from Hungary, and substantial German, Magyar, and Polish minorities. The new Yugoslavia had to weld South Slavs from Austria, Turkey, and Hungary, as well as little Montenegro, independent for more than a century, with Serbia, which had been fully sovereign only from 1878. The task was complicated by large Magyar, Italian, Albanian, and other minorities. The greatly enlarged Rumania had to forge a nation from small prewar Rumania, independent since 1878, and increments from Austria, Hungary, Russia, and Bulgaria, with Magyar, German, and other minorities. Albania, independent on paper only since 1912, had a relatively uniform population in terms of nationality, but had been subject to recent Italian, as well as the more ancient Turkish, influence, and lost to Yugoslavia almost half of her ethnic compatriots. For Hungary and Bulgaria, the losers, the problem was somewhat different—to create a system of politics for territories greatly reduced, in the case of Hungary, and much less than hoped for, and episodically achieved in the past, in the case of Bulgaria.

COLLAPSE OF DEMOCRACY

It is not surprising that in these circumstances, aggravated by international developments, almost none of these small states was able to erect a stable system of rule or to evolve a sound political tradition. Almost all started with the best of will to found a government on democratic foundations, but almost all had, by 1939, failed to achieve that goal. Lacking a tradition of genuine democracy, wracked by severe inner conflict between classes, nations, and religions, and plagued by continuing economic and social backwardness, the new nations did not possess the elementary conditions of a stable political community and especially one of democratic character. Their two decades of formative existence were lived, moreover, within an international context of extreme instability, arising from sharp territorial disputes with their smaller neighbors; the threat of German, Russian, and Italian expansionism; the clash of rival ideologies; the absence of a system of world security; and the ultimate breakdown of the international economic system. With the single exception of Czechoslovakia, the other states, from Poland to Yugoslavia, were eventually subjected to authoritarian government, often semi-fascist in character, each, however, with its own distinctive features.

Albania, for instance, after a few years of relative political freedom, was subjected after 1928 to absolute monarchy under

King Zog. In Yugoslavia, the centralizing constitution of 1920 was strongly opposed by the Croats, but was replaced by a royal dictatorship in 1929. In what is now East Germany, the democratic republic had been superseded by Nazi dictatorship in 1933, and all other parties ruthlessly destroyed. Bulgaria, Rumania, and Poland enjoyed some years of constitutional democracy, marred by coups d'état and infringements of parliamentarianism, but in the thirties succumbed to royal dictatorships under King Boris and King Carol, and presidential absolutism in Poland. Hungary, after brief communist rule in 1919, submitted to the authoritarian regency of Admiral Horthy, with a few "loyal" opposition parties preserving an appearance of democracy. Only in Czechoslovakia was a democratic republic maintained until 1938, although it was constantly threatened by the disaffection of Germans, Poles, Magyars, and even many Slovaks. In all these countries, two decades of independence had nonetheless offered a brief experience of political activity, had given some of the parties a taste of power, and others a tradition of opposition to arbitrary rule.

WAR AND ITS AFTERMATH

The years of World War II and of German expansion affected the political life of Eastern Europe in diverse ways. Certain countries, namely Czechoslovakia, Poland, and Yugoslavia, were literally destroyed, with "independent" puppet states created in Slovakia, Serbia, and Croatia (the latter including Bosnia and Herzegovina and, later, Dalmatia), and the rest of their territory subordinated directly to German (or Italian) rule. The remains of Yugoslavia, for instance, were placed under German, Italian, Hungarian, Bulgarian, or Albanian occupation and administration. The Czech rump was ruled directly by German authorities, as was the residuum of Poland, after the Soviet and German annexation of eastern and western territories. Other countries—Hungary, Bulgaria and Rumania—nominally allied with Germany, fell more and more under the control of the Reich, although preserving the forms of autonomous government and protecting themselves against the worst of Nazi terror. Indeed, two of them profited from the occasion to secure territories lost in 1919, Bulgaria at the cost of Greece and Yugoslavia, Hungary at the cost of Czechoslovakia, Rumania, and Yugoslavia. Rumania, however, although also an ally of Germany, suffered the loss of parts of Transylvania and the Dobrudja, but regained Bessarabia and added a new province of Transnistria, both at the expense of the Soviet Union. Albania, under Italian and later German occupation, seized territories previously belonging to Yugoslavia and Greece. Thus were old wounds reopened and new ones inflicted, aggravating further the national hostilities of the area.

Wartime political experiences widened the gulf between the nations. For some, the Germans were the most hated enemy, for others the Italians, and for still others, the Russians, or even their own closest neighbors. Some, the Poles, Czechs, and Serbs, in particular, suffered grievously at the hands of the Germans; others, such as the Hungarians and Bulgarians, much less. In some cases, notably Slovakia and Croatia, native fascist regimes, under Msgr. Tiso and Pavelić respectively, were fashioned, and collaborated willingly with the Nazi regime. Czechs and Serbs cooperated with the Germans to a lesser degree. Among the Poles, collaboration was almost nonexistent, and no puppet government was created. The states that retained their identity, such as Hungary, Bulgaria, and Rumania, were associated with Germany with varying degrees of reserve or enthusiasm, but sought escape from the war in the closing years. The extent of hostilities against the Russians varied, with the greatest effort expended by the Rumanians, a lesser amount by Slovaks, Hungarians, and Croatians, and least of all, by Czechs, Bulgarians, and Serbs. Rumania and Bulgaria joined Russia against Germany in 1944. Resistance to the occupant also varied considerably, reaching its maximum among Yugoslavs and Albanians, and attaining lesser extent elsewhere.

After 1945, the states of Eastern Europe were, somewhat paradoxically, in view of the changed political and diplomatic context, largely restored to their prewar form and dimensions. The legacy of the Paris peace of 1919, which had divided Eastern Europe into the satisfied and the dissatisfied, was therefore in the main perpetuated. The one great exception was Poland, which was shifted bodily about 125 miles westward, due to the loss of her eastern territories to the USSR and the acquisition of German territories in the west. Yugoslavia made some gains at the expense of Italy; Czechoslovakia ceded Ruthenia to the USSR; other minor territorial changes were incorporated in the peace treaties concluded in 1946. Great movements of peoples had occurred, especially the transfer of millions of Germans from Poland, Czechoslovakia, and other countries, and the exchanges of Slovaks and Magyars, Rumanians and Bulgarians, Yugoslavs and Magyars. Great human losses had also been suffered, especially by the Jews and the Poles. The peoples of the area emerged from the holocaust with varied wartime experiences, and with fresh sources of disunity added to the traditional ones.

4: Communism Ascendant

The roots of communism reach back to the late nineteenth and early twentieth centuries, when the doctrine of Marxism penetrated into Eastern Europe and resulted in the formation of social democratic movements. This occurred, however, at different times and took different forms in the contrasting milieux in which the various nations had their being. Some, for instance, were influenced more by the later Russian version of Marxism than by its original Western European source. Nor were the socialist political organizations equally successful in winning adherents, so that Marxism remained uneven in influence as well as divergent in content. Although its chief appeal among Germans, Czechs, Magyars, and Poles was to the workers of the industrialized areas and the cities, Marxism also exerted a strong attraction, especially in its more radical form, among the peasants of Eastern Europe, such as the Bulgarians and Serbians. The seeds of dissension and diversity were thus sown at the very outset.[1]

For the nations of the Habsburg monarchy, the main source of socialist thought was Germany, and the social democratic parties among Austrian Germans, Czechs, Magyars, and others were largely modeled on the German. By 1914, their socialism had become moderate and evolutionary, although more radical left wings also existed. The nationality strife in Austria-Hungary left its imprint on the socialist movement, so that, especially among the less-privileged nations, it assumed a decidedly nationalist hue that clashed with its original internationalism. Among the Poles, divided between three empires, the influence of Russian Marxism was the decisive one, but produced two divergent attitudes: one, personified by Rosa Luxemburg and the Social Democracy of the Kingdom of Poland and Lithuania, took a strongly international approach; the other, represented by the Polish Socialist party, followed a more nationalist line, favoring Polish independence. The Bulgarians came mainly under the influence of Russian social democracy, dividing into two wings, the "broads" and the "narrows," resembling the Mensheviks and Bolsheviks, and ultimately accepting the more revolutionary position of the latter. The Rumanians, too, owed their inspiration to Russian socialism but moved in a more moderate and nationalist direction. Among the South Slavs, socialism was derived from

[1] The only full histories of Eastern European communism are M. K. Dziewanowski, *The Communist Party of Poland: An Outline of History* (Cambridge, 1959), and Joseph Rothschild, *The Communist Party of Bulgaria: Origins and Development, 1883–1936* (New York, 1959).

many sources, and among the Albanians was almost nonexistent before 1914.

COMMUNISM ORGANIZES ITSELF

After the Russian revolution and the formation of the Soviet regime, communist parties were formed by the left-wing and radical elements of social democracy, and under the guidance of the newly formed Communist International, were fashioned on the Soviet model. In some cases, for instance, the Czechs or the Bulgarians, the whole or the bulk of the former social democratic movement joined the Comintern, but the more moderate elements were later weeded out. In other cases, only a radical wing affiliated itself with the Moscow-oriented organization. From 1920 on, the Comintern exercised the strictest control of the member parties, changing their leaderships almost at will, and laying down their basic strategy. Especially under Stalin, they became mere satellites of the Soviet party, obeying to the letter the dictates of Moscow. In most countries the communist movement was less an urban proletarian movement and more a party of oppressed social groups, especially the peasants in backward regions, but it was often led by urban intellectuals. Its appeal, although in theory international, was especially great among the Slavic nations, and within them, among certain groups such as the Macedonians, Ruthenians, or Slovaks, at a low level of cultural development.[2] Communism indeed exerted a special influence among national minorities, and often, as in Rumania and Czechoslovakia, had its strongest representation among these rather than the ruling national majorities. It had least attraction for the Germans, Magyars, Rumanians, or Turks, and among the Slavs, for the Poles. For some Jews, the communist movement represented a source of security and satisfaction, and in certain countries, such as Hungary, Jewish leadership was predominant.

The experience and the success of these Russified Leninist parties varied greatly. They were legally banned, and their leaders exiled, for most of the interwar period. Only in Czechoslovakia did the party enjoy a position of relative freedom, and although sometimes hampered by restrictions, acquired substantial political experience within a democratic system. By 1929, Comintern policy had reduced what was a mass movement to a small sectarian one, attractive in the main to the minorities. It was able, nonethe-

[2] See R. V. Burks, *The Dynamics of Communism in Eastern Europe* (Princeton, 1961), especially the conclusion.

less, to secure considerable electoral support between the wars, and after the adoption of the popular front policy in 1935, had a considerable appeal for the Czech nation. In Rumania, communism remained minuscule in membership and support. Albania had a few small communist groups, but no Communist party, between the wars. In Hungary, the attraction of Marxism was weakened by the experience of communist rule for a few months in 1919. Among Bulgars and Yugoslavs, on the contrary, although the parties were illegal during most of the period, they became influential spokesmen of peasant discontent. The Polish Communist party, which had some success among the minorities and less among the Poles, fell afoul of the Comintern in 1938 and was dissolved, and many of its leaders were liquidated in the purges. The German party was destroyed by Hitler, with some of its leaders escaping to Moscow.

At the outbreak of World War II, then, the position of the communist parties varied in the extreme, ranging from nonexistence in Albania, Germany, and Poland and almost total extinction in Rumania and Hungary, to a somewhat greater strength in Bulgaria and Yugoslavia, and maximum strength in Czechoslovakia. The policy of national unity in resistance to Naziism, although temporarily abandoned during the period of the Russo-German pact, was resumed after the involvement of the Soviet Union in the war and facilitated the establishment of good relations with other parties and movements. By this time, many of the leaders were in exile, mainly in Moscow, and were able to work with the Soviet authorities in wartime propaganda and postwar planning. Other leaders were in concentration camps or at home in underground movements. The extent of resistance and of partisan military activity differed greatly from country to country, reaching a high point in Yugoslavia and Albania, and representing a much less powerful force among Bulgarians, Czechs, Germans, Hungarians, and Poles. Most significantly, the top leaders of Yugoslav communism, headed by Tito, were not in Moscow, but were leading the partisan struggle in the field. The same was true of Enver Hoxha, the leader of the Albanian Communist party, which was formed only in 1941 under the direct guidance of Yugoslav emissaries.

POSTWAR STRATEGIES

In 1945, in the light of her military predominance in Eastern Europe, it lay within the power of the Soviet Union to transfer exclusive authority to the communist parties, to establish at once full-blown communism on the Soviet model, or even to annex the entire area. Taking into account the value of continuing diplomatic and military cooperation with Western governments, however, a different and more moderate strategy based on the prewar popular front policy had been worked out in Moscow during the war years, to the alarm of more left-oriented communists. Certain areas, notably the Baltic states, the eastern parts of Poland, Rumania, and Czechoslovakia, and part of East Prussia, were, it is true, to be directly incorporated in the Soviet Union. Beyond these zones, however, independent states were to be reconstituted, with the communists sharing power in differing degrees with noncommunists in coalition governments. The Yugoslav and Albanian leaders, somewhat out of touch with this planning, pursued more radical courses that brought the former into conflict with Moscow. Although the Soviet government had not been able to secure prior approval of its territorial claims from the Western Allies, it had won their consent, at the Teheran conference, to Soviet predominance in military operations in the region and in subsequent occupation of the countries liberated from Nazi rule, including Eastern Germany. Indeed, it had also gained acquiescence in a general sphere of Soviet influence in Hungary, Rumania, and Bulgaria. Although the Yalta conference of early 1945 proclaimed the principles of "joint responsibility" for the liberated areas and the right of the peoples to choose their form of government, the implementation of these principles in the face of Soviet paramountcy was bound to be difficult in the extreme.

As the Soviet armies rolled across Eastern Europe in pursuit of the retreating enemy in late 1944, it remained only to apply, according to the special situation of each country, the strategy worked out during the war.[3] Of the enemy states, Rumania and Hungary had taken an active part in military operations against the Soviet Union. After their defeat and surrender, these countries were placed under coalition governments, headed by Generals Sanatescu and Miklos respectively, and including a modest communist representation. In Bulgaria, which, although a German satellite, had been at war with the Soviet Union for a few hours only, power was seized by the Fatherland Front, and a government under Colonel Georgiev was formed, with more substantial communist participation. In East Germany, of course, the Soviet army was in exclusive control, with Berlin under joint allied

[3] See R. V. Burks' "typology of take-over" in Cyril E. Black and Thomas P. Thornton (eds.), *Communism and Revolution: The Strategic Uses of Political Violence* (Princeton, 1964), ch. 4.

occupation. No effort was made to form a government, although the communist leaders, headed by Ulbricht, returned to Berlin with the Red Army and organized a Communist party. Although the three other enemy countries were placed formally under interallied occupation, the major responsibility inevitably passed into the hands of the Soviet command, so that in succeeding months the ascendancy of the communists was facilitated. In Rumania, direct Soviet intervention, carried out by Deputy Minister of Foreign Affairs Vyshinsky in February, 1945, resulted in the forming of the Groza government, a coalition in name only, largely dominated by the Communist party. Western pressure at the Moscow conference in December, 1945, secured the addition of noncommunists but did not alter its fundamentally communist character. In Bulgaria, resignations by noncommunists during 1945 strengthened the communist position, and efforts by the West after the Moscow conference to broaden the government were unsuccessful. In Hungary, however, things moved in the opposite direction. The victory of the Small Holders party in a generally free election in November, 1945, led to the formation of a coalition in which the communists, although powerful, were not in complete control.

The treatment of the three "allied states," Czechoslovakia, Poland, and Yugoslavia, differed in form from that of the enemy states, but the actual result, in the case of Poland, was much the same. All three had ceased to exist during the war, although exiled governments in London claimed to represent their subjugated peoples. None had participated in military operations against the Soviet Union, although satellite governments in Slovakia and Croatia had done so. Two of them, the Poles and the Czechs, had formed military units within the Red Army. Among the Czechs at home, resistance had not been widespread, but a major revolt, in which communists and noncommunists cooperated closely, had occurred in Slovakia in 1944. The Czechoslovak government in exile, headed by President Beneš, enjoyed good relations with Moscow after 1941, and later concluded a military alliance and an agreement concerning the administration of territories occupied by the Red Army. The London exiles also reached a political accord with Czech and Slovak communists in Moscow, so that with the liberation of the country, a government of national unity, with substantial communist representation, but with a significant sharing of power by the traditional noncommunist parties, was formed under Beneš as President. The regime was forced to cede the eastern Ruthenian tip of the republic to the Soviet Union but was able to maintain the territorial integrity of the remainder.

The Poles were less fortunate. The London government in exile at first maintained diplomatic relations with the Soviet Union but became involved in serious disputes, particularly over the fate of the eastern areas of prewar Poland, annexed by the USSR in 1940. In 1942, Polish communists in Moscow sent agents to their occupied homeland to form a new Workers party, and the following year its leadership was assigned to Gomulka, a "native" communist, who had remained at home. When the Germans discovered the mass graves of Polish officers in the Katyn forest, and the Poles accused the Soviet authorities of their murder, the Russians broke off diplomatic relations with the London government. A largely communist Committee of National Liberation was then formed, with headquarters in Lublin. With the freeing of other parts of Poland, this provisional government, as it then called itself, recognized Soviet sovereignty in the eastern regions, and received in return the right to administer other liberated lands. As the Red Army advanced, the Home Army, organized by the London Poles, found itself treated as a hostile force, and the Warsaw revolt received no Soviet aid and was crushed by the Germans. Following the seizure of the devastated capital by the Red Army, and the expulsion of the German forces, the "Lublin government" was thus in complete command of the country. Only after the intervention of the Western powers at the Yalta conference in February, 1945, was the government reorganized as a coalition of five parties, including some representatives of the London Poles, in particular the peasant leader Mikolajczyk. The communists nonetheless retained their predominant influence. The Yalta conference recognized the Soviet seizure of the eastern lands and promised Poland territorial accessions in the north and the west.

Yugoslavia was a special case, differing from either Poland or Czechoslovakia. The exiled government in London, under King Peter, a coalition of the prewar parties, mainly Serbian in outlook, was rivaled at home by the partisan movement of Josef Brož-Tito, which included representatives of many prewar parties and all the nationalities of Yugoslavia, but was unquestionably communist in its leadership and program. A competing resistance army, headed by General Mihailović, minister of war in the London government, engaged in much fighting with the Titoist forces in what amounted to a large-scale civil war. As early as 1943, the communist-led movement had seized control of substantial territory, and had formed a provisional government. Receiving military aid from the Western governments, Tito's partisans were able to liberate a considerable part of former Yugoslavia, with a sizable contribution at the close of the war by the Red Army invasion of Serbia, including Belgrade. There was, however, no general Soviet occupation, so that with the withdrawal of the Russian armies, Tito's government was in full charge of the entire country. As a result of the Yalta conference, two representatives of the London government were added to the Tito regime without, however, seriously shifting the domestic balance of power.

The Albanian experience was unique. Occupied first by Italy, then by Germany, Albania had engaged in military operations against Yugoslavia and Greece and had annexed extensive territories of both. Rival partisan forces, as in Yugoslavia, waged war against each other and the occupants. The communist-led Liberation Front, under Enver Hoxha, was finally able in 1944 to seize power without any intervention by Soviet armed forces. There was no government in Western exile and no need therefore to make even a gesture to the West by the inclusion of noncommunists in the new regime. Complete communist rule, free of Soviet control but subject to marked Yugoslav influence, was established from the beginning.

THE STRUGGLE FOR POWER

By mid-1945, communism was well on the road to power in most of the Eastern European countries. The "old order" had been largely destroyed, both in the enemy states, where it had lasted until the war's end, and in the allied states, where it had been destroyed much earlier by foreign occupation. New political systems, sometimes without any links with the prewar regimes, sometimes, as in Czechoslovakia and Poland, with a tenuous constitutional continuity, had been established. Even more crucial, a fundamental realignment of forces had taken place with the rise to power of the communist parties, which had once been illegal or in permanent opposition, with the discrediting of many of the traditional governing parties and extreme rightist movements by their association with the prewar order or collaboration with the enemy, and with the emergence of new parties and new leaders in some of the old parties. Everywhere, coalition governments, based on national or people's fronts, had been formed, with the communists playing a significant, sometimes a decisive, role, and having the support of other left-wing elements. The more conservative forces were often rather uncomfortable partners in the coalitions and were increasingly forced into opposition. The end of military hostilities marked the beginning of intense conflict between the communists and their allies, on the one hand, who were seeking to accelerate social and economic change, even at the cost of democracy, and welcomed Soviet military and political aid, and the more moderate or conservative forces, on the other, who were trying to slow the course of reform and preserve freedom, and looked to the Western governments for moral and political support.

During the first phase of communist rule, that is, down to 1947 or 1948, a bitter struggle for power took place.[4] Taking full advantage of their positions of strength, and especially their control of the army, police, local governments, trade unions, and the mass media, the communists were able to undermine and ultimately destroy the other parties, whether in opposition or partners in coalition, by persecuting their leaders and splitting them internally. In the case of the social democrats, fusion with the Communist party was, with the aid of the socialist left wing, finally consummated. In Yugoslavia and Albania, the regimes were almost exclusively communist from the start, elections as early as 1945 documenting this fact. In Bulgaria and Rumania, the dominance of the Communist party was rapidly achieved, so that in elections in 1946, overwhelming victories for the government bloc were attained.[5] In Poland, Hungary, and Czechoslovakia, the process was slower, and ultimate victory for the noncommunists seemed not entirely excluded. In Poland, however, due to widespread terror against the Mikolajczyk party, a sweeping triumph of the communist bloc was scored in the elections of

[4] For fuller discussion of the initial phase, see Hugh Seton-Watson, *The East European Revolution* (3d ed., New York, 1956); Stephen D. Kertesz (ed.), *The Fate of East Central Europe* (Notre Dame, 1956); R. R. Betts (ed.), *Central and South East Europe, 1945–1948* (London and New York, 1950); Andrew Gyorgy, *Governments of Danubian Europe* (New York, 1949); A. Gyorgy, "The Internal Political Order," in Stephen Fischer-Galati (ed.), *Eastern Europe in the Sixties* (New York, 1963), chap. 6. The series *East-Central Europe under the Communists*, under the general editorship of Robert F. Byrnes (New York, 1956–57), is useful for the period up to 1955. Included are volumes edited by S. Skendi, *Albania;* L. A. Dellin, *Bulgaria;* V. Busek and N. Spulber, *Czechoslovakia;* E. Helmreich, *Hungary;* O. Halecki, *Poland;* S. Fischer-Galati, *Rumania;* R. F. Byrnes, *Yugoslavia.*

[5] On Rumania, see Ghita Ionescu, *Communism in Rumania, 1944–1962* (London, 1964). For other countries, see books cited in subsequent notes.

1947. In Hungary in the same year, noncommunist opposition still polled a strong vote, but was eliminated in subsequent months. Only in Czechoslovakia was a more or less genuine coalition maintained into 1948, when the crisis of February brought about a total shift in political power and the transformation of the coalition into a communist regime.[6] In East Germany, although several parties, including the Communist, came into existence under Soviet occupation, and increasingly exercised functions of administration in the provinces of the Soviet zone, political power remained with the occupation authorities until October, 1949, when the German Democratic Republic was formed. Although ostensibly a coalition, the regime was from the outset completely under communist control, as the elections in 1950 clearly revealed. The efforts of noncommunists and of Western governments to stem the tide of communism had proved vain in most of Eastern Europe. The fig leaf of national fronts and pseudo-coalitions could scarcely veil the reality of communist triumph.

The years prior to 1948 were characterized by radical change in all spheres of life in Eastern Europe, with industry nationalized, land tenure revised, the economy planned, the social-class structure overturned, national minorities expelled or transferred, and, as we have seen, the political patterns revolutionized.[7] This was, in communist doctrine, a "national and democratic revolution," with each country following its own "national path," distinct from each other and from the Soviet pattern. Certainly the revolution was not as purely communist or Soviet as might have been expected, and although exhibiting common features, varied in tempo and in form from state to state. Nonetheless, Yugoslavia and Albania had in fact largely skipped the "democratic" stage, and Bulgaria and Rumania had telescoped it severely, and had moved on toward more extreme goals without delay. The pace was slower in Czechoslovakia, Hungary, and Poland, reflecting not only differences in circumstance but also the participation of noncommunists in power, and the desire, perhaps genuine, of some communists for a moderate course and a less slavish following of Soviet commands and examples. As the tempo of

[6] See Paul E. Zinner, *Communist Strategy and Tactics in Czechoslovakia, 1918–48* (New York and London, 1963); Josef Korbel, *The Communist Subversion of Czechoslovakia, 1938–1948* (Princeton, 1959); H. Gordon Skilling, "The Prague Overturn in 1948," *Canadian Slavonic Papers*, IV (1960), 88–104.

[7] For fuller discussion of this and later stages, see the sources cited in footnote 4, as well as chapters 16, 17, and 18.

change increased in these states and the position of the Communist party was solidified, the differences among them lessened, the resemblance of the institutions of the so-called "people's democracies" to those of the Soviet system intensified, and the subordination to Soviet authority was more fully established. Communism of a national kind steadily declined in favor of a unified and uniform society throughout the area.

REVOLUTION BEGINS

The five years from 1948 until the death of Stalin in 1953 constituted a second and distinctive phase. Communist rule was complete everywhere, including Eastern Germany, with opposition forces eliminated and the coalitions and national fronts mere ornaments of a one-party system. Monarchies had become republics; old constitutions replaced by new ones; unicameral legislatures subordinated to centralized executive domination; civil liberties destroyed and religious freedom strictly curbed; nationalization extended and long-term planning introduced; collectivization of agriculture begun. This was, in the words of the communists, the "socialist" stage of the revolution and in many respects resembled the phase begun as early as 1945 in Yugoslavia and Albania. The approximation of all the people's democracies to the Soviet model was more and more effected, in no respect more strikingly than in the increasing terror, against communists and noncommunists alike, including a series of trials of communist leaders, first in Albania, then in Hungary and Bulgaria, and finally in Czechoslovakia and Rumania.[8]

Even in the heyday of complete Sovietization and Stalinization there were inevitable differences of policy and of practice, reflecting the distinctive circumstances of each state and the diverse viewpoints of communist party leaderships.[9] A striking example was the failure of the Polish regime to execute, or even to try, the former leader Gomulka, who was expelled from the Central Committee for "nationalist deviation" in 1949.[10] The outstanding anomaly was the case of Yugoslavia, the exponent of an

[8] See Z. K. Brzezinski, "The Patterns of Political Purges," in Henry L. Roberts (ed.), *The Satellites in Eastern Europe* (*The Annals of the American Academy of Political and Social Science*, CCCXVII [May, 1958]), pp. 79–87.

[9] Z. K. Brzezinski, *The Soviet Bloc: Unity and Conflict* (Cambridge, 1960), esp. chap. 3.

[10] For other distinctive features of Stalinism in Poland, see Richard Hiscocks, *Poland: Bridge for the Abyss?* (London, 1963), pp. 166–69.

extreme pro-Soviet line before 1948, but pursuing a course of its own after 1950. Basically communist in pattern, the Yugoslav "national path" nonetheless exhibited marked differences in the management of industry, in the treatment of agriculture, in local government, and in the interpretation of Marxism.[11] Above all, as a result of the break with the Soviet Union in 1948, Yugoslavia had vindicated its claim to be free of Soviet dictation and to follow an independent path. Whereas the other "satellites" were increasingly caught up in the web of Soviet controls, exerted through the Cominform, Comecon, and other bloc agencies, or through Soviet party, police, and other governmental links, the Yugoslavs stood alone and unfettered, a model of "national communism."

RELAXATION AND CRISIS

The death of Stalin in March, 1953, opened up a third phase in the life of the people's democracies, beginning with the so-called "thaw" or "new course," and culminating in the increasing spread of "national communism."[12] The events of the subsequent decade were the product of an interplay of Soviet policies and interventions in the satellites, and of native forces of discontent and rebellion, often aggravated by sharp differences within the communist leaderships. The period was characterized, not by evenness and continuity of development, but by zigzags, with temporary interruptions and frequent reversals. In varying degrees, however, the years witnessed a relaxation of the intense economic pressures, which had brought the economies of many countries to the verge of catastrophe, a lessening in the incidence of terror, and a certain loosening of the reins of cultural and intellectual control. In some cases, significant changes in the cadres of top

[11] For full discussion, see F. W. Neal, *Titoism in Action* (Berkeley, 1958); C. P. McVicker, *Titoism: Pattern for International Communism* (New York, 1957); and the more recent volume by G. W. Hoffman and F. W. Neal, *Yugoslavia and the New Communism* (New York, 1962). See also chapters 16, 17, and 18 below.

[12] For this development, see in particular Stephen D. Kertesz (ed.), *East Central Europe and the World: Developments in the Post-Stalin Era* (Notre Dame, 1962), and Brzezinski, *The Soviet Bloc: Unity and Conflict.* See also the symposium "The Soviet Satellite Nations: A Study of the New Imperialism," in *The Journal of Politics*, XX, 1 (February, 1958), and H. Ripka, *Eastern Europe in the Post-War World* (London, 1961). A good summary of this period is given by Robert Bass, "The Post-Stalin Era in Eastern Europe," *Problems of Communism*, XII, 2 (March–April 1963), 68–76.

leadership occurred, but nowhere, except briefly in Hungary, was the structure of communist power fundamentally altered. Just as the nature of Stalinism was not everywhere the same, so the reaction of the various states to Stalin's death and his later condemnation was not uniform and indeed showed impressive variations.[13]

Long before Khrushchev's assault on Stalinism, the very death of Stalin precipitated the first wave of change. Revolts occurred in Pilsen, Czechoslovakia, and in Berlin, in each case touched off by economic impositions, but were brought under control by concessions, and in Berlin by Soviet military force. The adoption of the "new course" in these and other East European states in the spring and summer of 1953 coincided with a similar program introduced by Malenkov in the Soviet Union. The slowest and slightest reactions came in Albania, Bulgaria, and Rumania. In Hungary and Poland, however, striking shifts of policy and in leadership occurred during the next three years, in the former case produced by drastic Soviet political interference, and in the latter, generated more by actions of the Poles themselves. In both countries, the role of the intellectuals was notable in creating an unprecedented political climate and pushing the regimes further along the road of change.[14]

The attack on Stalin at the Twentieth Congress of the CPSU in February, 1956, launched a fresh surge of reform. In Poland, continuing economic grievances produced a revolt in the city of Poznan, followed by lenient punishment of the ringleaders and serious concessions by the regime. The mounting crisis there and in Hungary reached a climax in the momentous events of October, 1956, which threatened the very existence of communism. In Poland, a tense confrontation between Gomulka, once again leader of Polish communism, and the Soviet chiefs, was resolved by a compromise, in which the new Polish leaders remained in command, relations with the Soviet Union were reframed on the basis of equality and autonomy, and revolutionary changes were introduced in the life of the country. In Hungary, however, where the impact of Stalinism had been most severe and the opposition to it most intense, the crisis got entirely out of hand,

[13] See the perceptive article by Edmund O. Stillman, "The Beginning of the 'Thaw,' 1953–55," in Roberts, *op. cit.*, pp. 12–21.

[14] For Poland, see Hiscocks, *op. cit.;* for Hungary, Paul E. Zinner, *Revolution in Hungary* (New York and London, 1962), and Ferenc A. Váli, *Rift and Revolt in Hungary: Nationalism Versus Communism* (Cambridge, 1961).

and culminated in open revolution, the breakdown of communist rule, and its restoration by direct Soviet military and political intervention.

Elsewhere there was no comparable revolt, and the previous policy of caution appeared to have been confirmed. Literary and intellectual ferment in Czechoslovakia, and more modest unrest in Bulgaria, in early 1956, were soon brought under control, so that these states remained stable and quiescent and weathered the storm in October. In Rumania, where a moderate policy had been launched as early as 1952, there was little unrest and no radical change in direction. In Albania and East Germany almost no serious modification of policy occurred. Yugoslavia, too, which had begun to evolve her own distinctive system much earlier, proceeded somewhat further along this path at the end of 1955 and in early 1956, and was not seriously shaken by the October events. The "fever," as Khrushchev once termed it, did not therefore spread from Warsaw and Budapest to the other capitals.

NATIONAL COMMUNISM

The five years after 1956 were years of consolidation and stabilization, but the "de-compression" or freeze-up varied from state to state. Although the events in Poland and Hungary led to the restoration of a harder line everywhere in the bloc, nowhere was there a return to outright Stalinism, except in Albania and to some extent in Eastern Germany. Even in Budapest, the post-1956 terror proved to be temporary and ultimately gave way to a moderate course more comparable to Poland than the other communist countries. In Poland itself, although a significant retreat was made from the advanced position of 1955–56, many of the October achievements were maintained, especially the decollectivization of agriculture, the agreement of the regime with the Catholic Church, the liberalization of intellectual life, and the relaxation of terror. Elsewhere a good many features of Stalinism remained, illustrated perhaps most strikingly by the renewed drive toward collectivization in Bulgaria, Czechoslovakia, Hungary, East Germany, and Rumania.

A new crisis came in 1961–62, with the renewed assault on Stalinism at the Twenty-second Congress of the CPSU, the expulsion of Albania from the bloc, and the mounting intensity of the Sino-Soviet conflict. This period, which will be dealt with more fully in the final chapter, was characterized by the ever-widening scope of national communism, in the sense of increasing differentiation among communist states and expanding freedom of action for each.[15] Poland, Hungary, and Yugoslavia, which had gone furthest in demolishing Stalinism, sought to maintain this status quo. Albania, Bulgaria, Czechoslovakia, East Germany, and Rumania, where the old order had been least changed, were reluctant to proceed along the path of reform, but, as later events in Czechoslovakia in 1963 and Rumania in 1964 demonstrated, were bound to feel the long-term impact. In a sense the people's democracies were returning to the "national path" of the immediate postwar period, but this time as a result not of coercion by Moscow but rather of their own independent choice. The imposed uniformity of the years 1948 to 1953 had been artificial in the extreme and likely, in view of the cultural, economic, geographic, and historic heterogeneity of Eastern Europe, to be ultimately explosive and destructive. Especially in the new climate after Stalin, there set in a nationalizing of communism, manifesting itself in ever more variation of policies and practices. The regimes continued to exhibit uniform features, too, but always expressed in a counterpoint of similarity and dissimilarity, of continuity and change. The removal of Khrushchev in 1964 did not check the trend toward national communism for which he had been so largely responsible, and led indeed to few significant alterations in Eastern Europe.

[15] See H. Gordon Skilling, *Communism National and International: Eastern Europe after Stalin* (Toronto, 1964); Adam Bromke (ed.), *The Communist States at the Crossroads: Between Moscow and Peking* (New York, 1965); William E. Griffith (ed.), *Communism in Europe: Continuity, Change and the Sino-Soviet Dispute* (2 vols.; Cambridge, 1964–), vol. 1; Fischer-Galati, *op. cit.*, esp. ch. 7.

PART TWO
THE PATTERN OF POWER

Introduction

The communist governments in Eastern Europe, like all others, are systems of power in which the rulers have control or influence over the actions of the ruled in the political sphere. Our concern must be to analyze the distribution of power and its exercise in these states. Who rules, that is, holds the ultimate power? How was (and is) that power acquired? How is it exercised and enforced? For what purposes is it employed? And is it in any way limited, or controlled, by the ruled? Answers to these and related questions will afford us a portrait of the "real constitution," in the sense of the actually existing structure or "anatomy" of power, that is, the pattern according to which power is habitually exercised by certain persons in certain ways for certain purposes. Because the power relations of any political system are constantly shifting and changing, our analysis must be a dynamic one, taking into account the evolution of each state in successive stages of communist rule. Moreover, within the context of the common features of all, the distinctive aspects of each of them, especially of Yugoslavia, must be examined.

In some countries of the world, the pattern of power is reduced to writing in the form of a fundamental or constitutional law, which, however, never gives a full or completely authentic picture of the actual anatomy of power and may give a misleading one. The unwritten constitution is equally, if not more, important, sometimes entirely replacing a written one. All constitutions are, moreover, subject to secular changes in the distribution of power, often without express amendment, as the result of the pressure of interests and social forces, and sometimes the arbitrary actions of certain persons or agencies. No government can be exclusively one of laws, and not of men. Only by a study of both the written *and* unwritten patterns of government, of the roles of men *and* of laws, can we penetrate to the real constellation of forces. Even if, as in the communist states, the written constitutions seem to have little influence on the actual working of the systems, and indeed seem to veil or camouflage the realities, they cannot be ignored. They give some information, however distorted, about the institutions and procedures of governing, and even more significant, a portrayal of the "ideal," the theoretical expression of the political system as its rulers wish to have it understood. Needless to say, the study of this "ideological" component must be supplemented by an analysis of the correlation of ideal to reality, and of the genuine relationship of ruler and ruled.

The possession of a written constitution must not be confused with the existence of a "constitutional" system. Many states *with* such a charter cannot claim to be "constitutional," and a few, notably Britain, *without* one, can with justice be so described. In contrast to an autocracy, a constitutional system is one of "limited power," in which the powers of government are shared among various organs, and between these organs and the people as a whole. Authority is exercised through regular procedures that cannot be arbitrarily ignored by individual participants in the political process. Moreover, the distribution of power cannot be easily changed or destroyed, and may be altered only by recognized methods. Normally, too, a constitutional state reserves to the people, or some part of them, certain rights that cannot be overridden by the established authorities and that can be protected by due process of law.

In spite of their elaborate constitutional documents, the Eastern European governments, like the Soviet, cannot be regarded as genuinely "constitutional." On the face of it, their charters distribute the functions of government among certain institutions, proclaim the basic rights of the citizens, and protect them against arbitrary action by their rulers. What is lacking, however, is that indispensable ingredient, namely, a relatively fixed sharing of power, which is protected by procedures and independent agencies capable of guaranteeing that no one oversteps his jurisdiction and arrogates prerogatives rightfully belonging elsewhere, and that no single holder of power amasses complete and unrestricted authority. Moreover, fundamental changes in the pattern may easily be made, with or without an amendment of the written provisions. What we have is a system of "total power," concentrated in the hands of a single party and its leadership, which effectively controls all the other organs of government and is not seriously limited in law or in fact. This is a government of men, not of laws, a system in which legal procedures and provisions play a minor role and may be manipulated, more or less at will, by the men who hold power.

This is not to say that the exercise of power in Eastern Europe is entirely without pattern. As in every state, there is a customary configuration of authority, indicating how and by whom decisions are made, a habit of behavior normally followed by the rulers, even if this differs radically from that set forth in the fundamental laws. Power is exercised by a ruling few, who occupy certain defined positions in the top organs of party and government. There is a conventional process of decision-making, largely monopolized by the rulers, but with a procedure of deliberation normally employed in the institutions of party and government. There is even a kind of representation of interests, by which the viewpoints of special groups are brought to bear on the making of policy. There is also a mechanism of enforcement consisting of agencies of administration, at the center and in the localities, which employ certain familiar practices of coercion and persuasion. All of this constitutes a regular design of action, which is, however, not securely safeguarded by enforceable rules, and is often ignored or altered with impunity. As in every state, too, there is an actual balancing of powers, especially noticeable since the death of Stalin, as various social forces and groups to some extent counteract each other and prevent the exclusive and unlimited dominance of one or the other. Group conflict, if not constitutional rules, may thus temper the absolute exercise of power.

5: Constitutional Forms

The communist governments in Eastern Europe were not slow to draft written formulations of the basic principles according to which their systems purported to operate. In the relatively short period of two decades, there has been a sequence of constitutions, often succeeding each other with astonishing rapidity. In all of these countries, there were initial transitional periods of varying lengths, during which institutions were created to carry on the business of government. In Bulgaria, Czechoslovakia, Poland, and Rumania, prewar constitutions were provisionally restored, although adapted to the new situation by wartime or postwar legal measures. In Albania, Hungary, and Yugoslavia, entirely new agencies of government were formed, without even a tenuous connection with the prewar systems. In Yugoslavia, these had already emerged in embryo in the liberated territories during the course of partisan action.

THE SEQUENCE OF CONSTITUTIONS

After a lapse of one or more years, constitutions were enacted in all the communist states, in varying degrees, amalgamating Soviet constitutional notions, indigenous national traditions, and democratic forms and procedures. In Poland and Czechoslovakia, in particular, the initial constitutions, reflecting the transitional nature of the period, were less Marxist in spirit and less Soviet in inspiration than might have been expected, and embodied important elements of precommunist patterns. Elsewhere, for instance, in Albania, Bulgaria, Rumania, and Yugoslavia, where full communist power was already established, the constitutions showed from the start a much clearer imprint of the Soviet model.

With several exceptions, the early constitutions were replaced by others that more accurately expressed the situation created by the termination of the multiparty coalitions. Those enacted in 1949 and after were much more clearly and admittedly influenced by the Soviet pattern, although, somewhat paradoxically, more by the Stalin constitution of 1936 than the Soviet charters of 1918 and 1924, which might have been considered more appropriate for an early stage of communist authority. As a rule, the later a constitution was introduced, the more radical was its break with past traditions and constitutional forms, and the more it reflected Soviet influence and Marxist thinking. The two exceptions were Bulgaria, where the strongly Soviet-type

CONSTITUTIONAL DEVELOPMENT*

	I *Initial Constitution*	II *Transitional Constitution*	III *Advanced Constitution*
Albania	1946		1950
Bulgaria	1944(1879)	1947	
Czecho-slovakia	1945(1920)	1948	1960
East Germany	1949		
Hungary	1946		1949
Poland	1947(1921)		1952
Rumania	1944(1923)	1948	1952 and 1965
Yugoslavia	1946	1953	1963

* Texts of the constitutions are not readily available in English. Detailed commentary is given in the series *East-Central Europe under the Communists*, ed. Robert F. Byrnes (New York, 1956–57), and in Vladimir Gsovski and Kazimierz Grzybowski, *Government, Law and Courts in the Soviet Union and East Europe* (2 vols.; London and The Hague, 1959). Standard Soviet commentaries are N. P. Farberov, *Gosudarstvennoe pravo stran narodnoi demokratii* (Moscow, 1949), and V. F. Kotok (ed.), *Gosudarstvennoe pravo stran narodnoi demokratii* (Moscow, 1961). A brief comparative analysis is given by C. E. Black, "The People's Democracies of Eastern Europe," in Taylor Cole, *European Political Systems* (New York, 1953). A fuller comparison, with the texts of some constitutions, is made by Samuel L. Sharp, *New Constitutions in the Soviet Sphere* (Washington, 1950). Full analysis of the Czechoslovak development is made in H. Gordon Skilling, "The Czechoslovak Constitutional System: The Soviet Impact," *Political Science Quarterly*, LXVII, 2 (June, 1952), 198–224; H. Gordon Skilling, "Czechoslovakia: Government in Communist Hands," *The Journal of Politics*, XVII, 3 (August, 1955), 424–47; and H. Gordon Skilling, "The Czechoslovak Constitution of 1960 and the Transition to Communism," *The Journal of Politics*, XXIV, 1 (February, 1962), 142–66. Successive Yugoslav constitutions, including the one of 1963, are analyzed by G. W. Hoffman and F. W. Neal, *Yugoslavia and the New Communism* (New York, 1962), chap. 13. For an interesting comparison of communist legal systems, including China, see John N. Hazard, "The Soviet Legal Pattern Spreads Abroad," *University of Illinois Law Forum*, Spring, 1964, pp. 277–98.

constitution of 1947 has not been replaced, and Eastern Germany, where the one introduced in 1949, "democratic" in form, has also not been superseded. Ironically enough, the changes in the political atmosphere occasioned by the death of Stalin and the trend toward de-Stalinization did not bring about the enactment of new constitutions, except in 1960 in Czechoslovakia where the Stalinist climate was still maintained. Elsewhere, for instance, in Hungary and Poland, measures were introduced to infuse greater life into the existing organs of parliamentary representation, without, however, a constitutional amendment or any basic alteration of formal institutions.

As a Soviet textbook has stated, the constitutions of the people's democracies were in a process of "uninterrupted development."[1] In some states, the fundamental laws have been modified by significant amendments, introduced by unanimous parliamentary votes, or the functioning of political institutions has been changed *de facto* without any legal alteration at all. The enactment of constitutions has been in any case extremely easy to effect, involving little more than basic decisions by the party hierarchies, legal formulation of the final documents by party-controlled parliamentary committees acting in secret, and subsequent ceremonial ratification by the parliaments. Only in the earlier stages in Bulgaria, Czechoslovakia, and Poland, were alternative proposals submitted by noncommunist parties, and controversial debates permitted. Since then, so-called "national discussions" of the drafts by the people at large have been intended mainly for propaganda purposes and have effected few, if any, significant alterations. This, and the fact that the process of revision has been swift but sporadic, and that some countries have not even bothered to revise their long-since obsolete constitutions, confirms how little meaning these fundamental laws have in the political life of the communist countries.

CONSTITUTIONS AND IDEOLOGY

The main purpose of the charters was ideological rather than legal, setting forth the prevailing theory of state and party at the time of their enactment, and requiring periodic alteration as doctrine changed.[2] As long as the "people's democracies" were interpreted, not as "dictatorships of the proletariat," but as regimes based on an alliance of several classes, the constitutions were designed to embody the theory that power belonged to "the people" as a whole, and deliberately omitted any idea of a dominant class or a ruling party. With the communist seizure of complete power, and the subsequent theoretical identification of the people's

[1] V. F. Kotok (ed.), *Gosudarstvennoe pravo stran narodnoi demokratii* (Moscow, 1961), p. 197.

[2] See Chapter 17 for fuller discussion of ideological questions.

democracies with proletarian dictatorships, the fundamental laws had to be revised to incorporate the concept of the sovereignty of the working or toiling people (proletariat and peasantry) and the notion of the Communist party as the vanguard or directing force. In this respect, therefore, the constitutions enacted at later dates were ideologically more "advanced" than the others.[3] In particular, the Albanian, Hungarian, and Rumanian charters, and even more strikingly the 1960 Czechoslovak document, gave unabashed expression to the ruling position of the working class and the Communist party, exceeding in this respect even the modest formulation of the Soviet constitution.[4] Strangely enough, however, some countries remained satisfied with their antiquated documents, and even the Polish constitution of 1952 made no allusion to the predominant role of the Communist party.

In similar fashion, the "socialist" character of these states was not at first proclaimed. As the constitutions were said to express in legal terms what had already been accomplished, they could not be regarded as charters of socialism in countries that were still laying the foundations of this system. At most they provided, as the earlier Soviet constitutions had done, a framework within which this goal could be fully achieved, and presumably would be replaced eventually, as in the USSR, by new constitutions. If the term "socialism" was used at all, it was as an objective of the future and not as an existing reality. The earlier, and even some later, constitutions referred to the economy as a mixed one, embodying three sectors—socialist, cooperative, and private—and governed by a general plan. Public property was that sector of industry which had been nationalized. Cooperative property was that owned by peasants' cooperatives, which had not yet been widely replaced by collective farms. Private property, notably the right of the peasants to own land, was also proclaimed. The constitutions did not, however, exclude a rapid socialization of the economy and the eventual elimination of the private sector, and became increasingly out-of-date as this process advanced. To date, however, only one state within the bloc, Czechoslovakia, has documented the achievement of socialism in a new constitution and renamed itself a "socialist republic." Other states that have completed the collectivization of agriculture and have advanced as far as Czechoslovakia on the road to socialism, for instance, Bulgaria, Hungary, and Rumania, have not followed suit. Two

[3] Sharp, *op. cit.*, pp. 18–22.

[4] Albania (1949), Art. 21; Hungary (1952), Art. 56; Czechoslovakia (1960), Art. 4; Rumania (1952), Art. 86.

of them, Rumania and Bulgaria, announced in the early sixties impending revisions of their constitutions in the light of the achievement of socialism, but did not proceed further, in all probability due to the uncertainty occasioned by the Soviet announcement of its intention to amend its constitution in line with the beginning of the transition from socialism to communism.[5]

Yugoslav constitutional development has also reflected the evolution of communist theory. Whereas most constitutions of Eastern Europe more and more resembled the Soviet, the Yugoslav moved in the opposite direction. Although the 1946 charter followed the Soviet pattern rather closely, more so indeed than other transitional constitutions, it was soon outmoded by the distinctive institutions Yugoslavia developed after its break with the USSR. Only in 1953, however, was a new charter, much less Soviet in spirit, introduced to codify the practices that had emerged after 1950. By 1963, the Yugoslavs felt it necessary to document the attainment of "socialism" and to describe their state as a socialist republic in a new constitution, which formulated an original system of government strikingly different from the more or less standard formulae of other communist countries. In a manner similar to others, however, the Communist party (renamed the League of Communists) was cited as "the organized leading force of the working class and working people," and "the fundamental initiator of political activity."

The Eastern European states were described, under their constitutions, as "people's republics." For some—Albania, Bulgaria, Hungary, Rumania, and Yugoslavia—this signified the abolition of the hereditary monarchy. Apart from this, the term gave no precise indication of the character of the systems, but was designed to distinguish them in theory not only from "bourgeois democratic republics," but also from the Soviet republics in the USSR. In fact, the distinctive character of the latter system, based originally on a hierarchy of soviets, had long since been superseded by institutions more "parliamentary" in form. Whatever the legal formulation might be in Eastern Europe, the reality was that the new republics had been from the beginning, or had soon become, communist or single-party republics. In most cases only one party existed. Where there was more than one, and a coalition government based on a so-called National Front, there were no opposition parties, and the satellite parties openly proclaimed their devotion to the ruling party. Ironically enough,

[5] In 1965, the projected constitution was formally approved by the Rumanian assembly.

even when constitutional endorsement of the privileged position of the Communist party was later given, the states were not identified as "soviet republics," as might have been expected in view of their approximation to Soviet reality.

THE FORMS OF GOVERNMENT

The hierarchy of institutions set up by the constitutions, even in their successive variants, was similar in all countries except Yugoslavia.[6] The difference was more in name than in substance. All had representative assemblies, directly elected by the entire population on the basis of unrestricted universal franchise, and endowed with the plenitude of legislative authority. In some instances, traditional names were retained, such as the Sejm (Poland), the Skupshtina (Yugoslavia), or National Assembly (Bulgaria, Czechoslovakia, and Hungary). Elsewhere they were called the People's Assembly (Albania), the Grand National Assembly (Rumania), or the People's Chamber (East Germany). Apart from Yugoslavia, the assembly was always unicameral. Under the 1946 constitution, the Yugoslav parliament consisted of two houses, one representing the individual republics; in the 1953 version, the latter was replaced by a Council of Producers, and in the latest, by an elaborate system of six chambers, to be discussed later.

Almost all, on the Soviet pattern, had a collective *Presidium*[7] which acted as the collegial head of the state, but which also possessed interim legislative authority in the form of the right to issue decrees; judicial functions in the interpretation of the laws; and, in some cases, the right to supervise local authorities. There were other variations. The Yugoslav Presidium, for instance, did not have legislative powers in the 1946 charter and was abolished entirely in 1953. In Czechoslovakia, the Presidium occupied a less important role, not serving as a collective presidency, and under the 1960 constitution no longer enjoyed the right of decree or of constitutional review. Some of these states also possessed a single-man presidency, combining it in various ways with the collective Presidium. Although this departure from Soviet practice was abandoned by Poland in 1952 and by East Germany in 1960, it was retained by both Czechoslovakia and Yugoslavia in their most recent constitutions.

[6] These institutions will be discussed more fully in later chapters.

[7] Called the Council of State in East Germany and Poland, and after 1960 in Rumania; Presidential Council in Hungary.

Apart from presidential or presidial functions, the executive power was exercised by a cabinet, usually called the Council of Ministers (in Yugoslavia, the Federal Executive Council), which was responsible to the assembly. In Czechoslovakia, the executive power was shared by the cabinet with the presidency, the powers of which were slightly reduced in the 1960 constitution. All of the countries had systems of courts and of local authorities, to be discussed later, which greatly resembled each other in their functions and in their relationship with the main political organs.

Constitutional commentary in Eastern Europe, as in the Soviet Union, has rejected the principle of the separation of powers as a bourgeois theory designed to obscure the fact of parliamentary impotence and executive predominance, and, hence, the reality of class rule. The Soviet doctrine of the "unification of power" was proclaimed by communist jurists as expressing the essence of their systems. True, there was an allocation of functions to separate legislative, executive, and judicial organs, but the authority of the last two was presumed to be derived from the legislature, which in turn embodied the will of the sovereign people. In fact, of course, as will be shown more fully in later chapters, the legislative assembly was in most cases largely ceremonial, always acting with unanimity, and was entirely controlled by the cabinet, the agency of executive authority. The courts, too, although ostensibly independent, were the creatures of the executive. The presidium of the assembly was also much less significant in fact than its wide array of powers would suggest. Moreover, the organs of government were fused together as a result of the total control of all of them by the Communist party. Although a separation of powers is not an indispensable feature of limited or constitutional government, its absence in Eastern Europe removed the checking and balancing of the various organs that might have helped to protect the rights assigned to them under the constitution. Nor was the representative system a guarantee of popular sovereignty. On the surface, a faultless system of representative democracy existed, without any restrictions on the suffrage. In fact, however, the single party dominated the process of nominations and elections, so that the assemblies were predominantly of one party, and expressed the will of that party rather than of the people. It might also be noted that the elaborate formulation of rights, including both civil and political, economic and national, did not in fact protect the citizens against arbitrary action by state or party or by other organizations, once again because of party control of the courts. Where the constitution itself did not, as in some cases, prohibit the "abuse" of these rights against the interests of the state, they might simply be ignored *de facto* without any recourse by the individual to an independent guarantor.

This concentration of authority was buttressed by certain other features designed to eliminate competing sources of power. All of the constitutions took for granted, without expressly stating it, the principle of civil supremacy over the military, thus eliminating the armed forces as a constitutional factor. The concept of an established church or religion was rejected, and the separation of Church and State was proclaimed. In fact, this meant the subjection of the former to the latter, since the churches were in the main financed and regulated by the government, and in some cases their leading dignitaries were imprisoned. Deprived of constitutional authority, the church, like the army, continued to be a real factor of potential, or actual, influence. The socialization of the economy, the progressive elimination of private enterprise, and the formation of a planned system signified that personal and corporate possessions were eliminated as sources of real power. Finally, apart from Yugoslavia, a federal distribution of authority was avoided, so that state rights or national autonomy did not challenge the centralized exercise of state power.

6: Party Realities

Real power in the "people's democracies" has rested, as we have seen, with the party of the communists, sometimes known, as in Bulgaria, Czechoslovakia, and formerly in Yugoslavia, as the Communist party, elsewhere masquerading under other names, such as the Polish United Workers' party (PUWP), or the Socialist Unity party of Germany (SED).[1] Even when the "leading role" of the communists was formally recognized, as in most of the constitutions drafted after 1949, the monopoly of power enjoyed, and the total domination of all organs of governments, was by no means fully revealed. The leaders themselves, however, were not averse to proclaiming the actual supremacy of their party. Klement Gottwald, for instance, at the Ninth Party Congress of the Communist party of Czechoslovakia in 1949 declared: "Today the Communist Party of Czechoslovakia incarnates the unity of our working class and its leading role in all spheres of our public life."[2]

THE PARTY STATUTE

Each of the parties had a "statute" or set of organizational rules, describing its structure and organs and setting forth the basic principles of its operation, which represented therefore a kind of secondary "constitution" of the political system.[3] Even in the

[1] Other titles were as follows: Albanian Workers' party (AWP); Hungarian Workers' (Communist) party (HWP), and after its October, 1956, reorganization, Hungarian Socialist Workers' party (HSWP); Rumanian Workers' party (RWP), renamed Rumanian Communist party (RCP) in 1965. The Communist party of Yugoslavia (CPY) in 1952 became officially the League of Communists of Yugoslavia (LCY).

[2] As quoted in H. Gordon Skilling, "Czechoslovakia: Government in Communist Hands," *The Journal of Politics*, XVII, 3 (August, 1955), 424–47. See the open admission of the leading position of the parties in Soviet textbooks, such as V. F. Kotok (ed.), *Gosudarstvennoe pravo stran narodnoi demokratii* (Moscow, 1961), pp. 87–91.

[3] None of these statutes, except that of the CPSU, is available in the English language, since, unlike the constitutions, they are not published and distributed for foreign consumption. They are not regarded as secret documents, however, and can be purchased, in the native language, in local bookstores. See, for instance, *Organisační řád Komunistické strany Československa* (Prague, 1949), and *Statut Saveza Komunista Jugoslavije* (Belgrade, 1958).

For the organization of the parties, see Carola Stern, *Porträt einer bolschewistischen Partei, Entwicklung, Funktion und Situation der SED* (Köln, 1957), esp. chap. IX; Edward Taborsky, *Communism in Czecho-*

early stages of communist rule, these charters, in contrast to the state constitutions, followed closely the model of the Communist party of the Soviet Union, and embodied what was called the Leninist organizational principles of "a party of a special type." Although they thus required less drastic and frequent modification, the statutes went through periodic revisions at successive party congresses, often copying the most recent alterations in the CPSU.[4] Some differences with the latter and among the several parties continued to exist, mainly, however, in nomenclature and wording, and without serious effect on the general method of work. Somewhat more meaningful were the changes in form and function of the Communist party of Yugoslavia, when it was renamed the League of Communists of Yugoslavia, although, as will be seen below, in many respects it continued to resemble the parties of the Soviet bloc. Like the state constitutions, the party rules did not accurately mirror either the manner in which the organs performed their functions or in which power was actually distributed between them and the members. In particular, the position of the party in the political system as a whole, as described, was fairly remote from the real situation. Nor were there serious limitations on the freedom of the leaders to make the basic decisions, or effective safeguards of the rights of the members and the various organs. Nonetheless, the statutes gave some information on the party's agencies and procedures, and when supplemented by a knowledge of the realities, indicated the pattern of action normally pursued in the conduct of public affairs.

Revisions of the statutes, like amendments to the constitutions, were mainly motivated by doctrinal considerations and the desire to reflect the successive stages of political and ideological development. Prior to 1948, for example, in the states where full

---

slovakia, 1948–1960 (Princeton, 1961), chap. III; G. W. Hoffman and F. W. Neal, *Yugoslavia and the New Communism* (New York, 1962), chap. 12; Richard F. Staar, *Poland, 1944–1962: The Sovietization of a Captive People* (New Orleans, 1962), chap. 9; the series *East-Central Europe under the Communists*, under the general editorship of Robert F. Byrnes (New York, 1956–57); Joseph Rothschild, *Communist East Europe* (New York, 1964).

For the legal status and the actual powers of the party in the USSR, see B. Meissner, "Party Supremacy: Some Legal Questions," *Problems of Communism*, XIV, 2 (March–April, 1965), 28–33.

[4] The 1965 revision of the RCP statute embodied several strikingly new clauses that differentiated it notably from the CPSU.

communist power had not yet been established, the party was described, not, in the customary Soviet terms, as "the vanguard of the proletariat," but, as in the Czechoslovak case, as "the leading force in the nation," and was linked with national and democratic traditions and with "progressive forces" throughout the world. Its position of political paramountcy was also less explicitly formulated. After 1948, however, these purportedly national mass movements were openly transformed into "Bolshevik" parties. The CPC, for instance, was defined in its 1949 statute as "the organized vanguard of the working class," linked by the bonds of "proletarian internationalism" with the working class of the world and inspired by "the world view of Marxism-Leninism," and its leading position in state organs and mass organizations was expressly stated. Still later, after the CPSU had in 1952 abandoned its own identification as a proletarian party and employed broader national terms, the other parties usually followed suit. In Bulgaria, for example, the party was defined as "a voluntary militant alliance of like-minded persons, organized by the working class, the toiling peasants and the working intelligentsia."[5] Somewhat paradoxically, the Yugoslav party, even after 1952, continued to call itself "the organized political power of the working class and the working people," and was said to be guided by "the theory of scientific socialism." The 1965 RCP statute retained the assertion of the primacy of the working class, but described the party as "the leading force of the people."

PARTY STRUCTURE

Structurally the parties were almost identical to each other, being fashioned on the pyramidal style of the CPSU. The foundation was formed by thousands of "basic" or "primary" organizations, created in factory, farm, or other institutions, wherever three or more communists worked together. This organization on the basis of "production" was preferred to that of "territory," although at various times some of the parties provided for primary units in neighborhoods or villages.[6] The intermediate level was formed by the district and regional organizations, consisting of

[5] The BCP statute of 1954. A similar formula was employed by the CPC in its statutes of 1954, 1958, and 1962.

[6] Such organizations were abolished by the CPC in 1952 but were continued in some of the other parties. In 1961, the CPSU, which had traditionally employed *only* the production principle, provided for the possibility of territorial organizations in villages and apartments.

PARTY STRUCTURE

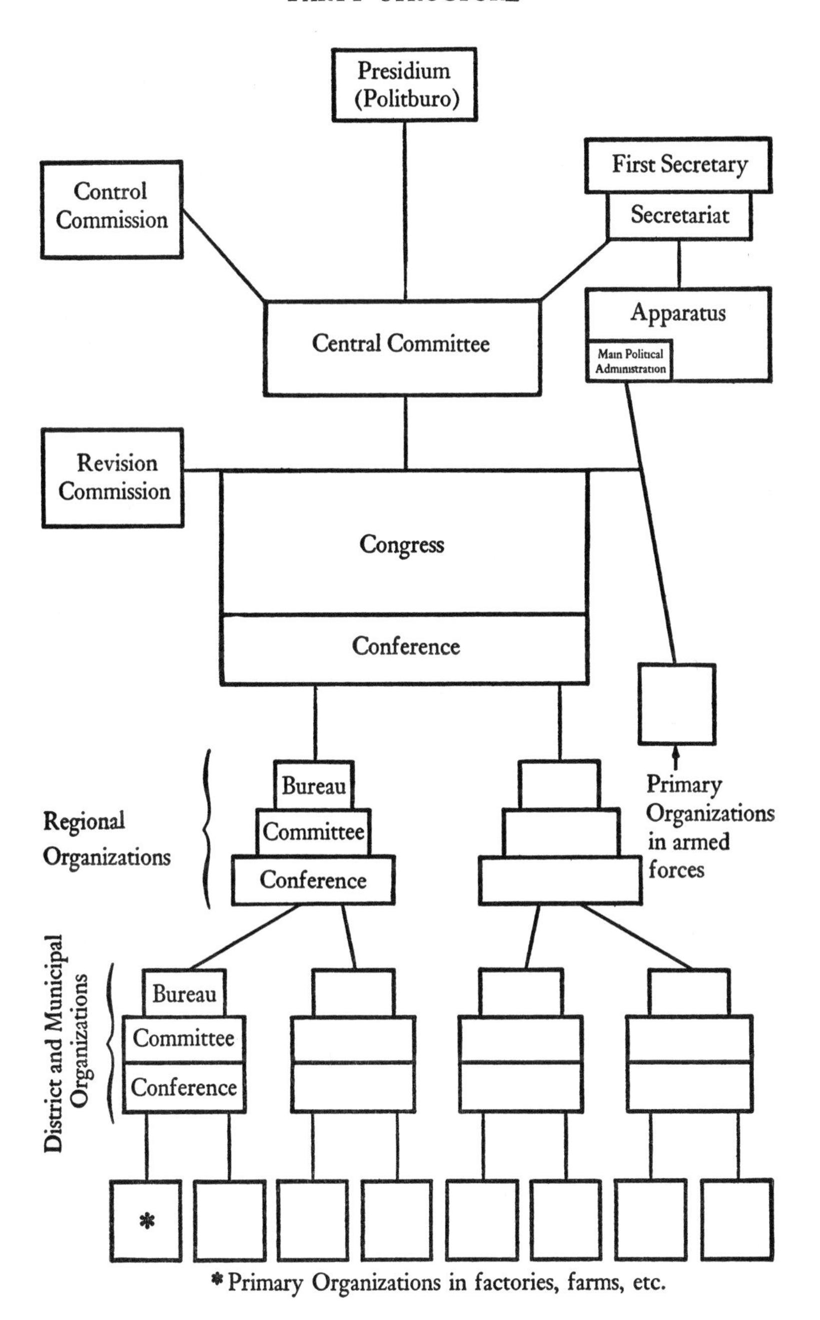

* Primary Organizations in factories, farms, etc.

annual conferences of delegates from primary and district bodies, respectively, and permanent executive committees headed by secretaries. At this level the structure was strictly territorial.[7] Above the districts and regions was the *Congress*, meeting at least every three or four years, and consisting of delegates from the inferior territorial units; it was regarded as "the supreme organ," determining fundamental policy. A *Conference* on a national basis could also be held when necessary, to deal with urgent problems. At the peak of the pyramid were the *Central Committee* and a cluster of smaller bodies that were in theory the creatures of the former, but were in practice its guides and directors. The Central Committee, consisting of about one hundred persons (full members and candidates), and meeting several times a year, was responsible for determining policy between congresses and managing the day-to-day work. The most important decisions were taken in its name. Its "plenums" were the occasions for the enunciation of key policies and their endorsement, and represented the successive milestones in the party's history.

The smaller agencies at the pinnacle, usually known as the *Politburo* (or *Presidium*)[8] and *Secretariat*, were "formed" by the Central Committee, normally by the unanimous adoption of a predetermined slate. Although their functions were not explicitly defined, and their exact relationship to each other was not clari-

[7] The parties usually subordinated their primary units in the armed forces directly to a Central Committee branch located within the Ministry of the Armed Forces and called the Main Political Administration. Until 1965, the RWP had similar arrangements in the appropriate ministries for party organizations in the police, railroads, state farms, and major socialist construction projects. After the revision of 1965, the Rumanian party subordinated the party units in the armed forces to the committees in the region and district, and to the Central Committee itself.

None of the parties copied the 1962 division of the regional committees of the CPSU (reversed after the fall of Khrushchev) into separate industrial and agricultural committees.

[8] The Politburo of the CPSU was renamed the Presidium in 1952 just prior to Stalin's death and has retained that designation ever since. The term had already been used by the CPC for some years, was changed to Political Buro in 1954, and changed back to Presidium in 1962. The Hungarian organ was officially called the Political Committee, but later resumed the term used by all the other bloc parties, namely, Politburo. The Yugoslav party, which used this term prior to 1952, adopted the name Executive Committee.

In 1965, the RCP renamed its Politburo the Permanent Presidium, retained the Secretariat, and established an Executive Committee, including all seven members of the Presidium and eight others. The Committee was to manage party activity between sessions of the Central Committee.

fied, there is little doubt that the main strands of power came together in these two bodies.[9] Before 1952, most of the parties, like the CPSU, possessed an organizational secretariat or bureau, presumably sharing duties of party management with the Secretariat, but they later followed the CPSU in abandoning this apparently superfluous piece of machinery.[10] Assisting these leading organs in the performance of their tasks was the *Apparatus* of the Central Committee, an administrative staff of many hundreds of full-time employees, under the direction of members of the Secretariat. At its head stood the *General Secretary*, concentrating, like Stalin, the main levers of the entire party mechanism in his hands. In the CPC, until 1951, and in the PUWP, until 1954, the party chairmanship was the key post, and was in each case occupied by the leading communist.[11] After the lapse of the general secretaryship in the CPSU (which is believed to have occurred just prior to, or right after, Stalin's death), its functions were exercised by what came to be called in the CPSU and in the other parties the *First Secretary*. Where the chairmanship existed, it too was dropped. The CPY was the only party to retain the term General Secretary, but the Rumanian party reintroduced it in 1965. Two other central organs of much less significance existed in all the parties, namely, the *Party Control Commission*, responsible for the enforcement of discipline on members, and the *Central Auditing* or *Revision Commission*, with the task of auditing financial resources and expenditures.[12]

Although the structure of the League of Communists of Yugoslavia was in the main similar, it was adapted to the multinational character of the state in a manner resembling the CPSU. In each of the six republics, a distinct party existed, with its own

[9] For further discussion of the two organs, see Chapter 8.

[10] For a short time after 1951, the CPC had two secretariats, one "political," and the other "organizational," presumably to eliminate the danger of an independent secretariat. Paradoxically, this change occurred at almost the same time the CPSU was abolishing its Orgburo and reducing its central organs to two. In 1954, the CPC conformed to pattern by eliminating the political secretariat.

[11] See Chapter 7. The office of chairman was abolished in the CPC in 1953 and in the PUWP in 1954. Until 1952, there was a chairmanship in the HWP, but it was an honorific position of little power.

[12] Again there has been some variation. The Albanians have had two separate agencies, an Auditing Commission and a Revision Commission. The CPC on the other hand, in 1962, for the first time combined the Auditing and the Control Commissions in one body. In 1965, the RCP replaced the Control Commission with a Control Collegium, with apparently reduced functions.

Congress, Central Committee, Executive Committee, and Secretariat. As in the Soviet Union, these were regarded not as independent but as integral parts of a single all-national organization, and were entitled to define their own "political tasks," but "on the basis of the political line of the CPY." Each of the six, working within the distinctive conditions of its own republic, guided and directed the republican state organs, and each was strongly represented in the party's central agencies. In subordinate national regions, such as the Kosmet or Vojvodina, there were no special party units other than those existing in all areas of local jurisdiction.[13]

In Czechoslovakia, there existed a Communist party of Slovakia (CPS), with its own local organizations and all-Slovak agencies, including a Congress, a Central Committee, and a Politburo (or Presidium), and until 1952, a Chairman and a General Secretary, and after that date, a Control Commission and a Secretariat, headed by a First Secretary. During the war years, and to 1948, the Slovak party had been entirely separate, although acknowledging the supreme direction of the leaders of the CPC. After fusion in 1948, the CPS was defined in the statute of 1949 (continued in 1962) as a part of the CPC and was said to "carry out the policy of the CPC in Slovakia in agreement with the decisions of the central committee of the CPC." The position of the Slovak branch has not, however, been a strong one in view of the predominantly Czech character of the membership and leadership of the party as a whole.

DEMOCRACY AND CENTRALISM

Ever since the formation of the communist parties, the fundamental axiom of their life and organization had been "democratic centralism," and this continued to be proclaimed in all current statutes, including that of the CPY. According to this principle, all higher organs were elected from below, and were accountable periodically to the organizations that had elected them. Members were supposed to enjoy the right, under the system of "inner party democracy," to participate in discussion of policy and to criticize the work of elected officers. At the same time, the decisions of the higher organs were binding on lower ones, and the strictest obedience of all members was required. A synthesis was

[13] This was also true of the Rumanian party in the Magyar Autonomous Region.

thus achieved, it was said, reconciling democratic participation and centralized voluntary discipline. In fact, under the pattern imposed by Stalin and his local counterparts, all the parties, including the Yugoslav, had increasingly become formidable, centralized managerial systems for the exercise of power by the top leaders, requiring the blind devotion of all members and functionaries. The lion's share, indeed a monopoly, of decision-making had passed to the politburos and secretariats, and especially to the leading party secretaries, who, like Stalin, arrogated to themselves the key role. Party congresses and central committees alike, although meeting more regularly than in the USSR, had become little more than sounding boards for publicizing decisions already reached in secret in the smaller central organs, and lacked any genuine share in policy-making. The central apparatus, headed by the First Secretary and the Secretariat, and the secretaries and their local offices at lower levels, provided a well-knit administrative network for transmitting directives throughout the country and mobilizing the actions of official institutions, mass organizations, and the general public, as well as the communist rank and file.

Since the death of Stalin, there has been a noteworthy effort to restore what were referred to as the "Leninist norms" of party activity, neglected during the period of "the cult of personality," as it became euphemistically called. After 1956, and more recently, after 1961, the stress has been on the collective principle of leadership and the democratic character of the parties, and changes have been made in the statutes to safeguard these tenets. An attempt has been made to render the election of officers more genuine, and to transform the Central Committee and other bodies into forums of meaningful discussion. In some of the parties, the rotation of leaders, which was adopted by the CPSU in its 1961 statute, has been introduced, although not at the topmost level, and in a gingerly and less definite manner.[14] It is difficult to know how much has been achieved in breathing more life and vigor into organs that had become largely extinct during the Stalinist period. Certainly the principle of party unity and dis-

[14] For instance, in 1962, the BCP asserted the principle of "systematic renewal" in party organs and of "continuity of leadership," without specifying, as the CPSU did, the proportions of new members to be elected each time. The CPC was no more explicit. The SED statute of 1962 made no mention even of the principle of rotation. Nor did the 1965 statute of the RCP introduce this feature.

cipline and the taboo on views contrary to the current "line" have been maintained, and effective authority continues to lie in the small bodies at the top.

PARTY AND STATE

The relationship of party and state organs, in large part obscured in the constitutions, is somewhat less camouflaged in the statutes, especially in their later versions. In the 1949 statute of the CPC, apart from referring to the fact that the party implemented "the leading role which belongs to the working class in the development of contemporary society," the only indication of its special position was that the Central Committee, and corresponding lower committees, were said to "direct the work of the communists" in the government, the National Assembly, other official agencies, and the mass organizations. In the current statute (1962), where the party is described as "the leading and directing force of society and state," its dominant role is emphasized by employing the Soviet formula that, at each level of the state administration, the appropriate party body (Central Committee, regional committee, and so on) "directs and supervises the work" of state institutions and mass organizations "through the medium of the communist and party groups" in them. The RCP statute of 1965 more openly announced that the party "guides the entire activity of the central and local organs" of the Republic. Even these provisions give only a pale reflection of the actual part played by the parties, which determine basic policy for the government agencies, control elections to the assemblies and other elected bodies, select personnel for the entire state administration, and supervise the official implementation of decisions at every level.

The position of the League of Communists of Yugoslavia has been greatly modified in theory, although it is uncertain how far it differs in practice from the other parties. When it was renamed in 1952, it was to abandon the "leading role" in society and to confine itself to "political and ideological education." The party's statute spoke of attaining its end by "political and ideological activity in all spheres of social and political life, and in all social organizations, organs and establishments." "Persuasion" was to replace "command." Party cells in government administration and in mass associations were disbanded, and communists were henceforth to exert their influence in such bodies as individuals. The party apparatus was to be greatly reduced. Meetings were to be open to the public. Voting was to be secret. Party democracy was to be restored. Lower organs, including those of the republics, were to enjoy wider authority. This was not, of course, intended to affect the one-party system, but Tito even spoke of the ultimate "withering away" of the party. This drastic change created great confusion in the ranks and a decline in enthusiasm, which soon caused the leadership to backtrack and to stress once again the need for discipline and unity, and the party's role of leadership. In the following year, Djilas, one of the top leaders, openly attacked many aspects of party life and eventually advocated the end of the Communist party and the establishment of a two-party system. His expulsion from the leadership and ultimate imprisonment ensued. In the spring of 1956, further steps were taken to tighten up party activity, including the restoration of *aktivs* in government agencies and mass organizations, and the insistence on discipline of members. Although it remained "a unique type of Communist party, different from what it had been prior to 1951," the League had by 1958 "reasserted its effective control over the direction of society."[15] Direct interference in the day-to-day life had been reduced, but the party leaders were unquestionably in control of the political system.

NATIONAL FRONTS

An unparalleled feature of the Eastern European states, contrasting with the Soviet system, is the so-called National Front, and, in some cases, the continued existence of noncommunist parties. Although none remain in Albania, Hungary, Rumania, and Yugoslavia, there are in Bulgaria, one, the Bulgarian Agrarian Union, and in Czechoslovakia, East Germany, and Poland, several such parties, presumably intended to link the regimes with sectors of the population not otherwise accessible to the communists.[16]

[15] For the above, see Hoffman and Neal, *op. cit.*, chapter 12. The citation is at pp. 209–10. See also Paul Shoup, "Problems of Party Reform in Yugoslavia," *American Slavic and East European Review*, XVIII, 3 (October, 1959), 334–50.

[16] In Czechoslovakia, there are the Czechoslovak Socialist party, the Czechoslovak People's party, the Slovak Freedom party, and the Slovak Renaissance party; in East Germany, the Christian Democratic Union, and the Liberal Democratic party; in Poland, the United Peasant party, the Democratic party, and the Catholic Znak group.

See Taborsky, *op. cit.*, chap. VII; Staar, *op. cit.*, chap. 13; Ernst Richert, *Macht ohne Mandat: Der Staatsapparat in der Sowjetischen Besatzungszone Deutschlands* (2d ed.; Köln and Opladen, 1963), pp. 218ff.

These parties have limited memberships and a minor representation in the assemblies, other elected bodies, and the governments; all publicly acknowledge the leadership of the Communist party and praise its basic policies. Their existence does not fundamentally alter the position of the ruling party, which is identical to that of the one-party systems elsewhere. The continuance of such splinter parties is an anomaly that may eventually be removed by their ostensibly voluntary liquidation.

The National Fronts are hardly more significant than the noncommunist parties.[17] Formed as broad alliances of antifascist parties during the war years, they emerged as the basis of postwar coalition governments and are officially regarded as important mass movements that follow the communist line and publicize it among the nonparty public. In some cases, they were in origin authentic groupings of independent parties, as in Czechoslovakia, Hungary, and Rumania, but in others, such as Albania and Yugoslavia, they were from the first communist-controlled formations, in which other parties, if included at all, were mere skeletons represented by a few leaders. In the course of time, all the fronts evolved into monolithic entities, with the inclusion of mass organizations such as the trade unions, and youth and women's associations, and with individual membership also provided for. Only in Czechoslovakia, Poland, and East Germany do the fronts still retain in part the form of a coalition of parties. The CPC statute of 1962, however, refers to the "voluntary grouping of the societal organizations in the National Front," led by the communist party, "the highest form of social and political organization." In Yugoslavia, in the reorganization of 1952, an attempt was made to increase the importance of the People's Front, which was renamed the Socialist Alliance of Working People.[18] It was said to be the main mechanism for putting communist ideas and policies into action. This assertion, and the duplication of the leadership of the Alliance and the League, made it difficult to distinguish the exact division of labor between the two. Technically, the League was to have no direct authority over the Socialist Alliance, but in fact the latter continued to be dominated by the former, and to follow the general policies laid

[17] They are variously called Democratic Front (Albania); Fatherland Front (Bulgaria); National Front (Czechoslovakia, East Germany, Poland); Patriotic People's Front (Hungary); People's Democratic Front (Rumania); the Socialist Alliance of the Working People (Yugoslavia).

[18] Hoffman and Neal, *op. cit.*, esp. pp. 179–82, 192–93, 208–9.

down by the League. It seems doubtful that the Alliance has any greater role than the fronts in other communist countries.

INTERNATIONAL OBLIGATIONS

The anatomy of power in Eastern Europe cannot be fully understood without reference to the crucial fact of the intimate association of the several communist parties with the CPSU, and indeed their earlier complete subordination to the mother party.[19] As "sections" of the Comintern, they had been required to model themselves on the Russian party and to accept the direction of the Comintern in all their activities. Even with their rise to power, the ostensible independence of the communist-ruled states was largely negated by the reality of dominance by Moscow. The CPSU was able to act decisively in the governance of these states, laying down the line of policy to be followed and determining the leadership of each of the parties. The party statutes, of course, never explicitly revealed subordination to the Soviet party, but in many cases still acknowledge it as the inspiration and model, refer to the individual party as an integral part of the international communist movement, speak of the necessity of proletarian unity, and in some cases recognize the CPSU as the vanguard of world communism.[20]

Soviet influence has been greatly modified by the rise of national communism. Successive acts of resistance by local parties, beginning with the Yugoslav in 1948, continuing with the Hungarian and Polish in 1956, the Albanian in 1961, and the Rumanian in 1962, demonstrated that Soviet control was by no means complete. Indeed, in Hungary, armed force proved necessary to effectuate it. Certain parties, such as the Yugoslav and Albanian, achieved complete independence.[21] Others, such as the Polish and Rumanian, while remaining in close association with the CPSU, vindicated their right to follow a course of their own. This was expressed forcibly in the 1965 revision of the RCP

[19] This will be dealt with more fully in Chapter 18.

[20] CPC statute (1962). Similar formulae were included in the Bulgarian, Hungarian, and East German statutes.

[21] The Yugoslav party, in its current statute, speaks of itself "as a part of the conscious socialist power of the international working class movement," but states that it "works for the development of internationalism, cooperation on the basis of equality of rights, and mutual understanding with communist and other working class parties and progressive movements of the entire world."

statute, which dropped the reference to its being an integral part of the world communist movement, and referred only to "ties of cooperation" with the other parties, based on "proletarian internationalism" and "the principles and norms of Marxist-Leninist relations." In another clause expressing the desire for autonomy of action, the RCP was said to base its activity on Marxism-Leninism, "applying it in a creative manner to the conditions and peculiarities specific to our country." Other parties, such as the Bulgarian and Czechoslovak, have not sought such a status, although they could do so but for the continued subservience of their leaders. Soviet power, needless to say, continues to be considerable, in all cases, but is exercised less by direct control and more by indirect persuasion and pressure.

PART THREE
THE HOLDERS OF POWER

Introduction

In all political systems there are, in Lasswell's term, "a ruling few," that is, a small group of persons who have more influence on the making of decisions than the mass of the population.[1] These are the "political leaders" or, as some have called them, the "power elite," constituting a relatively small minority of the total citizenry. Even in a democracy, only some thousands of persons qualify as belonging to the political elite, and in a dictatorship their number is still smaller.[2]

Who holds the power in the communist states of Eastern Europe? How do they reach their positions of advantage, and how are they displaced? What are the sources of their political influence? Which positions in the hierarchy of political institutions confer real, as opposed to apparent, constitutional authority? What features do the leaders have in common, in terms of social class, occupation, education, age, ethnic or national origin, or personal qualities? How do they share in the making of policy? How do they differ in the degree of their preeminence?

Political power may be "official," the result of occupying certain recognized offices, either elective or appointive, in the system. It may be unofficial or "actual," based on extra-constitutional assets, such as private wealth, social status, military force, special knowledge, or control of the means of communication. It may be, and more likely is, a combination of both official and actual power, with one or the other predominating. Leadership in the area of politics is not to be confused with membership in other elites, such as social, intellectual, or economic, although the latter may confer actual or potential political influence and there

[1] See Harold D. Lasswell, *Politics: Who Gets What, When, How* (New York, 1936, reprinted 1950), and Harold D. Lasswell, Daniel Lerner, and C. Easton Rothwell, *The Comparative Study of Elites: An Introduction and Bibliography* (Stanford, 1952).

[2] See Alfred de Grazia, *The American Way of Government* (New York, 1957), pp. 168–69, 284–86.

is usually an interlocking of memberships, and a high degree of interchange between the various elites. While recognizing the multiplicity of elites, we shall concentrate, in the chapters that follow, on the power derived from membership and office in the party.

In each society, political power is based on a unique synthesis of assets possessed by the leaders, and is exercised in distinctive ways appropriate to its history and culture. In Eastern Europe, individual or corporate property and social standing are less important than in Western democracies, but other unofficial assets have often outweighed or inflated the authority of public office. For example, the source of political strength may be command of some part of the party apparatus, either one dealing with a certain branch of work, such as cadres or propaganda, or one controlling a certain territorial jurisdiction, such as a region or district. It may be a high administrative position, such as a ministry or a local government authority, or the management of an enterprise or farm. It may be mastery of the instruments of coercion, such as the police or armed forces, or of the means of persuasion and indoctrination, such as a party school or newspaper. It may even be expert knowledge in certain fields, such as the scientific or economic, or individual talent, such as that of the teacher or writer. There is bound to be overlapping and some mutual counteracting of these various elements, as different leaders may not always have the same interests or act for a single common purpose.

In every society, there is always a gradation of political influence at any given time, and frequent changes in status as leaders rise and fall on the ladder of power. There are some leaders with very great, others with less, and many with only a modest, influence on decision-making. Mere membership in the party, for example, places a person in the lowest category of the communist elite, but gives him more power than the nonparty citizen. In Eastern Europe, as in the Soviet Union, there is a descending scale of influence, from the top leader, on his lonely pinnacle, and his closest associates—a dozen or more leaders in the Politburo and Secretariat; through an upper elite, consisting of heads of the central party bureaus or government offices, high police officials and generals, the main industrial executives, as well as the party leaders in cities and regions, all of whom are usually Central Committee members; and a middle elite including other important figures in industrial, military, and civil administration, lower officials in the central apparatus, and leading party functionaries in towns and districts; down to a still lower level of subordinate officials in army, administration, and party; and, finally, the rank and file of party members, whose power is limited to their own area of work and activity.

The people cannot directly govern themselves in any political system; they must allow others to rule on their behalf. These "representatives" may inherit their position or seize it through revolution, or they may be appointed or elected to office. How are the rulers of a communist society selected or recruited? Heredity plays little or no part. In the first instance, power is normally secured by revolution, or by the capture of the state with outside military and political aid. Once in office, communist leaders are not removed or replaced by a process of election, but mainly through designation. Even those ostensibly "elected" are, in view of the decisive influence of the single party on the electoral process, in effect appointed, although in a special manner. The bulk of power lies, in any case, not with those who sit in a representative assembly or even in a party conference, but with officials appointed to key positions in the party and government apparatus without benefit of balloting.

7: The Lonely Men

Through history, the mainspring of government has always been the so-called "executive power," representing, not as the term and traditional political science suggest, the mere carrying out or execution of decisions, but the exercise of supreme leadership. In the modern world, even where democratic procedures exist, the executive arm has remained a predominant feature of government, and has even advanced in recent times at the expense of the representative or legislative organs. Moreover, whatever the forms of government or the constitutional distribution of powers, there is always a chief executive, a single figure, bearing huge burdens of leadership and awesome responsibilities of policy-making. The American presidency, once described by Harry S. Truman as "the loneliest office in the world," has its counterparts in other countries, and most particularly in the office of the First Secretary, or Secretary General, of the Communist party of the Soviet Union. This is the loneliest of all pinnacles, as the occupant holds in his hand almost unrestricted authority over the key decisions for his party and country. The personalization of leadership in one man, pregnant as it is with the danger of abuse, seems to meet a need for a symbol of national unity and an effective center for coordinating the activities of the modern state.[1]

THE SUPREME LEADERS

In Eastern Europe, as in all communist states, the task of leadership has been concentrated in the hands of single individuals with great power. This was at first the result of an imitation of the Stalinist pattern in the USSR. In the years of the "cult of personality," the top communist in each country was elevated to an extraordinary level of absolutism and adulation, most pronounced in the autocracy of Rákosi in Hungary. As the Polish leader Gomulka expressed it after October, there had been created "a hierarchic ladder of cults," with Stalin at the top and the other communist leaders on the lower rungs, enjoying, within their own countries, "the borrowed light" of a national cult.[2] Of course, others shared in the making of decisions and their exe-

[1] See Alfred de Grazia, *Elements of Political Science* (New York, 1952), p. 374.

[2] *Trybuna Ludu*, October 21, 1956, quoted by Paul E. Zinner, *National Communism and Popular Revolt in Eastern Europe* (New York, 1956), p. 228.

cution, even under a Stalin or Rákosi, but their power was almost totally derived from the omnipotent ruler and was overwhelmingly eclipsed by him. Even in certain countries, especially Poland and Yugoslavia, where there was a greater reality to the collective leadership of a ruling team, one figure, Bierut and Tito respectively, stood out as first among equals.

Since the death of Stalin, it is claimed, the "cult of personality" is dead, and the principle of "collective leadership" has been restored. The supreme power is supposed to be shared by a group of persons, especially by the Central Committee, in a manner modeled on the style of Lenin's leadership. Nonetheless, the predominant position of a single man has not disappeared, although the conditions of his exercise of power have changed substantially. He no longer wears "the robes of infallibility and wisdom," to use Gomulka's words in the speech quoted above, and has ceased to be the object of sycophantic worship. Yet his position is powerful and far outranks that of his closest associates, and in some cases, such as that of Ulbricht in East Germany and Gheorghiu-Dej in Rumania, has been accompanied by lavish praise. Official communist theory recognizes the need for such "leading comrades," and for the acceptance of their authority.[3] Rule by one man, although but an example of a universal tendency toward the personification of power, seems to be a peculiarly inherent and inescapable feature of communist government.

Supreme leadership in Eastern Europe presents a curious and variegated pattern, sometimes exhibiting considerable continuity but often remarkable transiency and mutability. The leaders of some parties, for example, Tito, Hoxha, or Gheorghiu-Dej, had long and unbroken careers at the top. In Hungary and Bulgaria, the men presently in power succeeded distinguished postwar predecessors, Rákosi and Chervenkov, now vilified as Stalinist. Indeed, in the case of Hungary, all the main leaders of the past, Béla Kun, Rákosi, Nagy, and Kádár, have at one time or another been in disgrace, and only Kun and Kádár have since been rehabilitated.[4] Similarly, the Polish party, most of whose leaders were liquidated in the purge of the thirties, is headed by a man who was in disrepute for eight years. In Rumania, all the prewar heads have been discredited and condemned by the party.

[3] See the defense of Ulbricht and his authority in *Neues Deutschland*, November 24, 1961.

[4] See William O. McCagg, "After Rákosi, Disgrace and Rehabilitation," *Survey*, No. 40 (January, 1962), pp. 124–32.

EASTERN EUROPEAN LEADERS

Country and Name	BEFORE 1953		AFTER 1953	
	Top party post	*Top government post*	*Top party post*	*Top government post*
Albania (AWP)				
HOXHA	SECY. GEN., 1941–54	P.M., 1946–54	1ST SECY., 1954–	(M. Shehu, P.M., 1954–)
Bulgaria (BCP)				
DIMITROV	CHMN., later SECY. GEN., 1945–49*	P.M., 1946–49* (Kolarov, P.M., 1949–50*)		
CHERVENKOV	SECY. GEN., 1950–54	P.M., 1950–56	1ST SECY., 1950–54	P.M., 1950–56 (Yugov, P.M., 1956–62)
ZHIVKOV			1ST SECY., 1954–	P.M., 1962–
Czechoslovakia (CPC)				
GOTTWALD	SECY. GEN., 1929–46 CHMN., 1945–51 SECY. GEN., 1951–53*	(Fierlinger, P.M., 1945–46) (Beněs, Pres., 1945–48) P.M., 1946–48 PRES., 1948–53* (Zápotocký, P.M., 1948–53)		

SLÁNSKÝ	SECY. GEN., 1946–51			(Široký, P.M., 1953–63) (Zápotocký, Pres., 1953–57*)
NOVOTNÝ			SECY. GEN., 1953–	PRES., 1957– (Lénart, P.M., 1963–)
East Germany (SED)				
ULBRICHT	DEPUTY CHMN. to 1950 SECY. GEN., 1950–53 (Pieck) } Chrmn., (Grotewohl) } 1950–53	(Pieck, Pres., 1949–57*) (Grotewohl, P.M., 1949–64*)	1ST SECY., 1953–	CHMN. ST. CNCL., 1960– (Pieck, Pres., 1949–57*) (Grotewohl, P.M., 1949–64*) (Stoph, P.M., 1964–)
Hungary (HWP; after 1956 HWSP)		(Dalnoky-Miklos, Tildy, F. Nagy, Dinnyes, and Dobi, P.M., 1944–52)		

* Died in office.

NOTE: Names and posts of top leaders are capitalized, and their posts are not enclosed in parentheses.

EASTERN EUROPEAN LEADERS (*cont'd.*)

Country and Name	BEFORE 1953		AFTER 1953	
	Top party post	*Top government post*	*Top party post*	*Top government post*
Hungary (cont'd.)				
RAKOSI	SECY. GEN., 1944–53	P.M., 1952–53	1ST SECY., 1953–56	
NAGY				P.M., 1953–55 (Hegedus, P.M., 1955–56) P.M., Oct.–Nov., 1956
GERÖ			1ST SECY., July–Oct., 1956	
KÁDÁR			1ST SECY., Oct., 1956 1ST SECY. (HWSP) Nov., 1956–	P.M., Nov., 1956–58; 1961–65 (Muennich, P.M., 1958–61) (Kallai, P.M., 1965–)
Poland (PUWP)				
GOMULKA	SECY. GEN., 1943–48		1ST SECY., 1956–	
BIERUT	CHMN., 1948–54 SECY. GEN., 1948–54	ACT. HD. OF ST., 1944–47 (Osobka-Morawski, P.M., 1945–47) PRES., 1947–52 (Cyrankiewicz, P.M., 1947–52)	1ST SECY., 1954–56* (Ochab, 1st Secy., Mar.–Oct., 1956)	P.M., 1952–54 (Cyrankiewicz, P.M., 1954–) (Zawadzki, Chmn., Cncl. of St., 1952–64*)

		P.M., 1952–54 (Zawadzki, Chmn., Cncl. of St., 1952–64*)		(Ochab, Chmn., Cncl. of St., 1964–)
Rumania (RWP; RCP before 1948 and after 1965)		(Groza, P.M., 1945–52)	(Apostol, 1st Secy., 1954–55)	
GHEORGHIU-DEJ	SECY. GEN., 1945–53	P.M., 1952–55	1ST SECY., 1955–65*	P.M., 1952–55 CHMN., ST. CNCL., 1961–65* (Stoica, Chmn., St. Cncl., 1965–) (Stoica, P.M., 1955–61)
CEAUSESCU			GEN. SECY., 1965–	(Maurer, P.M., 1961–)
Yugoslavia (CPY, then LCY)				
BROŽ-TITO	SECY. GEN., 1937–	P.M., 1945–53	SECY. GEN., 1937–	PRES., 1953– PRES., EXEC. CNCL., 1953–63 (Stambolić, Pres., Exec. Cncl., 1963–)

* Died in office.

INTERLOCKING OF POSITIONS

Top communist figures have almost always occupied the party posts of Secretary General or First Secretary, innocuous titles masking the reality of power exercised by their bearers. In most states, at least after the solidification of power and the ousting of rival parties, there was a personal fusion of the party and government hierarchies, with the leader occupying both the secretaryship and the prime ministership or presidency. The real power lay with the crucial party post, usually the secretaryship, and power based on state offices was derivative and subordinate. Only exceptionally, in Poland and Czechoslovakia, did the leading figures (Bierut and Gottwald respectively) hold another party position, namely that of Chairman, as well as the state presidency, and shared power in the party with a Secretary General, Gomulka and Slánský respectively. In Poland, this was terminated with the elimination of Gomulka from all positions in 1948, the abolition of the general secretaryship, and the assumption of the party chairmanship by Bierut. In 1952, when the presidency was abolished, Bierut became Prime Minister, too. In Czechoslovakia, the conflict between the authority of state and of party was at least one of the major causes of Slánský's removal in 1951 and his execution the following year. Thereafter, Gottwald, until his death in 1953, occupied the pinnacles of both state and party, as President and Secretary General. His successor in the latter post, Novotný, at first shared power with the new President, Zápotocký, but after the latter's demise, assumed the two positions.

In most countries, this merging of the highest government and party positions was regarded as exemplifying the cult of personality and was abandoned in the period of de-Stalinization, although there were variations in the pattern of action, and there has been a countertendency at work.[5] Kádár and Zhivkov, for instance, later resumed the premiership. In several cases, in particular that of Tito and, after 1957, of Novotný, the party chief has continued to hold the highest governmental post, the presidency. In Poland, the First Secretary, Bierut, abandoned the premiership to someone of lesser stature, a practice continued by his successor, Gomulka. In Albania, Hoxha, who had been Prime Minister, Minister of Foreign Affairs, and Minister of

[5] See A. Gyorgy, "The Internal Political Order," in Stephen Fischer-Galati (ed.), *Eastern Europe in the Sixties* (New York, 1963), pp. 176–80.

People's Defense, gave up these posts in 1953 and 1954. In East Germany, Ulbricht, who had never held the highest government office, continued as First Secretary without interruption. Gheorghiu-Dej, Secretary General from the first, became Prime Minister in 1952, temporarily relinquished the party post in 1953, but resumed it again within two years, continuing also as premier until 1955. In 1961, he assumed the post of Chairman of the newly-created State Council or collegial presidency. When a similar post was set up in East Germany, Ulbricht took it over, for the first time combining governmental and party positions. Paradoxically, the greatest concentration of offices was in Yugoslavia, where Tito occupied not only the chief party and government posts, but also the chairmanship of the Executive Council, command of the armed forces, and the leadership of the People's Front. The Yugoslav constitution of 1963 provided for the separation of the two top government posts, but Tito continued as President and Secretary General.

The case of Hungary and Bulgaria was, after 1953, somewhat different, since the position of the First Secretary was counterbalanced by that of Premier, and a bitter struggle for power ensued. In these two countries, Rákosi and Chervenkov, who had long held both the key posts, relinquished one of them to Nagy and Zhivkov, who assumed the premiership and the first secretaryship respectively. After Chervenkov's removal, Zhivkov, as the First Secretary, did not at first assume a state position. As events turned out, this was the first step down the ladder for Chervenkov, who was successively demoted in the following years and finally eliminated altogether. Gheorghiu-Dej, who had taken the same risky course in Rumania, was able soon to reclaim the first secretaryship. In Hungary, the period of "dual rule" between the heads of party and state were years of deadly conflict.[6] Rákosi, who had retained the first secretaryship and given up the lesser post of Premier, was able to make a temporary comeback with the ouster of Nagy in 1955, but was himself removed as First Secretary in 1956. After the revolution, Kádár reverted to the earlier procedure of combining the secretaryship and the premiership in one person, but in 1958 conformed to the more general practice when one of his subordinates became Prime Minister. Three years later, however, he resumed the premiership but relinquished it again in 1965.

[6] See Ferenc C. Váli, *Rift and Revolt in Hungary: Nationalism Versus Communism* (Cambridge, 1961), pp. 100, 104–6, and p. 81 below.

SELECTION OF LEADERS

The process by which an individual secured his place among the seats of the mighty, sometimes moving directly from communist prison to Politburo and Secretary General's office, and sometimes suffering degradation from supremacy to powerlessness, and even imprisonment or execution, was an obscure and mysterious one, defying scholarly analysis. Certainly it was not democratic or subject to fixed rules and procedures. None of the leaders was popularly chosen as First Secretary. The elevation to the presidency or other high elective office was an *ex post facto* ratification of the power already possessed as chief of the party. None of the leaders was limited to a defined term of office, and there were no provisions for an orderly succession. The choice of the leader and the determination of his successor were in the hands of the Presidium and Secretariat, both operating in a secret manner, and with a large but indeterminate influence normally being exerted by Moscow and the CPSU leadership. In times of great crisis, the replacement of one leader by another was a product of tidal waves of popular resistance and discontent, and direct and decisive intervention by Moscow in the internal affairs of a given party. Although backstairs intrigue in "smoke-filled rooms" is not unknown in democracies, the communist counterpart is much more hidden from view, and is ultimately decisive, without any subsequent endorsement by popular vote.

The initial postwar appointments in Eastern Europe were no doubt largely the work of Moscow, although with some exceptions. Several of the leaders, Dimitrov, Gottwald, Rákosi, and Ulbricht, had spent the war years (indeed, many prewar years too) in the Soviet capital, and were the choice of the CPSU. All except Ulbricht had been appointed party chiefs by the Comintern in the twenties and thirties, as had Tito, who, however, was not in Moscow during the war. Gheorghiu-Dej, who had been in prison for eleven years prior to 1944, was put in charge of the Rumanian party in the first days of Soviet military occupation. Gomulka, however, acquired the leadership at home in 1943, at a time when the Polish party was probably out of touch with Moscow. Hoxha was no doubt selected by the Yugoslavs when the Albanian party was formed under the former's auspices.

In later changes of leadership, the part played by the CPSU was probably great, although it cannot be documented and was often affected by indigenous forces. The removal of Gomulka and Slánský, for instance, was the climax of a bitter struggle within the Polish and Czechoslovak parties, with Moscow either proposing or approving the dismissal of the defeated rivals and placing the final seal of approval on Bierut and Gottwald. In the same way, the replacement of the powerful Chervenkov by Zhivkov, and the succession of Novotný to Gottwald, must have occurred either at Moscow's instigation or with its sanction. In the cases of Tito and Hoxha, however, Moscow was unable to supplant them by more subservient leaders. In the crisis in Hungary after the death of Stalin, Rákosi's first demotion, the appointment of Nagy to the premiership, Rákosi's later resumption of full power, and, still later, his supersession by Gerö were all the product of direct intervention by Moscow, either by the summoning of Hungarian leaders to Moscow, or by visits to Budapest of leading Soviet statesmen.[7] These changes also reflected domestic events and, ironically enough, the influence of Tito, who held a series of conferences with Khrushchev at that time. The selection of Kádár in the revolutionary days at the beginning of November, 1956, remains shrouded in mystery. Although a member of the dissident Nagy government, Kádár, at a critical moment of resistance to the USSR, traveled to the nearby Soviet city of Uzhgorod and returned to Budapest as the Moscow-selected leader, to be imposed by armed force after the liquidation of the Nagy regime.[8]

Death of a leader, or his removal while still alive, sometimes touched off, or was the product of, a bitter struggle for power, although normally not so protracted as in the Soviet Union, because of Moscow's decisive influence on the choice of a successor. In the Hungarian crisis after 1953, however, the party was divided into sharply opposed wings, represented by the two rivals for office, and the CPSU leadership was also subject to internal strains and conflicts. At first, Moscow's support, during Malenkov's regime, was thrown to Nagy, but after the fall of the former, was transferred to Rákosi. As a result of growing disaffection in Hungary and the insistent pressure of Tito, Rákosi was dropped in favor of Gerö, who was in turn cast aside in favor, first, of Nagy and, finally, of Kádár. Nagy's rise to power reflected, it would seem, the increasing opposition of top party cadres to the former leader, and the mounting demand for Nagy as his replacement, while Moscow hesitated long before

[7] *Ibid.*, pp. 1–8, 91ff., 155–62, 236–37, 285, 302.

[8] *Ibid.*, pp. 370–73; Paul Zinner, *Revolution in Hungary* (New York, 1962), pp. 324–26, 331–34.

abandoning the veteran Rákosi. In a somewhat similar way, the re-admission of Gomulka to the party in 1956, the appointment of Ochab as Bierut's successor on the latter's death in March, 1956, and his replacement by Gomulka, as the crisis deepened, reflected the rising tide of popular discontent and the party's dissatisfaction with the earlier leadership rather than Moscow's pressure. The ultimate selection of Gomulka as First Secretary, although formally occurring after negotiations with Khrushchev and other Soviet representatives in Warsaw, had already been made by the Central Committee immediately before the arrival of the Soviet emissaries, and was a genuine election by secret ballot.[9]

CAREER PATTERNS

It is not easy to find a common denominator in the lives of the topmost communist leaders, or to identify a clearly defined career pattern in their rise to supreme power. Few men can aspire to the leadership of a Communist party or regime, and "rules of availability" limit the choice substantially. Almost none had achieved high rank or reputation in other fields, either governmental, military, or intellectual. All had passed the test of life-long devoted service to communism, and were marked by their ability to survive in the internal political struggle of the party and the world communist movement. All had been willing to accept the dictates of their former chiefs and of Moscow, or, in some cases, to defy the one with the support of the other. Some had led their party in the prewar period; others were appointed to the top posts during the war or immediately thereafter; still others were postwar successors. Some were workingmen with little education (Bierut, Dimitrov, Gheorghiu-Dej, Gomulka, Gottwald, Kádár, Novotný, Tito, Ulbricht, and Zhivkov); others were of the middle class, with some higher education (Chervenkov, Gerö, Hoxha, Nagy, Rákosi, and Slánský). Some, such as Slánský and Gottwald, and to a lesser degree Ulbricht and Gomulka, had had experience with the political processes of a democracy, but most had been more familiar with authoritarian rule in their home countries. Many had suffered long prison terms, some, such as Rákosi, Gheorghiu-Dej, Gomulka, Tito, and Bierut, under prewar regimes, and a few, Slánský, Gomulka, and Kádár in particular,

[9] See Richard Hiscocks, *Poland: Bridge for the Abyss?* (London, 1963), pp. 173, 197–98, 208–9, 220; M. K. Dziewanowski, *The Communist Party of Poland: An Outline of History* (Cambridge, 1959), p. 278.

during the Stalinist period. Many, including Kádár and Slánský before their own arrests, had shared the responsibility for the conduct of terror. Some were men of considerable intellectual ability and personal charm and enjoyed a certain charisma of leadership. This was especially true of Dimitrov, Gheorghiu-Dej, Hoxha, Rákosi, and Tito. Others—Gottwald, Kádár, Novotný, Ulbricht, and Zhivkov—were dull and colorless, lacking in distinction. Some, such as Gomulka, although not of intellectual stature or popular style, exercised a considerable appeal because of the prestige of their performance in national crisis.

Of the original leaders, a good many had perforce spent long years in Moscow, and had worked in the Comintern or other Soviet organizations. Dimitrov, the most distinguished, had been Secretary General of the Comintern from 1935 to 1943, and was its chief spokesman during the popular front period. He had gained worldwide notoriety by his courageous defense at the Reichstag fire trial in Leipzig. Rákosi, a member of the Béla Kun communist regime in 1919, had been an important officer of the Comintern in the early twenties, but was confined to Hungarian prisons after 1924. Like Dimitrov, he had gained fame through public appeals on his behalf throughout the world. Bierut, Gottwald, Tito, and Ulbricht were also long-time Muscovites.

Others were what may be called "home" or "native" communists, with little or no residence in Moscow or close association with the Comintern. This was especially true of Gheorghiu-Dej, Gomulka, and Hoxha; the last was one of the few "western" communist chiefs, having lived in France for many years between the wars. Some, including Tito and Ulbricht, had been participants, or closely involved, in the Spanish Civil War.

A few, notably, Tito and Hoxha, and, to a lesser degree, Kádár and Zhivkov, acquired fame and influence as leaders of partisan struggles, or as heads of strike movements, such as Gheorghiu-Dej. Gottwald had won some popularity by his prewar resistance to the Munich settlement and his wartime radio campaign against the German occupation. Some gained widespread support in later years by virtue of resistance to Moscow's policy, in the first rank Tito, Gomulka, and Nagy, and more recently Gheorghiu-Dej.

The successors to the original leaders were usually men of a similar generation, having been party members from the twenties and having had careers as illegal or revolutionary workers. Some, such as Nagy, Gerö, and Chervenkov, had lived for fifteen to twenty years in Moscow; others, Kádár and Zhivkov, were involved in underground movements during the war; Novotný spent the war years in a German concentration camp. Most of them also had postwar experience in government and party posts, but two, Zhivkov and Novotný, were pure *apparatchiki*, having held no public offices. Future successors are likely to be similar to these two, products of the apparatus who have worked their way up that ladder to the top, a managerial type comparable to the new generation of Soviet leaders.[10]

The key to the attitudes taken and the roles played by the various leaders is not so much their inclusion in particular categories such as those given above, but rather the personality, undefinable and often unpredictable, of the man in question, and the circumstances of time and place. "Muscovites," such as Nagy and Tito, have resisted the Soviet Union; "home communists," such as Novotný, Zhivkov, Kádár, and until lately Gheorghiu-Dej, have been devotedly pro-Soviet. A "westerner" and "home communist" such as Hoxha was for years "Muscovite" in outlook and in action, and remains strongly anti-Western in spite of his break with the USSR. The course of events in Poland and Hungary in 1955–56 was greatly influenced by the contrasting personalities and capacities of a Gomulka and a Nagy, and the remarkably different roles played by two "Muscovites," Ochab and Gerö, the former ready to turn over power to Gomulka, and the latter anxious to continue the course of his predecessor, Rákosi. The ability of some persons, such as Novotný or Ulbricht, to remain in power was partly a consequence of the absence in these countries of a Tito or Gomulka, capable of making an independent stand. Yet later, under different circumstances, both Tito and Gomulka, models of "home communists," demonstrated their ability to give full and warm support to Soviet policy.

BURDENS OF OFFICE

Once in power, each of the communist chiefs assumes a burden and acquires a power far beyond anything assigned to him by the constitution or even the party statute. As will be discussed more fully in succeeding chapters, his is the decisive leadership in formulating the main lines of public policy and making the vital decisions; his are the powers normally assigned elsewhere to a chief-of-state, such as the president, or the head of a government, such as a prime minister, including the deter-

[10] Such a man was N. Ceausescu, who succeeded Gheorghiu-Dej in March, 1965. During the war he had been in prison in Rumania.

mination of foreign and military policy; the direction of the administration of both government and party; and the carrying out of the ceremonial tasks of head of state. True, the burden is lightened by the fact that the decisions are coordinated with, or subordinate to, the rulers in Moscow, although this is no longer true of Tito and Hoxha, and has become decreasingly so in other cases as well. Moreover, in carrying out his functions as chief executive leader, each shares his power in some undefined and largely unknown way with a circle of top associates, to be discussed in the next chapter, but is not seriously hampered by the broader, representative bodies of party and government. Each has his own style of leadership, varying according to his personality and conditions, and no longer modeled, as was once the case, on Stalin. Following certain well-established habits and procedures, the leaders make their long addresses to Central Committee and Congress, to assembly or other mass meetings, and make party and state visits to communist and other capitals of the world as the spokesmen of their party and their nation as a whole, and as the personal embodiment of their own brand of communism.

8: The High Command

Even under Stalin, the monopoly of decision-making in the hands of one man was, to some extent, an optical illusion. Personal rule of a modern state by a single leader is impossible in any real sense. Even the most powerful chief executive is necessarily surrounded by associates who are more than mere policy-implementers but have a share in the shaping of policy. Such "political executives" are not necessarily elected, and may indeed hold no public office at all, serving merely as personal advisers of the chief executive. In communist countries, they are as likely to hold high party offices as governmental posts. Although close to the chief, and having an inordinate influence on his decisions, they may not share a collective responsibility with him, as do the cabinet ministers of a parliamentary democracy, but act rather as counselors, more in the style of the ministers of the Russian tsar. However democratic, or however autocratic, no system can dispense with such persons, numbering perhaps a dozen or two in the most intimate circles around the chief executive, or several hundreds in the broader group of key officials and consultants.

THE INNER COUNCILS

In communist countries, the functioning of the chief executive is shrouded in obscurity and difficult to assess. There may well be persons among his close friends or relatives, or intimate advisers, who function as *éminences grises;* there may be a "brain trust" or "kitchen cabinet," whose counsel carries great weight. Before 1956 in Hungary, for instance, Rákosi's personal secretariat was a decisive force. In a wider orbit, the top leaders may turn to the higher officers of the central party apparatus and its sections, and to the heads of government departments and agencies, for detailed assistance in the formulation of public policy. In this shadowy land of consultation behind the scenes, the recommendations of various Soviet advisers, including the ambassador or visiting delegates of the CPSU, may be influential, or even, as in Stalin's day, decisive, in those countries still accustomed to look to Moscow for guidance. The greatest influence, however, belongs to the members of the topmost party organs, the Politburo (or Presidium) and the Secretariat, numbering twenty to thirty persons, and the Central Committee, totaling two or three hundred. The degree to which the supreme leader will avail himself of their advice and the manner in which they will be associated with the taking of decisions will, of course, vary greatly with his personality and with the conditions of time and country.

Although these highest agencies fell into disuse during the Stalinist period, they have been restored as important organs of policy formation since his death and the revival of "collective leadership." Although the Central Committee is officially described as the main vehicle of collective leadership, the two smaller bodies are in fact much more influential. The relationship of Politburo and Secretariat, and of their individual members, to each other and to the supreme leader, is a peculiar one, varying in each country and each period, and not easily subject to systematic analysis. The Presidium or Politburo[1] is presumably the place where fundamental matters of policy are settled, although the degree to which its final decisions are based on real participation, and whether they are taken by majority vote, is impossible to determine. The First Secretary is normally "first among equals," if not the all-powerful figure in this team, and may override the majority or a powerful minority. There is likely to be an inner core of three or four persons, the most intimate associates of the chief, who arrogate to themselves the lion's share of authority. No doubt, too, there are individual members who carry greater weight than others, such as a Marshal Rokossovsky in the Stalinist days in Poland, or, in the Yugoslav corps of leaders, a Ranković or Kardelj, to whom Tito has turned over important responsibilities. Still others may be largely of decorative value, as in the case of Professor Nejedlý, in his later years, in the Czechoslovak leadership.

The smaller Secretariat,[2] composed of the so-called secretaries who work exclusively within the party apparatus, may play a part much greater than might be indicated by its apparently subordinate administrative functions. During the Stalinist days, indeed, its place was usually more important than that of the Politburo. Even now, the position of the First Secretary as boss of the Secretariat is one of considerable strength and is the basis of his power in the party. Through him the Secretariat may be in a position to influence, or even dominate, all other organs,

[1] For an analysis of the Polish Politburo, see Richard F. Staar, "The Political Bureau of the United Polish Workers' Party," *American Slavic and East European Review*, XV, 2 (April, 1956), 206–15.

[2] See Richard F. Staar, "The Secretariat of the United Polish Workers' Party (PZPR)," *Journal of Central European Affairs,* XV, 3 (October, 1955), 272–85.

including the Politburo. At moments of crisis, however, the leading secretary may lose his control and be ousted by a group within the Politburo, as happened to Slánský, Chervenkov, and Rákosi.

The exact role of the Politburo is further obscured by the fact that it represents a kind of fusion of the topmost pinnacles of party and state. Whereas the Secretariat consists exclusively of party *apparatchiki*, who hold no governmental posts, the Politburo normally includes not only persons with high party position, usually in the Secretariat, but also top government officials, including the Prime Minister, some deputy prime ministers, and certain cabinet ministers, and sometimes the heads of other important organizations, such as the trade unions.[3] In this way, the Politburo may be regarded as a forum for discussing and reconciling the interests of party, government, and other institutions. At certain times, one or the other of these interests may dominate the Politburo, excluding, or discriminating against, the rest. Normally, however, the real source of power is membership in the Politburo, and appointment to high government positions, even the presidency or the premiership, merely transfers to those posts the authority of the party leaders. Some members of the Politburo, such as deputy prime ministers, without specific departmental portfolios, supervise certain spheres of government activity and the relevant ministries. In most situations, therefore, the Politburo serves as an effective instrument of control by the Communist party over the administrative centers of government.

PERSONAL BACKGROUNDS

The members of Politburo and Secretariat vary greatly in their career backgrounds. Due to the relatively short period of communist rule, there has not yet emerged in the Eastern European countries the more or less homogeneous class of "professional bureaucratic politicians" that has been described with reference to the Soviet leadership.[4] Studies of leadership in Eastern Europe indicate a greater representation of what have been called "revolutionaries," that is, persons who were active in the prewar and

[3] Richard F. Staar, "Third Congress of the Polish Communist Party," *American Slavic and East European Review*, XIX, 1 (February, 1960), 63–73.

[4] See Z. K. Brzezinski and Samuel P. Huntington, "Cincinnatus and the Apparatchik," *World Politics*, XVI, 1 (October, 1963), 55ff., and esp. p. 71.

LEADING POLISH COMMUNISTS, OCTOBER, 1959

Name	*Position*
* Albrecht, Jerzy	Director, CC‡ Justice Commission
† Cyrankiewicz, Jozef	Prime Minister
*† Gierek, Edward	First Secretary, Katowice Province
*† Gomulka, Wladyslaw	CC First Secretary
* Jarosinski, Witold	First Secretary, Warsaw City–Province
† Jedrychowski, Stefan	Chairman, Economic Council
*† Kliszko, Zenon	Chairman, PUWP Parliamentary Club
† Loga-Sowinski, Ignacy	Chairman, Central Council of Trade Unions
* Matwin, Wladyslaw	First Secretary, Wroclaw Province
*† Morawski, Jerzy	Director, CC Education and Science Department
† Ochab, Edward	Minister of Agriculture
† Rapacki, Adam	Minister of Foreign Affairs
† Spychalski, Marian	Minister of National Defense
*† Zambrowski, Roman	Director, CC Peoples Councils Department
† Zawadzki, Aleksander	Chairman, Council of State

* Member, Secretariat
† Member, Political Bureau
‡ Central Committee

SOURCE: Richard F. Staar, "Third Congress of the Polish Communist Party," *American Slavic and East European Review*, XIX, 1 (February, 1960), 72.

wartime movement, although, needless to say, with the passage of time these are gradually being replaced by communists with experience attained exclusively since the seizure of power.[5] For

[5] In addition to the articles by Staar, already cited, and his book, *Poland, 1944–1962* (New Orleans, 1962), see also the mimeographed studies made by Radio Free Europe, *The Communist Leadership in Eastern Europe*, I, Bulgaria; II, Poland; III, Czechoslovakia (Munich, 1959), and Radio Free Europe, *The Rumanian Workers' Party on the Eve of its Third Congress* (Munich, 1960). Also D. A. Tomasic, *The Communist Leadership and Nationalism in Czechoslovakia* (Washington, 1960); D. A. Tomasic, "The Rumanian Communist Leadership," *Slavic Review*, XX, 3 (October, 1961), 477–94; D. A. Tomasic, "Political Leadership in Contemporary Poland," *Journal of Human Relations*, IX, No. 2, pp. 191–206. Biographical material is also given in the series *East-Central Europe under the Communists*, under the general editorship of Robert F. Byrnes (New York, 1956–57), and Joseph Rothschild, *Communist East Europe* (New York, 1964).

example, in 1959, of 31 heads of the Czechoslovak party, at least nine were active prewar communists, and of these, most had studied in Moscow for several years. Six had spent the war in Moscow; one in England; six had been in German concentration camps; and five had been active in the underground movement. Of the total of 31, 18 had spent the bulk of their postwar careers as party functionaries, two had served in the trade union movement, and 15 had held ministerial or other government posts. In more recent years, additions to the high command have come increasingly from the ranks of the postwar apparatus, and are beginning to resemble the Soviet prototype. A somewhat similar pattern was evident in the Bulgarian and Rumanian parties, with an even heavier concentration of "revolutionaries" of working class origin. In both cases, however, the rise of the *apparatchik* who had little or no connection with illegal activity before or during the war, and was better educated, was noticeable.

The leading corps is in fact even more diverse than so far suggested. Some, as just noted, are prewar revolutionaries, with years of imprisonment, partisan or underground experience, or participation in the Spanish civil war; others are postwar communists, *apparatchiki*, without revolutionary background and with experience largely in the period of communist rule. Some are more party-oriented, others more government-oriented, as a result of holding positions primarily in one or the other system. Some (usually the majority) are workers and peasants in origin, with little or no education; others are middle class, with some higher education. Some have specialized knowledge and experience, sometimes in police and security work, or in military service; sometimes in economic management and planning, or in diplomacy; occasionally in intellectual activity; although these together form a small minority compared with the generalists with varied experience in either government or party work, and sometimes in both. Some few are former social democrats; most are life-long communists, often from their youth on. Some are Stalinists in the sense of having been in power during Stalin's lifetime; others entered on their main careers after his death. Some are more nationalist in their interpretation of communism; others more international or Sovietophile. In some cases, nationality differences, for instance, between Czech and Slovak, or between the various peoples of Yugoslavia, are a significant factor, with Czechs predominating in the CPC leadership and a more equitable distribution of nationalities existing in the multinational CPY. In the Rumanian and Hungarian, and, to a lesser extent, the Czechoslovak and Polish, parties, the proportion of Jewish leaders was quite high until the Stalinist purges eliminated most of them.[6] These categories are, of course, seldom clear-cut and may often overlap, even in the same person. Such diversity, and the natural uniqueness of human beings, are bound to produce sharp differences, or at least nuances, in their approach to questions requiring decision.

One of the most important differentiations among the communist bosses was that between the "Muscovites" and the "home" or "native" communists. Almost all the parties, with the exception of Albania, had a Muscovite wing, made up of those who had passed the war years in Moscow and had often studied or worked in the USSR prior to the war. This was particularly true of the Bulgarian party, many of whose leaders had spent much of the interwar period in the Soviet Union. Important members of the Czech and Slovak, German, Hungarian, and Rumanian leading cadres had been in Moscow during the war. In contrast, most of the top commands also included persons who had remained at home, taking part in the underground movement, or who were confined in prison and concentration camps. This was notably true of the Albanians and Yugoslavs, but also of individual leaders in the six other countries. Some of these had never been in the USSR for any extended period. "Home" communists were fewest among Czechs and East Germans. "Westerners," who had lived in the West for some years, usually during the war, were another element in some parties, especially the Czech, Slovak, and Hungarian.

THE CLASH OF FACTIONS

In spite of an appearance of monolithic unity at any given time, the high command was almost always riven by deep divergences of outlook and sharp conflicts over policy. Even during the Stalinist period, when unorthodox views, such as liberal or national communism, were stamped out, the profound diversity of viewpoint inevitably affected the course of events, and played its role in bringing Stalinism ultimately to an end. In particular, the sharply opposed factions within the Hungarian and Polish leaderships, especially between the "national communists," and the "Muscovites," had far-reaching effects on the post-Stalin crisis

[6] R. V. Burks, *The Dynamics of Communism in Eastern Europe* (Princeton, 1961), pp. 165–70.

and its outcome.[7] There were also cleavages between the two groups in Bulgaria, Rumania, and Czechoslovakia, although they did not produce the same serious consequences. In other countries, there was a greater unanimity of outlook, notably in Yugoslavia, where the close collaboration of the leaders during partisan days acted as a strong bond after the assumption of power. Even there, however, after the break with the Soviet Union, two pro-Soviet leaders, Hebrang and Zhujović, had to be purged, and Djilas, second in line, broke with Tito in the early fifties and was excluded from the top ranks.

Since the death of Stalin, the changed atmosphere in most of the communist countries has permitted freer expression of divergences, and in some cases a sharp clash of opposing factions, within the ruling group. The main division has been among the so-called Stalinists, reluctant to see serious modification of the old system, the de-Stalinizers, seeking to "liberalize" and "nationalize" communism, and still others urging a middle-of-the-road course. In Poland, Hungary, and, to a lesser degreee, Bulgaria, the leadership has tended to adopt a "centrist" position, seeking to excommunicate, not only the so-called "rightists" or "revisionists," but also the "leftists" or "dogmatists."[8] In Albania, Czechoslovakia, East Germany, and Rumania, there have been few if any "liberals" or "revisionists" among the leading cadres, and the veteran Stalinists have remained largely in control. In Yugoslavia, groupings have emerged within the high command, largely on the question of how far the regime should proceed in liberalizing the economy and decentralizing administration, and how far it should maintain its "national" stance or adopt a more conciliatory attitude toward the Soviet Union. This has been linked with nationality questions, some leaders such as the Serb, Ranković, favoring a tougher and more centralist course, and

[7] See, for instance, William Griffith, "The Revolt Reconsidered," *East Europe*, IX, 7 (July, 1960), 12–20. On the Polish internal split, see M. K. Dziewanowski, *The Communist Party of Poland* (Cambridge, 1959), pp. 173–74, 272–74, 278, and Richard Hiscocks, *Poland: Bridge for the Abyss?* (London, 1963), pp. 111–13, 139, 207, 222, 251. On Hungarian factions, see Paul E. Zinner, *Revolution in Hungary* (New York and London, 1962), pp. 83–87, 146–47, and also Paul Kecskemeti, *The Unexpected Revolution: Social Forces in the Hungarian Uprising* (Stanford, 1961).

[8] For the internal politics of certain countries, see J. Ptakowski, "Politics in Poland," *East Europe*, XI, 12 (December, 1962), 18–25; Z. M. Szaz, "Kadar's Politics," *East Europe*, XI, 10 (October, 1962), 2–11. The division into Stalinists and "liberals" does not always accurately describe, nor fully exhaust, the differences within the ruling elite.

others, such as the Slovene, Kardelj, and the Croatian, Bakarić, favoring autonomy and greater liberalism, and a "national path." Tito himself seems to have adopted something of a middle-of-the-road position between the competing groups.[9]

PURGES AND TRIALS

There is a constant ebb and flow of leaders, and the line between power and impotence is sometimes thin indeed. Frequent changes are made in the composition of Politburo and Secretariat, and in the highest government and party posts, sometimes through the appointment and removal of leading figures in a manner not unlike that of all political systems, but sometimes more dramatically through the crisis and purge so characteristic of communist government. Important as this process is, it remains one of the most mysterious aspects of communist politics. Ostensibly elected by the Central Committee, the members of the Politburo and Secretariat are in fact presumably selected by the First Secretary and an inner group of his colleagues. In some cases, considerable influence may still be exerted by the CPSU. In critical moments, as in Poland in 1956, the choice may be much more genuinely made by the Central Committee.

In Stalinist days, removal from the highest office was often accompanied by trial and execution, or at least denunciation and the loss of all posts. Following the Soviet-Yugoslav break in 1948, a series of purges occurred throughout East Europe, resulting in the removal and frequently the liquidation of persons accused of Titoism and other deviations and crimes. In certain countries, notably Albania, Bulgaria, Czechoslovakia, Hungary, and Rumania, the expurgations were violent, involving the execution of prominent figures, such as Xoxe, Kostov, Rajk, Slánský, and Clementis, and Luca and Pǎtrǎşçanu. In other cases, especially that of Gomulka in Poland, Merker in East Germany, and Djilas in Yugoslavia, the procedure was less bloodthirsty, and was limited to exclusion from high office and imprisonment. Although the charges against the deviators were many, and the issues frequently obscure, the purges were principally directed against those who

[9] G. W. Hoffman and F. W. Neal, *Yugoslavia and the New Communism* (New York, 1962), pp. 493–504; V. Meier, "Der Soldat und die Kompanie—Die politische Probleme der jugoslavischen Kommunisten seit 1958," *Osteuropa*, XIII, 7/8 (July–August, 1963), esp. pp. 458ff.; and V. Meier, "Die Frage der Nationalitäten und die Nachfolge Titos," *Osteuropa*, XIV, 1 (January, 1964), 39–46.

were in any way suspected of nationalist resistance to Soviet policy. This was especially true of Merker, Gomulka, Rajk, Pătrăşçanu, and perhaps also of Kostov. In other instances, however, they were mainly aimed at "Muscovites," such as Pauker and Luca in Rumania and Slánský in Czechoslovakia. In Albania, Xoxe was charged primarily with Yugoslav sympathies. Although Titoism and "national communism" were the accusations most often leveled, the trials also struck at certain groups, such as former social democrats, "Westerners," "Spaniards," or, especially in Rumania and Czechoslovakia, Jews or "Zionists," and in the latter country, Slovaks.

In the post-Stalin period, significant political purges have continued to take place, sometimes directed against persons presumably guilty of excessive nationalism or liberalism;[10] sometimes, against those considered Stalinist or dogmatist.[11] The main Slovak trials occurred in Czechoslovakia in 1954, and as late as 1962, Barák was sentenced to a lengthy term in prison. The Djilas imprisonment in 1955 was followed by re-imprisonment in 1962. The execution of Pătrăşçanu in Rumania in 1954, of Nagy in Hungary in 1957, and of Belishova in Albania in 1960 indicated that physical liquidation continued to be the form of punishment in certain countries. It is still possible for a person to be suddenly deprived of all power, and even of freedom, by a turn of the wheel of political fortune, as demonstrated by the experience of Djilas in Yugoslavia, Barák in Czechoslovakia, or Yugov in Bulgaria.[12] Conversely, in the post-Stalin period, some men moved from seclusion and complete ostracism, even from prison cells, almost directly to high party office, as, for example, the associates of Gomulka and Kádár.

[10] For instance, Chankov (1957) and Taskov (1959) in Bulgaria; Chisinevski and Constantinescu (1957) in Rumania; Dahlem, Zeisser, Herrenstadt, and Ackerman (1953) in East Germany; Belishova (1960) in Albania; Djilas (1955) in Yugoslavia; and Zambrowski (1963) in Poland.

[11] For example, Čepička (1954) in Czechoslovakia; Rákosi and Gerö (1962) in Hungary; Yugov (1962) in Bulgaria; Bacílek and Široký (1963) in Czechoslovakia; Berman, Minc, Nowak, and others (1956) in Poland.

[12] After severe criticisms of party methods, Djilas, who had been second in command to Tito, was expelled from the Central Committee and from the Executive Committee, in 1954, and resigned from the party. In 1955, as a result of books published abroad, he was sentenced to successive terms of imprisonment. Barák, who had for more than a decade been a Politburo member and Minister of the Interior, was first demoted and then tried and imprisoned on charges of embezzlement. Yugow was suddenly and without warning removed from the Politburo and from the premiership in 1962.

CONTINUITY AND CHANGE

The sequence of major purges and the natural course of deaths and replacements have had a marked effect on the continuity of leadership. In Albania, the top command was almost entirely renewed after 1945, with Hoxha alone remaining from the original team. Between 1952 and 1964, however, there has been almost no change in the Albanian leading corps.[13] Of the Rumanian Politburo (18 members) in 1948, only 6 were left in 1960.[14] Rumanian cadres, after severe purges before and after Stalin, have been quite stable since 1957. In the Bulgarian case, the opposite trend has prevailed since 1951. Of the 12 full or candidate members of the Politburo in that year, only 4 were left in 1964. Of the 1951 Secretariat of 6, only one, Zhivkov, remained, although one other was in the Politburo.[15] The Czechoslovak leading corps, greatly shaken by the Slánský case, remained largely the same throughout the later fifties, but has undergone substantial changes since 1963, with the removal of some of the older veterans.[16] The SED command has been much altered since 1949. Only 4 of the 1949 Politburo (9 members) were left in 1957; only 6 of the 1950 (15) in 1964. Of the 11 secretaries in 1950, only 2 remained in 1964, although 3 others had been elevated to the Politburo.[17] Apart from the 1948 expulsions and the case of Djilas, there has been a remarkable continuity in the Yugoslav party elite.

Needless to say, the biggest upheavals occurred among the Hungarian and Polish cadres. In the former case, the HWSP, newly-formed after the revolution, had an almost entirely new high command.[18] Of the total of 26 persons in the Secretariat,

[13] J. F. Brown, *Background Notes to Albania's Party Congress* (Munich: Radio Free Europe, 1961), p. 35. Up-to-date lists of party leaders are given in Radio Free Europe, *Soviet and Satellite Party-Government Line-up* (Munich), which appears at regular intervals.

[14] *The Rumanian Workers' Party on the Eve of its Third Congress*, pp. 11–12.

[15] D. Nemoff, *The Bulgarian Communist Party* (New York: National Committee for a Free Europe, 1951), pp. 24ff.

[16] Of the Czechoslovak Presidium in 1949 (22 members), only 6 were left in 1954 and 5 in 1959. Of the 7 members of the 1949 Secretariat, none were left in 1954. Of the 1964 Politburo (11 members), only 4 were members in 1954, and only 5 in 1959. Of the 1964 Secretariat of 7, only 2 remained from 1954 and 5 from 1959.

[17] Carola Stern, *Porträt einer bolschewistischen Partei* (Köln, 1957), charts following pp. 326 and 334.

[18] See the detailed listing and analysis of Paul Detré, "Personnelle

and Political and Organization Committee, in 1952, only 3 remained in the provisional Directing Committee of February, 1957, together with Kádár, who had been eliminated in 1951. Five years later (1962), the Politburo was largely the same, only 2 having been dropped in the meantime. The 6 members of the Secretariat in 1962 were mainly new to this body, only 2 being left from 1957. In the Polish party, there has been somewhat more continuity, but substantial changes resulted from the crisis of 1956. In 1959, only 4 of the 12 persons in the Politburo had been members in 1954; only 1 of 9 in the Secretariat had been members in 1954.[19]

THE PROCESS OF POLITICAL PURGE

The explanation of the purges and trials is difficult and differs from country to country and period to period. In some respects, the process of purge and counterpurge is a kind of parallel, in a one-party system, of the struggle over power and policy in other governments, and a surrogate for the procedure of election and appointment used for the rejuvenation of leadership in more democratic systems. It provides a "mechanism of change," facilitating and justifying a shift in policy and a change of leaders.[20] The purge reflects, however, the special problems of leadership in a centralized and monolithic party, where an elite rules and strict discipline is demanded.[21] Decisions on basic policy are bound to create strains within the inner circle, as men react variously to the situation and to proposed solutions. Apart from such genuine differences, the purge may mirror a struggle for power among persons jealously aspiring to a place at the top of the ladder, and sometimes representing diverse groups within society. In the past, purges were often linked with similar events in the Soviet Union, and were indeed imposed on the local parties by the mother party.

Veränderungen in den Führungsgremien der ungarischen Kommunisten," *Osteuropa,* VIII, 4 (April, 1958), 259–266; see also P. Detré, "Der neue innenpolitische Kurs in Ungarn vor und nach dem VIII. Parteikongress," *Osteuropa,* XIII, 2/3 (February–March, 1963), 179–80.

[19] See G. Rhode, "Der Dritte Parteitag und das II. ZK—Plenum der polnischen KP," *Osteuropa,* IX, 10 (October, 1959), 625.

[20] See Adam Ulam, *Titoism and the Cominform* (Cambridge, 1952), for an excellent study of the early purges in Eastern Europe, especially pp. 145, 189, 190, 192–93, 205–8.

[21] Stern, *op. cit.,* discusses the general factors making for purges, as well as the specific situation in East Germany. See especially pp. 109–12, 119–30, 163–69.

Differences over policy and the struggle for power are, in a communist country, explained in ideological terms, with each disputant claiming doctrinal orthodoxy and charging his rivals with deviations and even criminal actions. No doubt these bitter internecine struggles do sometimes lead to opposition, and even to conspiracy and counterrevolution. There will in any case be suspicion and fear of such treachery by those who hold power. In some cases, however, as has been admitted in the post-Stalin period, the charges were trumped up, and the trials were total fabrications. The victims, even though dead, have been exonerated and rehabilitated. At the time the purges had served the useful purposes of finding scapegoats for regime failures, of excluding rivals from the leadership, of justifying policies introduced by the regime, and of stimulating actions required of party members. The drastic penalties of the past are not so common, and removal of individuals may occur without denunciation and punishment, but the purge seems likely to continue as an instrument for settling the struggles over policy and power which are not easily handled in a system permitting only one party, and requiring strict unity of thought and action.

9: *Apparatchiki*, Activists, and the Rank and File

The communist political elite embraces, in addition to the high command discussed in the preceding chapter, several hundred other "leading cadres," many thousands of middle or lower cadres or "activists," and tens of thousands of rank and file members, all of whom exert an influence over the affairs of society far greater than that of the ordinary citizen. Most prominent are the "*apparatchiki*," engaged full time in party work, and serving as paid functionaries in the central offices, or in branches in the regions, districts, cities, or large basic organizations. Other leading cadres occupy influential positions in state administration, local government, or mass associations, such as the trade unions and women's and youth organizations. Still other "activists," while not employed by state or party, exercise considerable influence by virtue of their work in a particular functional sphere or territorial jurisdiction. Even rank and file members, the basic cadres of the party, although continuing to work in their trades or professions, enjoy a political status superior to that of the population at large.[1]

The power of most of these is a reflected one, their authority derived from above and transmitted downward to others. Only a few of them, at the center, carry any appreciable weight in the decisions taken at the higher levels of government. On the whole, their influence is confined within territorial or functional bounds, and rests largely on their responsibility to implement policy within their jurisdiction. Within that realm, and subject to the authority above, all are "political leaders," who have substantial control over the actions of others and perform roles, in miniature, somewhat comparable to that of the top command over its broader field. With power goes a heavy burden of re-

[1] The distinction between an "*apparatchik*" and an "activist" is taken to be that the former is a full-time, paid functionary, and the latter a part-time volunteer. However, the term "active" is a loose one, which embraces also party members who hold paid offices in nonparty organizations, including the state itself, and even nonparty persons playing a prominent role in public activities. The term "cadres" is an even more generic term, including all persons at the disposal of the party, whether for work in party or government, or for after-hours activity. If these form the "hard core," in the terms of R. V. Burks, the "soft periphery" includes voting supporters, partisan fighters, and party members who are inactive or "opportunist." See R. V. Burks, *The Dynamics of Communism in Eastern Europe* (Princeton, 1961), pp. 8–16.

sponsibility, and even significant risks and dangers, but also prestige, special rights, and some economic and social privileges. There is also a high rate of turnover, and at times, the effect of purges is felt so that power may be evanescent and fleeting.

THE CENTRAL COMMITTEE

The membership of the Central Committee affords a good picture of the power elite at the upper and middle levels, including, as it does, not only the leader and his closest associates in the Politburo and Secretariat, but also the most prominent party and government officials from both the center and the regions. Although the committee itself, as a collective body, does not in fact exercise the power ostensibly belonging to it under the party statute, it represents a gathering of the most powerful persons from various walks of life, including, in addition to the party and government representatives, leading figures from the military, industrial, and intellectual sectors of society. A high proportion of the Central Committee, perhaps about a half, may be regarded as the "hard core" who run the country, occupying the crucial party and government posts.[2] Each of the others, within his own field, has considerable influence over the making of decisions, and even more, the carrying out of the policies formulated above. Taken together, they also constitute a substantial pool of future topmost cadres.

As in the CPSU, the Central Committee in the communist parties of Eastern Europe consists in the main of professional full-time politicians and governmental bureaucrats, more or less equally represented.[3] In a study of the Polish Central Committee elected in 1956, the conclusion was drawn that 44 held positions in the top party leadership and the central apparatus, or were provincial party secretaries, and 50 held positions in the central and provincial government administration.[4] The party contingent

[2] See Richard F. Staar, "The Central Committee of the United Polish Workers' Party (PZPR)," *Journal of Central European Affairs*, XVI, 4 (January, 1957), 379–81. Of the 127 members in 1956, Staar distinguished a "hard core" of over 40 persons.

[3] See Z. Brzezinski and Samuel P. Huntington, "Cincinnatus and the Apparatchik," *World Politics*, XVI, 1 (October, 1963), 61ff.

[4] Staar, *op. cit.*, pp. 371–83. A somewhat similar analysis of the Rumanian Central Committee was made by D. A. Tomasic, "The Rumanian Communist Leadership," *Slavic Review*, XX, 3 (October, 1961), 489–92. Of 17 regional secretaries, 13 were members of the Central Committee; of 24 cabinet ministers, 19 were members.

included the Politburo members and the secretaries of the Central Committee; 15 of the 19 provincial secretaries; section directors or deputies and other officials in the apparatus; officers of the main party schools, chief editors, and so on. The government contingent included members of the State Council and the Council of Ministers (the Prime Minister, deputy prime ministers, other ministers, and deputy ministers), state planning heads, Sejm officers, high officials of the ministries of National Defense and of Public Security, and representatives of the judiciary. The balance of 33 included nine from the mass organizations, such as the trade unions and youth league, four from local government, and others—theoreticians, writers, scholars, and a lone collective farm chairman. The profile of the Czechoslovak Central Committee over the period from 1946 to 1958 was somewhat the same, with, however, a substantial representation of industrial and agricultural administrators, an important component whose weight increased considerably in the later period.[5]

A classification on the basis of social class, occupation, and duration of party membership reveals interesting characteristics that may well be typical of other parties. Although the Czechoslovak Central Committee could not by any means be described as exclusively proletarian, either in social roots or occupation, those who were workers in origin always formed at least half the total, and in 1954 and 1958 exceeded 60 per cent. Farmers constituted an extremely small proportion, never more than 5.9 per cent, and reached a low of 2 per cent in 1958. The two other groups, intelligentsia and white-collar workers, taken together, represented a substantial segment, running from 25 per cent in 1954 to a high of 44 per cent in 1949, almost exactly equaling the ratio of workers in that year.

The Central Committee of the Czechoslovak party was even less proletarian in character when the membership was analyzed in terms of current occupation (see table, page 101, top). It should be noted that persons engaged in industry and agriculture were performing administrative, not manual, tasks, so that workers and peasants may be said not to be represented at all. Even in countries predominantly agricultural, such as Albania, Poland, and Yugoslavia, the majority of Central Committee members was primarily middle class, both in social origin and in current occupation, and workers predominated over peasants.[6]

[5] Daniel Kubat, "Patterns of Leadership in a Communist State: Czechoslovakia 1946–1958," *Journal of Central European Affairs,* XXI, 3 (October, 1961), 305–18.

[6] Burks, *op. cit.,* p. 21.

OCCUPATIONAL MAKEUP OF THE CZECHOSLOVAK CENTRAL COMMITTEE, 1946–58

	CC ELECTED AT CONGRESSES (IN PERCENTAGES)			
Occupation	*VIII* *1946*	*IX* *1949*	*X* *1954*	*XI* *1958*
Party administration	33.9	29.5	26.8	34.7
Industry, construction, transportation, and trade	16.4	12.5	16.9	15.6
Farming and forestry	1.5	4.7	6.2	8.1
Government and local administration	22.3	27.1	26.8	19.0
Mass organizations	13.4	17.0	12.5	10.8
Education, sciences, and arts	11.8	6.9	5.4	6.9
Army and police forces	0.7	2.3	5.4	4.9

SOURCE: Daniel Kubat, "Patterns of Leadership in a Communist State: Czechoslovakia 1946–1958," *Journal of Central European Affairs,* XXI, 3 (October, 1961), 314.

In the early postwar years, veteran communists, their membership dating before the seizure of power, usually predominated. In Czechoslovakia, two-thirds of the Central Committee at the congresses in 1946 and 1949 were prewar or wartime party members; even in 1958, they still constituted 43 per cent of the Central Committee.[7]

LENGTH OF MEMBERSHIP OF THE CZECHOSLOVAK CENTRAL COMMITTEE, 1946–58

	CC ELECTED AT CONGRESSES (IN PERCENTAGES)			
Date of membership	*VIII* *1946*	*IX* *1949*	*X* *1954*	*XI* *1958*
1921–May, 1945	62.7	67.4	54.5	42.9
May, 1945–February, 1948	37.3	25.6	41.9	51.7
After February, 1948	—	7.0	3.6	5.4

SOURCE: Daniel Kubat, "Patterns of Leadership in a Communist State: Czechoslovakia 1946–1958," *Journal of Central European Affairs,* XXI, 3 (October, 1961), 314.

[7] Staar, in his analysis of the 44 persons designated as the hard core of the Polish Central Committee in 1956, concluded that the overwhelming majority of them, 84 per cent, had been party members prior to 1938! Most of them had had careers since the war, primarily in party work.

More and more in the later period, after 1954, the old guard was replaced by a new type of younger socialist leader with a proletarian background and less formal education, but with party training, usually of a specialized type, who had come up through the channels, not of government service, but of party administration or industry.[8]

Nationality plays a role in countries of ethnic heterogeneity, such as Czechoslovakia, Yugoslavia, and Rumania. In the first, there has always been a heavy predominance of Czechs in the Central Committee, accurately reflecting their proportion of party membership, but far exceeding their ratio in the total population.[9] In multi-national Yugoslavia, the representation of the various national groups in the Central Committee is relatively equitable, with 46 Serbs, 29 Croats, 21 Slovenes, 16 Macedonians, and 15 Montenegrins, as well as eight from other minority groups.[10]

As in all top party bodies, there is a constant process of change in the Central Committee. In spite of their high status and substantial power, the members are always expendable, and may be removed at will. The composition mirrors the shifting alignments of the various groups within the elite. At almost every party congress there is a considerable turnover, as some leave, others are promoted from the status of candidates, and others enter the committee for the first time. Even between the congresses, there are removals and co-optations. Of the total of 337 members of the four Central Committees studied in Czechoslovakia, two-thirds of them were elected only once; one-fifth were elected to two terms; and only one-eighth elected three or four times.[11] Periods of purge, of course, bring even more radical and wholesale replacements. Between the ninth and tenth congresses

[8] Kubat, *op. cit.*, pp. 311–12.

[9] In 1962, of 97 full members, 18 may be identified as Slovaks. Of 50 candidates, nine were Slovaks. See page 110 for nationalities of party members.

[10] G. W. Hoffman and F. W. Neal, *Yugoslavia and the New Communism* (New York, 1962), p. 494. D. Tomasic in "The New Class and Nationalism," *Journal of Croatian Studies*, I (1960), 53–74, argues the thesis of a Serbian-Orthodox dominance in the CPY, but his evidence rests largely on his identification of Montenegrins as Serbs, and Macedonians and "Yugoslavs" as Orthodox, thus giving the combined Serb-Orthodox group 57.8 per cent in the 1958 Central Committee. In fact, if each group is taken separately, the Serbs are underrepresented on the Central Committee in terms of their share of the population as a whole, and the Slovenes, Macedonians, and Montenegrins are greatly overrepresented.

[11] Kubat, *op. cit.*, p. 307.

of the CPC, for instance, only six members were reelected (of 112 appointed). The change in the Hungarian Central Committee in the wake of the revolution was also drastic. In the small committee of 36 in 1957, 25 were entirely new. In 1957, only 10 members of the 1952 committee (87 full and candidate members), plus Kallai and Kádár, who had been purged in 1951, were left.[12]

Other parties have preserved greater continuity in their Central Committees. For instance, in the Bulgarian party, of 35 full members (26 candidates) in 1952, 19 of each were still members or candidates in 1958.[13] Surprisingly, in view of the crisis of 1956, the Polish leadership also remained relatively stable. At the third congress in 1959, 62 per cent of the 1954 Central Committee were re-appointed; only 13 of the new Central Committee had not been members in 1954, and of these, several had been earlier members purged in 1948.[14]

OTHER MEMBERS OF THE POWER ELITE

There are hundreds of other leaders who occupy important positions in government, party, or other administrative hierarchies, and who exercise an influence on a national scale. Although not members of the Central Committee, they may aspire eventually, when fortune smiles upon them, to become candidates and even to enter the inner circle. These include cabinet ministers or their deputies; high officials in government departments; leaders of the trade unions and other mass organizations; high-ranking officers of the armed services and the police; and other public servants in radio and television, and so on. Even more important are several hundred topmost functionaries or *apparatchiki* in a cluster of key party agencies grouped around the Central Committee apparatus.[15] These include the members of the Party Control Com-

[12] See Paul Detré, "Personnelle Veränderungen in den Führungsgremien der ungarischen Kommunisten," *Osteuropa*, VIII, 4 (April, 1958), 259–66, and R. Gabor, *Organization and Strategy of the Hungarian Workers' (Communist) Party* (2d ed.; New York: National Committee for a Free Europe, October, 1952), p. 40.

[13] See D. Nemoff, *The Bulgarian Communist Party* (New York: National Committee for a Free Europe, 1951), and Radio Free Europe, *The Central Organs of the Bulgarian Communist Party After Its Seventh Congress* (Munich, 1958).

[14] G. Rhode, "Der Dritte Parteitag und das II. ZK—Plenum der polnischen KP," *Osteuropa*, IX, 10 (October, 1959), 623. See also Staar, *op. cit.*, pp. 382–83.

[15] A somewhat similar cluster exists in all the parties, including the CPY. See Hoffman and Neal, *op. cit.*, p. 192.

mission, the Central Revision Commission, and those in other influential institutions, such as the publishing house, the official daily newspaper, the monthly theoretical journal, the magazine for party functionaries, the Higher Party School, the Institute for Party History, and usually an Institute of Social Sciences. Most of the parties follow the East German example in having standing or provisional commissions, subordinate to a Secretary, and consisting of apparatus members and representatives of scholarship, the public service, and mass associations. In the East German case, too, each of the Politburo members has a personal staff, and there is a common office serving both Politburo and Secretariat.[16]

Most strategically located on the ladder of power, however, are the highest officials in the Central Committee apparatus, who head up the main departments of this powerful administrative organism. The SED in 1957 may be taken as illustrating the general pattern, which is everywhere closely modeled on the Soviet party, but, as in the USSR, is subject to frequent reorganization. Those employed in the SED apparatus numbered about 2,000 persons, of whom 1,000 were termed "political functionaries." Apart from the secretaries, each of whom was responsible for several branches of work, each department was directed by a chief, with several section heads under him. Some, but not all, of these leading officials were members of the Central Committee. Departments covered all spheres of party work proper, as well as public affairs in general.[17]

LOCAL FUNCTIONARIES

Away from the center, great power rests in the hands of the outstanding cadres of regions, districts, cities, and other areas of jurisdiction (such as the republics in Yugoslavia), and of the basic party organizations. In Bulgaria, for instance, of over 425,000 party members in 1950, it was estimated that there were, in addition to 2,000 at the center, approximately 55,000 cadres at the lower levels, either serving as functionaries of the party or working as officials in local government, in the local offices of administration, army and militia, or in mass organizations.[18] Fuller data showed that the *apparatchiki* proper in the Czechoslovak party in 1962 included the following:

[16] Carola Stern, *Porträt einer bolschewistischen Partei, Entwicklung, Funktion und Situation der SED* (Köln, 1957), pp. 269–77, 338, 347–52.

[17] See Chapter 12, pp. 147–48, n. 18, for a listing of the departments of the Polish apparatus.

[18] Nemoff, *op. cit.*, p. 31.

Members and candidates of party committees in the regions and in Prague (Category A)	570
Members and candidates of party committees in districts, areas, and other towns (Category B)	4,583
Chairmen and secretaries of basic organizations (Category C)	45,851
TOTAL MIDDLE AND LOWER CADRES	51,004

An even wider circle of persons enjoying substantial influence embraced the members of the committees of basic organizations (Category D), numbering about 293,000, or roughly 19 per cent of the entire membership.[19] Of the total membership of 1,680,000, then, the leading activists numbered almost 350,000 persons.

Who are these local activists and *apparatchiki?* In the early years, many of them were persons with prewar and wartime communist activity, often illegal, but more and more they are recruited from postwar members and from the lower ranks of the apparatus. Long years of membership are, however, normally required, even for election to committees—for instance, in the Czechoslovak party, seven years for regional, five for district, committees. Most of the leading cadres in the CPC are communists with 15 or more years of membership: 75 per cent of Category A above; 63 per cent of Category B; and 47 per cent of Category C. Carefully supervised, especially by the cadre offices at their own and the next higher level, such persons have been sifted and screened, moved from assignment to assignment and post to post, promoted or demoted, and if they make good, have moved from the ranks of activists to that of *apparatchiki,* and then up and up in the apparatus. Many of them have had periods of special education, either for a few months in regional and district schools or, for higher cadres, a year or more at the Higher Party School. An increasing number have had university or secondary education. A large proportion of them are of working-class origin: 70 per cent in Category C, and over 75 per cent in Category B. In their present occupations, however, most are of the middle class; a smaller proportion are workers; and a much smaller group, collective and individual farmers, as the following table indicates:

[19] For this, and data cited in following pages, see the unsigned article, "Some Details About the Communist Party of Czechoslovakia," in the CPC organ, *Život strany,* No. 24, December, 1962. Staar gives similar figures for the Polish party in 1950, with a total of 54,300 party workers at lower, middle, and higher levels. See his *Poland, 1944–1962* (New Orleans, 1962), pp. 170–74.

COMMUNIST PARTY OF CZECHOSLOVAKIA—PARTY ACTIVISTS

Current occupations	CATEGORY A %	B %	C %	D %
Workers (including those in services)	17.9	20.4	36.0	37.4
Collective and individual farmers	11.4	12.0	5.6	7.2
White-collar employees*	63.3	60.2	40.6	39.0
Others (including housewives, pensioners, and so on)	7.4	7.4	16.9	16.4

* The original categories given were engineers and technicians, working people trained in economics, public workers, teachers and professors, and administrative officials.

SOURCE: *Život strany*, December, 1962.

The party bureaus or executive committees at these lower levels are somewhat like miniature Politburos, including in their ranks persons at the head of the local party secretariats, as well as leading figures in local government, mass associations, and the like. Thus, in the SED county (Bezirk) organizations, the membership of each bureau was as follows:

First Secretary	1
Second Secretary	1
Other secretaries (heading departments of Agitation and Propaganda, Economics, Agriculture, and Culture and Education)	4
Chairman of District Party Control Commission	1
First Secretary of city leadership	1
Chairman of local county council	1
Chairman of county trade union council	1
Head of the county administration of the State Security Service	1

Among the candidate members were several party secretaries in districts (Kreise) and in large factories or farms, and secretaries of the youth association.[20]

Of the local functionaries, the most powerful are the first secretaries within each jurisdiction. "Like the Soviet *obkom*, *gorkom*, and *raikom* secretaries," writes Taborsky about the CPC, "they are the key political figures on all territorial levels. They are the nabobs of the communist system engaged full time

[20] Stern, *op. cit.*, table after p. 352.

in directing and controlling, on behalf of their superiors and under their watchful supervision, not only the Party apparatus but also the machinery of government in the area assigned to their jurisdiction."[21] In the basic party organizations, the chairmen occupy a similar position of supremacy. The secretaries are experienced veterans, with ten years' membership required for regional, and eight for district, secretaries, under the latest CPC statute. Usually proletarian in origin, they are often persons with substantial education, either higher or secondary. Under Stalin, they were "little kings" within their respective areas, often holding many posts and exercising a virtual monopoly of power. At present the cult of personality is condemned at the lower levels as well as at the highest, and the principle of collective leadership is proclaimed. Although it is difficult to ascertain to what extent their power is shared with their colleagues, there is little doubt of their continuing importance.

The power of the local cadres, including that of first secretaries, is not independently acquired or exercised, but entirely derived from above. The principle of democratic centralism that suffuses the whole system treats the functionaries as elected officers, responsible to the bodies choosing them. In the post-Stalin days, there is in all probability a more genuine process of election, with a secret ballot, and a more effective system of accountability. The principle of "rotation" of officers at all levels, introduced recently in some of the parties, is supposed to increase the democratic and responsible character of the leadership, and may indeed assure a greater circulation of the elite. Nonetheless, rotation can also be a device, not really new, for facilitating the replacement of lower officials at the will of those above. In any case, the centralizing aspect of democratic centralism is paramount, with the real responsibility flowing always upward to the next level, and ultimately to the apex. Secretaries of every rank are carefully selected and schooled, and their appointments are subject to the endorsement of the superior level. They are usually members, in a kind of "reverse representation," of the superordinate body as well, so that the entire system forms "a chain of interlocking secretariats" or a "secretarial axis," which insures monolithic unity and the quick execution of instructions from on high.[22]

[21] E. Taborsky, *Communism in Czechoslovakia 1948–1960* (Princeton, 1961), pp. 61, 65.

[22] Tomasic, "The Rumanian Communist Leadership," pp. 492–94. The regional secretaries, for instance, are usually members of the Central Committee; the district secretaries, of the regional committee; and so on.

THE RANK AND FILE

The position of the rank and file member is set forth in the party statutes, with a detailed listing of his rights and duties. Although since the death of Stalin an effort has been made to broaden his rights, he is probably still unable to affect greatly the decisions even of his basic group, and has little or no influence over the course of action at a higher level. Duties are also heavy, since the

PARTY MEMBERSHIP (INCLUDING CANDIDATES)

	End of War	*1948*	*1954*	*1958–65*
AWP	700 (1943) 2,800 (1944)	45,382	48,644 (1956)	53,659 (1961)
BCP	15,000 (1944)	463,701	455,251	493,255 (1958)
CPC	27,000 (1945)	2,418,199	1,489,234	1,680,819 (1962)
SED		1,773,689 (1949)	1,413,313	1,610,679 (1962)
HWP (HWSP)	2,000 (1945)	1,500,000	864,607 100,000 (Dec., 1956)	490,000 (1962)
PUWP	20,000 (1945)	1,500,000	1,297,000	1,023,425 (1959) 1,494,105 (1963) 1,614,273 (1964)
RWP (RCP)	1,000 (1944)	900,000	595,398 (1955)	834,600 (1960) 1,450,000 (1965)
CPY (LCY)	140,000 (1945)	448,175	700,030	857,537 (1959) 1,030,040 (1965)

SOURCES: *East Europe*, IX, 12 (December, 1960), 8; G. W. Hoffman and F. W. Neal, *Yugoslavia and the New Communism* (New York, 1962), p. 197; Carola Stern, *Porträt einer bolschewistischen Partei, Entwicklung, Funktion und Situation der SED* (Köln, 1957), p. 282; and the volumes in Robert F. Byrnes (gen. ed.), *East-Central Europe under the Communists* (New York, 1956–57): S. Skendi (ed.), *Albania*, p. 84; L. A. Dellin (ed.), *Bulgaria*, p. 130; E. Helmreich (ed.), *Hungary*, p. 125; O. Halecki (ed.), *Poland*, pp. 123–24; S. Fischer-Galati (ed.), *Rumania*, p. 76; and V. Busek and N. Spulber (eds.), *Czechoslovakia*, p. 70. Latest data are taken from official announcements as reported in the local presses.

member must obey decisions of the party, and perform all assignments given by his superiors. Members form "cells" or "aktivs" in the organizations to which they belong, and seek, with their fellow communists, to give effect to party policy. The member's power is greatest in relationship to nonmembers, and in his place of work or neighborhood. Nonmembers, especially if they are experts, are more and more drawn into important tasks, so that the difference in power between them and members is to some extent reduced. Nor are all party members equally active or powerful; many may be apathetic and inactive. Party membership does, however, bring with it added authority and an ability to influence the actions of others, as well as the burdens and risks of responsibility.

At the close of the war, most of the East European parties were small in size, but have since developed into mass parties. In the early years, there were campaigns for members, and the rules of admission were not strict. The fusion of social democratic and communist parties brought in many newcomers. The peak was usually reached in 1948 or 1949. Thereafter, admission was more selective and made on an individual basis, with a period of candidacy required, and with other requirements differing according to social class.[23] The parties carried through periodic screenings of members, eliminating tens of thousands during each check-up for ideological deviations or personal inadequacies. Political purges resulted in mass exclusions. The crisis of 1956 in Hungary led to the disintegration and subsequent reforming of the party, much smaller in size. There has been a constant turnover in the ranks in all the parties, and there are large numbers of ex-communists in every country.

Although, as in the CPSU, admission is carefully regulated and subject to stringent rules set forth in the statutes, the parties have in most cases attained massive dimensions, often representing a high ratio of the total population. The CPC, which has been the largest party in Eastern Europe, included in its ranks in 1962 roughly 17.5 per cent of all adults over 18 years old.[24] It was a relatively old group, with only 9.2 per cent of the members 26 years or younger, and over two-thirds dating their membership back to 1948 or earlier. Although most were therefore veterans,

[23] The RCP in 1965 was the first party to abolish entirely the candidacy and eliminate all differences in requirements based on class.

[24] Full details are given in *Život strany*, December, 1962. For the Polish party, see Staar, *Poland, 1944–1962*, chap. 10. See also Burks, *op. cit.*, p. 51.

only 1 per cent had been members prior to 1945, so that it was primarily a postwar party. Women constituted only 27 per cent of the membership, an underrepresentation common to all communist parties. Most significantly, Slovaks were only 17.5 per cent of the total, and Czechs, 79.9 per cent as compared to ratios of the total population of 28 per cent and 66 per cent respectively.

The rank and file of the parties were less predominantly middle class than the leading middle and lower cadres discussed above, but were by no means exclusively or even predominantly proletarian. Usually no single class represented a majority. In certain parties, notably the Albanian and Bulgarian, the largest group was of peasant origin, approximately 67 per cent and 40 per cent respectively. In the early years after the war, the Yugoslav party showed a similar composition. In the others, the largest group, forming, however, only a plurality, was normally of working-class origin, running from 40 per cent to as high as 50 per cent. It is extremely hard to draw hard and fast conclusions, however, as data refer sometimes to social origin and sometimes to current occupation. The information available for the CPC, for instance, indicates that in 1962, 62 per cent of the members were of working-class background, but only 36 per cent were workers by current occupation. Farmers constituted a ratio of only 6.6 per cent, a low proportion characteristic of most of the parties, except the Albanian and the Bulgarian. Persons with engineering, technical, and economic qualifications formed 14.6 per cent of the total.[25] Increasingly important has been the ratio of state employees and persons of various white-collar or intellectual occupations, occasionally mounting to a proportion as high as, or higher than, that of the workers. Many of these, as Burks has put it, were "self-tutored professionals" who had climbed, via the movement, into the ranks of the middle class.[26]

[25] *Život strany*, December, 1962.
[26] Burks, *op. cit.*, pp. 35–37, 187, and p. 52 for data as of 1947–48.

PART FOUR
THE PROCESS OF GOVERNING

Introduction

It is the central purpose of any government to establish a general framework of public policy for the community over which it has power, and to enforce this policy on the individual members of that community. Through an infinite series of particular decisions, a government formulates a set of binding norms or obligations which in some fields impose certain limits on the conduct of citizens; in others, protect their freedom of action; and in still others, afford them specific opportunities and assistance. The scope of policy-making will vary greatly from one time to another, and from society to society, in some cases embracing a relatively small, in others, such as the communist, a very large, sector. The processes by which decisions are effected will diverge, as will the forms in which they are expressed. Different, too, will be the locus of the ultimate power to decide. In every political system, however, the making of such decisions is a crucial function, indeed the very *raison d'être*, of government.

Traditional political science focused on the "legislature" as *the* law-making institution, from which presumably emanated all the major measures of public policy. In many states, laws, either as constitutional norms or as ordinary statutes, are important. Decisions need not, however, take legal form at all, and may be established through institutions not endowed with legislative power. This is especially true of communist systems, where, as we have observed, the position of the legislature, although vaunted in theory, is in actuality circumscribed, and the power of decision-making assumed by other instrumentalities.

It would be misleading in the analysis of any political system to focus exclusively or even mainly on formal institutions, and in particular on the legislative bodies. Seldom, if ever, does any institution of government fully perform the functions officially assigned to it. Our aim should be to reveal the real process of making authoritative decisions, whether in the shape of laws or not, and whether promulgated by legislatures or by other bodies.

Who makes the key decisions in communist societies? Who takes the initiative in raising a problem for consideration and suggesting a solution? Who takes part in the process of deliberation and in what manner? How and in what form are the final decisions made?

Most countries in the past, and many even in the twentieth century, have dispensed entirely with legislatures and have depended on the executive arm for the making of policy. Only with the rise of representative government in the nineteenth century was the circle of decision-making widened, and executive decrees or fiats increasingly replaced by statute and law. Even in the modern democratic state, there has been recently an attenuation in the authority of legislatures, as executives have arrogated more and more of the power of policy formation.[1] In no country in fact is the legislature the exclusive law-making body, even if it is so described in the constitution. The initiative in enacting laws often comes from a president or other executive officer, and the law as finally determined is the result of a highly political process, reflecting the interplay of forces within and outside the legislature, and departing substantially from the procedures set forth in legal theory.[2]

An idealized picture of democracy suggests that the "people" rule, that is, that the population as a whole makes the crucial political decisions. In fact, in all systems, almost without exception, the people do not exercise their power directly, but do so through "representatives" who govern on their behalf. Whether elected or not, the rulers "represent" the ruled, even if only in the sense that the former themselves determine the interests of their subjects. Only in a democracy is it assumed that they carry out the will of the people as expressed *by* the people; the electoral system and parliament are designed to effect this. Yet even in a democracy, many leaders are appointed to office, and represent the people more indirectly than popular myth suggests. Even where there are elections, the representatives seldom if ever merely passively reflect the people's will, but always use their own judgment in carrying out their mandate, and themselves exert an influence on public opinion. In the most perfect democracy, the genuinely representative character of the system may

[1] J. Meynaud, "The Executive in the Modern State," quoted by Roy C. Macridis and Bernard E. Brown (eds.), *Comparative Politics: Notes and Readings* (Homewood, Ill., 1961) p. 343.

[2] Alfred de Grazia, *Elements of Political Science* (New York, 1952), pp. 328, 342.

be distorted or limited by such factors as public apathy or misinformation, by the irrational factors affecting voting behavior, and, not least, by the extraordinary role played by parties and leaders in the crystallization of opinion, and in the nomination and election of candidates. Although the voters have the final choice between rival candidates, and hence have some influence on the determination of public policy, the "people's choice" is not as pure and unsullied as sometimes assumed.

In any case, in all countries, the "people" and the "individual" participate in politics primarily through organized groups, varying in their interests and in their capacity to give effect to them, and differing, too, in their organizational structure and in their members' ability to influence group policy. In some cases, certain groups representing narrow or partial interests will be able to impose their wishes on the country as a whole. In others, many groups will have to reconcile their separate concerns in a more general "public" interest. Political systems differ widely in the manner in which group interests are expressed and compromised, or, to use the terms suggested by Almond and Coleman, "articulated" and "aggregated."[3] Certainly a representative assembly is not the only agency for discharging such tasks. The administrative hierarchy may also play a significant part in sorting out the many demands placed before the government and working out a viable and satisfactory policy. Parties often play an important role in this process as do pressure groups, and other less formal associations with political interests.[4]

In a democracy, competing parties normally perform important functions in choosing representatives for the elected branches of government, in mediating conflicting interests, and in crystallizing a "public" opinion. Their primary purpose may be the expression of fundamental political principles; or the attainment of power, or more likely, some combination of both. Whether "principled" or not, parties and individual politicians are usually brokers of ideas and interests, working out a program attractive to the voters, and to some degree embodying it in public policy, if they are elected. In fulfilling their role, the parties decisively affect the entire system of politics, and in particular the relationship between the "people," or specific groups, and their representatives, and exert a crucial influence on the

[3] Gabriel Almond and James Coleman (eds.), *The Politics of the Developing Areas* (Princeton, 1960), pp. 33ff.

[4] Henry Ehrmann (ed.), *Interest Groups on Four Continents* (Pittsburgh, 1958).

making of decisions. Parties are not, however, essential features of a political system, as has been demonstrated throughout history by authoritarian rule in its many manifestations. Even a democratic system may dispense with competing parties and operate with a single dominant party, with no parties at all, or with other variations too numerous to mention.[5]

Communist government has been traditionally analyzed largely in terms of "outputs," that is, the manner in which decisions are made and enforced, but increasing recognition is given to the "inputs," characteristic of every system, including the assertion of group interests as the raw materials of the decision-making process. Since competing parties do not exist, and one party dominates, other means must be found for "sublimating" the influence and the demands of society, and evolving a policy for the community as a whole. A representative body exists, as do organized groups such as the unions. Yet the party alone has the right, and the power, to determine the "real interest" of the people as a whole, as opposed to what may seem to them to be their interests, and occupies a "strategic" position which enables it to subordinate the lesser interests to a broader "social" interest.[6]

[5] Fred I. Greenstein, *The American Party System and the American People* (Englewood Cliffs, N.J., 1963), pp. 62ff.

[6] See J. Djordjević, "Interest Groups and the Political System of Yugoslavia," in Ehrmann, *op. cit.*, pp. 202, 204–5, 220–22.

The Making of Decisions

Communist constitutions normally provide that the legislative authority shall rest exclusively with elected parliaments or assemblies, and shall not be shared with any other bodies. Legal theory in these countries claims that other binding measures, such as administrative decrees or court decisions, are based on, and in harmony with, the legislative statutes, and these in turn rest on the constitutional foundations of the state. There is thus a hierarchy of legal norms embracing fundamental laws; ordinary statutes; decrees or resolutions of the parliamentary Presidium, and of the cabinet; ordinances and directives of individual ministers; court decisions; and even to some extent, customary law.[1] Law is therefore assumed to occupy a key place in society, and the law-making body to have a crucial role in creating the basic obligations of citizens. In reality, however, the executive has increasingly displaced the parliament, and, as in other systems of absolutist rule, has become a preeminent agency of decision-making. But even more significant is the domination of the party, its top organs and its leaders, which in practice, and even in communist theory, is the main architect of public policy.[2] Moreover, "laws" or their derivatives comprise but a small part of the general framework of compulsory rules binding the citizen. Although decisions other than laws are important ingredients of policy-making in all states, the extralegal component of the communist system has a vastly wider scope than in democratic societies.

THE ASSEMBLIES

In communist countries, the legislature has normally acted only on the most important measures, such as enactment and amendment of the constitution, certain fundamental legal codes and basic statutes, the annual budget, and the long-term plan. Even

[1] See the analysis of sources of Hungarian law in Vladimir Gsovski and Kazimierz Grzybowski (eds.), *Government, Law and Courts in the Soviet Union and Eastern Europe* (2 vols.; London and The Hague, 1959), I, 310–15. For some recent developments, see K. Grzybowski and J. L. Alder, "Eastern Europe: Legislative Trends," *Problems of Communism*, XIV, 2 (March–April, 1965), 122–31.

[2] See Chapter 5, pp. 52–54. For an excellent analysis of the decision-making process in East Germany, see Ernst Richert, *Macht ohne Mandat: Der Staatsapparat in der Sowjetischen Besatzungszone Deutschlands* (2d ed.; Köln and Opladen, 1963), esp. chap. 2.

in these matters, its role is purely formal and does not involve really independent acts of deliberation and decision. For one thing, as will be seen more fully in the next chapter, the assembly is handpicked by the ruling party, and is not representative of the populace, so that its members cannot bring the views and interests of the public or of special groups to bear on proposed legislation. The assembly is completely controlled by its officers (the chairman, the Presidium, committee chairmen, and others), and its legislative output is largely predetermined by the cabinet or the Presidium. Sessions are short in the extreme, two or three days several times a year. Debates in plenary session involve statements in favor of the legislation by selected spokesmen, without opposition or fundamental criticism, normally without amendments, and with unanimous approval the foreordained outcome, thus emptying the decision of all real content. Committees, although sometimes numerous, have never enjoyed the right to introduce legislation.[3] Even committee discussion, although permitting detailed examination of, and perhaps technical changes in, the bills under consideration, has been largely without meaning, since these bodies are also dominated by the ruling party and no opposition exists. Certainly during the Stalin period, the representative assembly in all the countries of Eastern Europe served in the main as a "rubber-stamp" for decisions taken elsewhere, and as a kind of educational forum for its members and the public at large. Although the parliament performs other functions, to be discussed elsewhere, it cannot be regarded as significant in the forming of public policy, or even in the deliberative process.[4]

Much more powerful than the legislative assembly as a whole, but falling far short of the rights assigned to it in theory, is the Presidium of the assembly, or as it is called in certain countries, the State Council. Although possessing a wide range of functions, only its part in law-making is relevant here. In most cases, it has enjoyed the right, between sessions of the assembly, to issue

[3] The Czechoslovak National Assembly has had a large number of committees, including credentials, constitutional law, foreign affairs, budget and the economy, agriculture, public welfare and health, and cultural affairs, and earlier, defense and state security. In 1960, separate committees for the budget and the plan, and for industry, were created. E. Taborsky, *Communism in Czechoslovakia, 1948–1960* (Princeton, 1961), pp. 252–53.

[4] See Richert, *op. cit.*, chap. 8, esp. p. 227, and Taborsky, *op. cit.*, chap. XI. See also H. Gordon Skilling, "Czechoslovakia: Government in Communist Hands," *Journal of Politics*, XVII, 3 (August, 1955), 434–39.

decrees that have legal validity, subject, however, to later ratification by the assembly. As assembly meetings are few and brief, and confirmation merely a formality, the bulk of the legislative power in effect gravitated into the hands of the Presidium. Even constitutional amendments were adopted in this manner. The Presidium usually enjoys, but seldom if ever exercises, the right to give a legally binding interpretation of the constitution and other laws. Although such a body no longer exists in Yugoslavia, and in Czechoslovakia has a more limited function, it has emerged elsewhere, on the Soviet model, as a key agency for giving formal enactment to certain measures. Yet in spite of appearances, it does not begin to compare with the Council of Ministers or the top party organs in legislative initiative. The fact that it is often headed by a nonparty personage, who serves as honorific "president,"[5] and that its other members are usually not high-ranking communist leaders, testifies to its largely ceremonial position.

During the post-Stalin thaw, especially in Poland and Hungary, the failure of the parliaments to fulfill their constitutionally provided tasks was openly admitted, and some attempts were made to enhance their importance in law-making. In Hungary, as a result of the revolution, such efforts came to nothing. In Poland, even before October, steps were taken to enlarge the role of the Sejm, and in particular to enliven the work of the committees.[6] After October, Gomulka referred to "the elevation of the role of the Sejm to that of the supreme organ of state power" as of great importance in the process of democratization.[7] Although it never assumed the role thus envisaged, it did become a more significant factor in public life. Not only were the elections to the Sejm made more meaningful, but its actual functioning became more effective. It has met more often, and for longer sessions, lasting sometimes several months. Its legislative output has been greater, and that of the Council of State less. Although the general debates in plenary sessions have remained largely per-

[5] This was once true of Rumania and still is of Hungary. In Czechoslovakia, the chairman has usually been a former social democrat. In some countries, Bulgaria and Poland, for instance, a leading communist has held the post. In East Germany and Rumania, the chairmanship of the State Council was assumed by the First Secretary of the party, Ulbricht and Gheorghiu-Dej respectively, thus increasing the significance of this post.

[6] Gsovski and Grzybowski, *op. cit.*, Vol. I, pp. 303–6, 351–61.

[7] Speech by Gomulka, *Trybuna Ludu*, October 21, 1956, given in English in Paul E. Zinner (ed.), *Communism and Popular Revolt in Eastern Europe* (New York, 1956), pp. 235–38.

functory, critical opinions are sometimes expressed, and even occasional negative votes are cast, and abstentions occur. Although most bills are still initiated by the government, some have been submitted by private members. The parliamentary committees have carried on frank and sometimes heated discussions, and have been able in some degree to influence legislation.[8]

In other countries, there has been talk of the need for open and critical debate, and for a genuine parliamentary process. The new constitution in Czechoslovakia in 1960, heralded as a landmark in democratic development, in fact did not alter seriously the role of the National Assembly.[9] In 1964, proposals were made by the CPC to give greater reality to the sessions of the National Assembly and the Slovak National Council, with more frequent and longer meetings and more active committees. Although this may have led to some improvements, it seems doubtful that the position of the legislature will be fundamentally changed as long as elections are purely formal, and as long as a single centralized party persists, and other parties are only decorative.

Even in Yugoslavia, the situation has been similar, with administrative decrees more important than legislative enactments, and the executive dominating the actual process of legislation. After 1954, and later, in the 1963 constitution, steps were taken to give the Federal Assembly greater authority to draft laws and to issue directives binding on administrative agencies. Parliamentary debate in the Skupshtina remained, however, less spirited than in the Polish Sejm, and its sessions were seriously affected by the fact of an overwhelming communist majority.[10] In 1964, an appeal made by E. Kardelj, the Assembly chairman, for more "independent" conduct by this body seemed to produce some results, and a year later it forced the government to make many amendments to the plan before it was formally approved.[11]

[8] See Chapter 11, and Richard Hiscocks, *Poland: Bridge for the Abyss?* (London, 1963), pp. 203–5, 219–20, 272–76. See also V. C. Chrypinski, "Poland's Parliamentary Committees," *East Europe*, XIV, 1 (January, 1965), 16–24.

[9] See H. Gordon Skilling, "The Czechoslovak Constitution of 1960 and the Transition to Communism," *Journal of Politics*, XXIV (1962), 152–53.

[10] See Gsovski and Grzybowski, *op. cit.*, Vol. I, pp. 457–58; G. W. Hoffman and F. W. Neal, *Yugoslavia and the New Communism* (New York, 1962), pp. 220–21, 459.

[11] *Christian Science Monitor*, February 24, 1965. See also R. V. Burks, "Yugoslavia: Has Tito Gone Bourgeois?" *East Europe*, XIV, 8 (August, 1965), 8.

THE GOVERNMENTS

In most countries, the executive or government plays a crucial part in formulating policy and making laws, usually drafting and submitting the major projects to the legislature for ratification. In communist countries, the cabinet is indeed not a "mere executive," but an organ of "leadership and decision-making." It is chiefly responsible for initiating legislation, which is assured of automatic approval without fundamental, or even minor, changes. Moreover, as in other countries, the cabinet may issue decrees or ordinances for fulfilling the purposes of a law, and for carrying out day-to-day operations. In view of the long periods of inactivity of the legislature proper, this is a source of legal compulsion more important than formal statutes, and thus ranks with the power of the Presidium of the assembly to issue decrees. Between 1950 and 1953, for instance, in the DDR, as compared with 60 laws, over 1,000 ordinances, cabinet decisions, and executive orders were issued, not infrequently bypassing existing statutes and introducing basically altered policies. The entire New Course in early 1953 was so introduced.[12]

To "govern" is more than to "legislate," however, especially in a communist society. The executive branch has a crucial position in adumbrating the entire framework of policy, being responsible for formulating long-term plans, the annual budget, and the major lines of military and foreign policy. The initial "declaration of government policy" becomes the major expression of the "political will" of the state, setting the limits and molding the content of all legislative activity. Legislation thus becomes a secondary matter, reduced to dealing with "bagatelles of the second and third rank."[13] Central importance attaches to the plan, with its systematic determination of the shape of the economy and the distribution of investment, of labor, and of the national income. Even the constitution may be thought of as subordinate in significance to the provisions of the plan. The government statement itself can be flexibly interpreted, modified, and even bypassed, when conditions require a new policy. Much power belongs therefore to the executive in making the "general will" a "concrete practicable will," applying it in detail to the actual

[12] See Richert, *op. cit.*, chap. 4, for an analysis of the executive in East Germany; see also Chapter 12 below.

[13] Richert, *op. cit.*, p. 90.

conditions of society, through legislative or administrative means, and making it obligatory for all.[14] Although this role of the executive is not entirely foreign to a democratic system, in communist societies it is greatly enhanced by the absence of opposition within the assemblies, and the resulting impotence of these bodies as organs of critical and partisan debate.

In spite of what has been said above, the position of the government is not in fact quite as powerful as suggested. For one thing, it has usually become too large for effective action, numbering as many as 30 to 40 ministers, chairmen of commissions, and so on. In almost all communist countries, there has emerged a smaller inner cabinet, or Presidium, made up of the Prime Minister, the deputy premiers, and sometimes several other important ministers.[15] Always dominated by the party, with most of its members also belonging to the Politburo, this body may include spokesmen of other parties where they exist. It represents thus a personal union of party and state at the apex of administrative power, and provides a committee of leadership for the government comparable to the Politburo on the party level. It performs the indispensable function of coordinating the measures taken by the state; its individual members often hold no portfolios but supervise several cabinet departments.

The exact position of the cabinet and its Presidium is somewhat more difficult to define in states where a President or a State Council exists. As will be seen in a later chapter, in Czechoslovakia and Yugoslavia, where an individual presidency continues, "executive" power is shared by the cabinet with the chief of state, and the status of the former is thereby reduced and is subordinate to that of the President, the Prime Minister, and its own Presidium.[16] When, in East Germany, a Council of State was formed and placed under Ulbricht as chairman, this body, and even its smaller "bureau," came to rival in some degree the Presidium of the Council of Ministers. Perhaps in Rumania, too, the Council of State, headed until 1965 by the First Secretary, Gheorghiu-Dej, displaced some of the authority of the cabinet Presidium. Nonetheless, in East Germany at least, the cabinet, with its extensive administrative apparatus in its many departments, and the collective role of its Presidium, seems to have remained more powerful, especially in economic fields, and the

[14] *Ibid.*, pp. 84, 91.

[15] *Ibid.*, esp. pp. 94ff.

[16] Taborsky, *op. cit.*, p. 200.

State Council, with its small administrative staff, has been quite restricted in its law-making activities.[17]

THE PARTY AND DECISION-MAKING

The position of the cabinet and its Presidium has to be understood within the familiar context of the supreme position of the ruling party. The government's declaration of policy is normally based on the program of the National Front, proclaimed before the election of the assembly, and this in turn is formulated by the dominant Communist party. This is "the general line," which is binding on all public agencies, parliament and executive included. The "political will" formulated by the cabinet is thus the "party will," and sets out the basic directives for action in all spheres. The government and administration are therefore reduced to "instruments" of the party, and the executive, which is supposed to be secondary to the representative assembly, is in fact subordinate to the nonrepresentative party. The government, although certainly "one of the integrating parts," is not "the key to the system of rule."[18]

The dominating role of the party in the making of policy is effected in various ways: sometimes, as we have seen, by the personal union or fusion of the peaks of party and state, especially in the cabinet Presidium; sometimes by laying down general principles of policy and leaving it to parliament and cabinet to implement them in statutes or ordinances; sometimes through joint government-party decrees or decisions, issued in the name of the Council of Ministers, the Central Committee, and occasionally also the Presidium of the Assembly, or even the National Front.[19] But the party may also issue directives of its own, with detailed regulations, say, concerning agriculture or industry, or proclamations concerning cultural life, binding directly on those affected, without the intermediary of legislative or administrative action. Such party commands, as well as the joint government-party decrees, are certainly the equivalent, in all respects, of "legisla-

[17] Richert, *op. cit.*, chap. 3 and pp. 102–4.

[18] *Ibid.*, pp. 26–27, 40, 82, 86.

[19] In the DDR, it was formally announced in 1960 that henceforth, joint decisions of Politburo, Council of Ministers, and Council of the National Front would be issued on essential questions; this was largely superseded by the formation of the State Council, which became the main channel of government-party policy declarations. See *ibid.*, pp. 36ff., 51–52, 75–76, 83.

tion," without requiring action by the duly authorized lawmaking organs.

Earlier chapters (6 and 8) have intimated that the crucial power of decision-making, ostensibly belonging to the party as a whole, in fact adheres only to its topmost organs, and in particular, to its supreme leader. According to party statute and theory, policy is set by the Congress, meeting every few years, and in the interim, by the Central Committee, meeting several times annually. The sessions of these bodies are occasions for long, detailed reports by the First Secretary or other high party men, and for decisions on policies to be pursued by party and state in the forthcoming period. These proposals are presented, however, ready-made and automatically endorsed by unanimous vote after a purely nominal debate. Proceedings are normally in secret, with edited verbatim reports published later in book or pamphlet form. Since the Stalin period, these organs have met more regularly, and discussion has perhaps been somewhat freer. It seems doubtful that the members, in spite of their constitutional right to take part in free and businesslike discussion, are able to question proposals or seriously to influence the final outcome, any more than the members of the elected state assemblies. Yet the reports and the decisions emanating from these organs, although not couched in legal form, are more important than legislative statutes, or the constitution itself, in determining the framework of compulsion binding on party members and citizens alike. Indeed, any major speech by a leading functionary constitutes a set of imperatives for action no less obligatory than the much rarer legislative statute.

Notwithstanding the above, the exact relationship of the topmost organs in decision-making is not as clear and simplified as at first appears. The assumptions that party and state are sharply separated from each other, that the former makes policy and the latter implements it, do not fully correspond with the complicated realities, according to which the party constantly interferes in the state sphere, the state works through and with the party, and both are intermingled in a unique method of policy-making strikingly different from noncommunist states.[20]

No doubt the key part in the process is played by the members of the party's Presidium and Secretariat, and by the officials of the apparatus. However, an important advisory role is taken by the state administration and its appropriate departments, and

[20] *Ibid.*, pp. 28–29, 53, 62–64.

the highest civil servants exert an imponderable influence on the final molding of policy. In some countries, there exist commissions that are deliberately designed to bring together influential and expert persons from both party and state, as well as from other spheres. It is likely, too, that important Central Committee decisions are formulated only after close consultations with government organs and outside experts.[21] The interlocking of party and state takes different forms in the individual countries, and depends on personalities and the peculiar circumstances, and may vary in each field of government activity. No doubt, as communism becomes more "national," the reality of decision-making will be increasingly varied and will depart still more from the standard models traditionally used by political analysis.

THE CHANGING PROCESS OF POLICY-MAKING

The process of communist decision-making is veiled, then, in uncertainty and difficult to define. Many things are not known, both as to the actual agencies that participate, and still more, as to the informal procedures by which conclusions are reached. Problems are stated, solutions suggested, and decisions made, without regard for formal channels of law-making, by a small circle of decision-makers occupying the strategic posts at the top of the party and state hierarchies. In large part, especially during the Stalin period, decisions were emanations of the arbitrary will of the supreme leader, who drew upon his few closest associates for counsel. Apart from this "personal" component in decision-making, there was a crucial "Soviet" element, a tendency to follow the guidance of the USSR in fundamental policies, and to copy its institutions and procedures.

Personal whims of a single leader, or explicit directives from Moscow, although not entirely absent, are yielding in varying degrees to the "collective" and the "national" aspects of decision-making. Even in the post-Stalin era, there continued to be a certain rhythm of action, with some Eastern European states following Soviet examples, a few months later, as, for example, in the dissolution of machine tractor stations, the decentralization of management, or party intervention in cultural life. The basic determinations are, however, more and more within the province of the local party and do not rest exclusively on Soviet commands.

[21] *Ibid.*, pp. 32–36, 50–51.

The knowledge of a wider circle is being drawn upon in the formation of a policy designed to serve national interests. This has heightened the "rational" element in decision-making, with the leaders drawing upon the experts, in the cabinet and in the administration generally, for specialized technical advice. There is still an "ideological" element, since the ideologues are consulted for "partisan" or "doctrinal" counsel, and for theoretical justification of the ultimate decisions. No doubt there is continuing tension between "state" and "party," or to put it in other terms, between rational requirements and doctrinal imperatives. Yet the distinction is not clear-cut, as all concerned are communists, or procommunist in outlook; the experts are not unaffected by ideological considerations, and the party officials are often themselves specialists, interested also in efficiency. Moreover, neither is totally immune to the inchoate trends of public opinion and of group interests, which may set limits or impose influences on the development of public policy.

Interests and Their Representation

Communist society is depicted by its own supporters as homogeneous, with one class, the proletariat, supreme, embodying and expressing the interest of the people as a whole. It is assumed that a single or dominant party, that of the working class, best knows the "real" interest of the people, that it has no special interests of its own, and that there can be no legitimate group interests other than those defined by it. This excludes the notion of conflicts within the working class and its unified party, or between these and rival classes or groups, except with the former exploiting classes or the enemies of the existing social and political order. Somewhat contradictorily, however, it is also argued that there is a democratic deliberation on public policy, and that the ultimate decisions reflect a consensus arrived at through the interchange of differing views. Even more paradoxically, it is assumed that the "representative" assembly is also capable of expressing the will of the sovereign people.[1] In fact, as we shall see in this chapter, the interplay of group forces and the process by which social conflicts are resolved is much more complicated than the above doctrines of "party leadership" and the "representative" system suggest.

SOCIAL GROUPS

Communist society, in spite of its monolithic appearance and the claims of homogeneity cited above, is in fact as complex and variegated as any other. Certain social classes, which existed prior to communist rule, have indeed been eliminated: large land owners, large property holders in industry and commerce, and even many small proprietors, such as tradesmen, craftsmen, and peasants. The social groups that remain have been radically transformed in character and status. The peasants, having in most countries lost the ownership of their land, are grouped together in collective farms. The workers continue to labor as before in factories and mines, but as these are nationalized, they have become employees of the state. Neither of these two classes in fact "hold power," as official theory and the constitutions proclaim. Authority has passed into the hands of a "new class," to use the term introduced by Djilas, the "political bureaucrats," who, due to their dominant position in the party, and its preeminence in the

[1] Ernst Richert, *Macht ohne Mandat: Der Staatsapparat in der Sowjetischen Besatzungszone Deutschlands* (2d ed.; Köln and Opladen, 1963), p. 27.

state, occupy the seats of power. Not owning property in their own right, the members of this class, according to Djilas, control the property of the nation as a whole, and as a result derive special economic and social benefits and are able to dominate the entire life of the nation.[2]

Other groups exist, however, whose role is also more important than that of the mass of workers and peasants, and who challenge, sometimes successfully, the political bureaucrats or *apparatchiki.* There is a second "new class," as the Rumanian, Dumitriu, has termed it, a "middle class," which includes the managers of lesser factories and the heads of state farms and collective farms as its backbone, but also skilled workers, technicians, scientists, professional people, artists, and writers.[3] This class may be identified as the "intelligentsia," although its ranks include many social groups in addition to the "creative intellectuals" in art and science.[4] Not having the power to command, nor enjoying the same social privileges as the *apparatchiki,* nonetheless these strata have their own values and interests, and are increasingly able to bring these to bear on the making of public policy.

Other classes of lesser power include the growing numbers of administrative and office workers; small manufacturers and tradesmen, and agricultural laborers, all greatly reduced in number since the war; peasant-workers and peasant-clerks, who work both in industry and on the land; and in Yugoslavia and Poland, many small farmers owning their own land.[5] In an even broader sense, society is divided into amorphous categories distinguished by factors such as nationality or religion, profession or level of income, and type or location of employment. Whether organized or not, and whether united in outlook or not, these special interests make their claims on the institutions of government and must be reckoned with by those in power.[6]

[2] Milovan Djilas, *The New Class* (New York, 1957), esp. pp. 39, 43–47. See also Wayne S. Vucinich, "The New Society," in Stephen Fischer-Galati (ed.), *Eastern Europe in the Sixties* (New York, 1963), chap. 1.

[3] Petru Dumitriu, "The Two New Classes," *East Europe,* X, 9 (September, 1961), 3–6, 30–33, and "The Lonely Managerial Class," *East Europe,* X, 12 (December, 1961), 22–27.

[4] Cf. Jan Szczepánski, "The Polish Intelligentsia: Past and Present," *World Politics,* XIV, 3 (April, 1962), 406–20. Szczepánski, however, includes the party *apparatchiki* in the category of the intelligentsia, and calculates the total membership as over 2,000,000.

[5] See Jan Szczepánski, "Poland's Class Structure," *Polish Perspectives,* VII, 7–8 (July–August, 1964), 66–75.

[6] The role of social forces other than class and of organized "interest groups," in communist systems was recognized by J. Djordjević, "Interest

INFLUENCE ON POLITICS

The exact relationship between such social forces and public policy is difficult to define in any country. Like all others, communist society is a complex organism of diverse economic, social, and cultural groups, each with its own "selfish" values and interests, and each with sharp internal differences, and all inescapably in conflict with one another. Powerful as the communist leaders are, they can hardly insulate themselves entirely from the impact of society. Under Stalin, governments were able, at least for a time, to mold it arbitrarily in the shape desired, although group pressures were sometimes able to thwart the most coercive of measures. The tempo of collectivization, for instance, varied considerably from country to country, in part reflecting passive resistance by the peasantry, and culminating in certain countries in its abandonment. Religion, too, was able to continue to exert a profound influence, and to frustrate the efforts at total governmental control. In the freer atmosphere after Stalin's death, social forces have been less easy to stifle or to direct, and the converse reaction of society on government has become increasingly evident. Direct pressure was applied, for instance, by the workers in Pilsen or Poznań, by strikes or demonstrations, or in East Berlin and Budapest, by open revolt, and after the uprising was crushed in Hungary, by a general strike of some weeks duration. Similarly, during the "thaw" of the past decade, in certain countries, the writers, intellectuals, and students, as groups and as individuals, have been able to express their views and interests more overtly, and even to create a kind of public opinion capable in some cases of affecting government action. In the long run, secular trends, such as, say, the desire of writers for greater freedom of expression or of the people as a whole for more and better consumers' goods, may inexorably produce changes in official attitudes.

More relevant for political analysis than broad general groupings of a sociological character are the organized groups that claim to express the interests of the former and to exert pressure on government for their implementation. In communist countries,

---

Groups and the Political System of Yugoslavia," in Henry W. Ehrmann (ed.), *Interest Groups on Four Continents* (Pittsburgh, 1958), pp. 197–228, 292–94; and by M. Lakatoš, "On Some Problems of the Structure of our Political System" (in Slovak), *Právny obzor*, No. 1 (1965), pp. 26–36. See H. Gordon Skilling, "Interest Groups and Communist Politics," to be published in *World Politics*, April, 1966.

there are many such associations, including the societal organizations, as they are called—the trade unions, youth leagues,[7] women's committees, Soviet friendship societies, and peace movements, and a host of lesser bodies in specialized fields, such as the unions of writers, painters, composers, former partisans, and so on. Known in Stalin's time as "transmission belts," they were regarded as crucial links between the party, whose task was to lead, and the people, who were to be led. Although intended to provide the leaders with information on the attitudes of diverse sectors of society, they were admittedly more important as a means of implementing policy, and had little or nothing to do with its formulation. Efforts have been made, in Czechoslovakia, for example, to make them vigorous exponents of group interests and to strengthen their influence over policy-making.[8] They still, however, serve mainly as a channel for governmental and party pressure on society. Strict control over them is effected by the party's cadre system, which mans the offices of each major organization with trustworthy activists, and through the medium of party members working among the rank and file. Power is concentrated, according to the principle of democratic centralism, in the higher echelons, so that each organization has tended to stand, not for the special interests of its membership or of a broader social group, but rather for a general public interest as conceived by the party and its spokesmen within that organization.

It is hard to estimate the degree to which specific interest groups have exerted a notable counterinfluence on the policy-makers. During the worst days of Stalin, there was perhaps only a kind of underground pressure hardly more definable than that of the amorphous social forces themselves. In times of crisis, the mass associations have only occasionally emerged as political factors, as in the case of the writers' unions in Poland and Hungary, which in 1955 and 1956 asserted their autonomy and became powerful pressure groups challenging the party itself. More significant were *ad hoc* organizations, such as the Petöfi club, a forum for intellectuals in Hungary during the thaw, or the workers' councils created in the revolt itself, and in Poland, the Club of the Crooked Circle.[9] In more recent times, in Czecho-

[7] On the Polish youth movement, see Richard F. Staar, *Poland, 1944–1962* (New Orleans, 1962), chap. 12.

[8] See Lakatoš, *op. cit.*, and his "The Societal Organization and the Interests of the Workers," *Hospodářské noviny*, March 26, 1965.

[9] F. A. Váli, *Rift and Revolt in Hungary* (Cambridge, 1961), pp. 253, 330–32; Richard Hiscocks, *Poland: Bridge for the Abyss?* (London, 1963), pp. 188–90, 232–33.

slovakia, through the congresses of the Union of Writers and its journals and newspapers, the writers were able to raise such sensitive issues as de-Stalinization and the rehabilitation of victims of the Stalinist purges, and even to push the government in the direction desired. Professional and scholarly associations, such as those of the economists and the lawyers, openly discussed alternative methods of dealing with urgent economic and legal problems, and created a climate of opinion favorable to change. As in the case of the writers, the experts were not necessarily unified in their thinking and were concerned not merely with a special group interest of their own, but with broad matters of public concern. The party exerted much control over the course of the debate and remained the decisive factor in the ultimate outcome. Nonetheless, in freer communist states such as Poland and Hungary, and more recently in Czechoslovakia, a wider array of interests has been brought into the arena of public discussion.

Polish Catholicism has presented a special case, unique in Eastern Europe, constituting not only a social force of great magnitude, but a highly organized group of considerable political influence. Since the October days in 1956, there has existed almost a balance of power between party and Church, personified by Gomulka and Cardinal Wyszynski, respectively. Tension has persisted, and the Church has been subjected to many official restrictions and to the competition of government-sponsored Catholic organizations.[10] Nonetheless, the Catholics have remained strong, with their many churches, newspapers, such as *Tygodnik Powszechny*, *Znak*, and *Wiez*, a university in Lublin, publishing houses, and discussion clubs, and they constitute a remarkable force in intellectual and religious life. The so-called "Znak" group of Catholic intellectuals, suppressed during the Stalin period, emerged after 1956 as a political factor unique in the communist world, with deputies in parliament and representation on parliamentary committees and in the State Council. Although ready to accept the existing political and social system and the foreign and domestic policies of the regime, they reject Marxism, proclaim openly their adherence to a Catholic world view, and defend their religious interests in legislative matters. They have also made themselves a more general pressure group for democratization and for strengthening the power of parliament. They have ventilated grievances by raising questions in the Sejm or intervening with the administration, and have sought to

[10] Staar, *op. cit.*, chaps. 14 and 15.

remedy defects in legislation, even to the point of abstaining or voting against specific measures.[11]

More powerful than the groups so far discussed are those whose position is institutionalized as part of the administrative machinery, but whose interests may be distinct and even in conflict with each other. The Soviet counterparts have been called the "policy groups"[12] and include the highest state officials (ministers and planners), the managers of industrial enterprises, specialists in agriculture, and the military and police, all of whom, by virtue of their official positions, are able to influence the formulation and implementation of policy. To some extent, they defend the views of an extensive social group, such as the "managers" or the "military"; to some extent, the standpoint of a particular department or enterprise. Some segments of the public administration, such as the army and the police, which hold the instruments of violence in their hands, may exercise undue power as they did during the Stalin period, but may be strictly subordinated to the party and the bureaucracy as they are at present.

ELECTIONS AND REPRESENTATION

It might be assumed, on the face of it, that the representative assemblies would offer an effective means of transmitting the people's will, and of expressing the interests of the major groups. In all the communist countries of Eastern Europe, parliaments are elected on the basis of universal suffrage. The franchise is usually open to all citizens of both sexes 18 years old or above, without discrimination as to religion, race, or creed, or any of the class exclusions that existed in the early days of Soviet rule.[13] Almost to a man, the voters, in sharp contrast to their counterparts in many democratic states, exercise their privilege of voting. With

[11] See Adam Bromke, "The 'Znak' Group in Poland," *East Europe*, XI, 2 (January–February, 1962), 15–20, 11–15 respectively. This group is not to be confused with "Pax," a "progressive" or procommunist Catholic organization, which has played an even more unusual role as a quasi-political organization and also as an economic enterprise, with extensive commercial and industrial undertakings. It was allotted three seats in the Sejm in 1961. See the same author's "From 'Falanga' to 'Pax'," *Survey*, No. 39 (December, 1961), pp. 29–40.

[12] Z. K. Brzezinski and Samuel P. Huntington, *Political Power: USA/USSR* (New York, 1964), p. 196.

[13] Only in Rumania, under the 1952 constitution, were members of certain classes excluded. See Vladimir Gsovski and Kazimierz Grzybowski (eds.), *Government, Law and the Courts in the Soviet Union and Eastern Europe* (2 vols.; London and The Hague, 1959), I, 393.

the exception of Yugoslavia, parliamentary deputies are elected directly, from territorially defined constituencies, almost identical in size of population, and without special privileges for workers or peasants. (For Yugoslavia, see pp. 132–34.) The composition of the assembly normally mirrors the social structure of the population, with workers, peasants, intellectuals, and party and state officials included, although not in a strictly proportionate manner. Other refinements, such as "instructions" from voters to the deputy, his duty to report periodically to his electors, and the right of the latter to recall him from office, seem to insure an almost perfect form of representation.

The assemblies, which were once classified among the "transmission belts" of the proletarian dictatorship, have in fact hardly exerted more influence than the mass associations, perhaps even less as compared with the trade unions.[14] In most countries, there are no competing parties, or even alternative candidates, and hence no genuine choice for the voter. Even when other parties exist as links between the Communist party and certain specific groups, such as Catholics, intellectuals, or peasants, they have no independent opportunity to express their special interests.[15] Normally the National Front prepares a single list of candidates, with the total equal to the number of seats to be filled, and with a fixed quota for each party or mass organization. Where there are single-member constituencies, nominations are made by the party or mass organizations and multiple candidacy is not excluded. Registration of candidates is, however, in the hands of an electoral commission controlled by the leading party, and inevitably results in a single candidate appearing on each ballot.[16] A communist majority in the assembly is therefore preordained. As a consequence, both the campaign, although characterized by intense "agitation" by party propagandists, and the actual casting of ballots on election day are rendered meaningless. The right to

[14] For a description of German elections, see Richert, *op. cit.*, pp. 198ff.; of Czechoslovak elections, E. Taborsky, *Communism in Czechoslovakia, 1948–1960* (Princeton, 1961), pp. 235–251; of Polish elections, Richard F. Staar, "Elections in Communist Poland," *Midwest Journal of Political Science*, II, 2 (May, 1958), 200–18, also given in his *Poland, 1944–1962*, chap. 4. See also Daniel Kubat, "Communist Use of the Czechoslovak Parliament Since World War II," *Slavic Review*, XX, 4 (December, 1961), 695–700.

[15] See Chapter 6, pp. 65–66. In Hungary a multiparty system, established under Nagy on October 30, 1956, lasted four days.

[16] Kádár, in a speech made on February 11, 1965, spoke of the future desirability of multiple candidates for all elected bodies.

scratch a candidate is exercised by a few, but without any effect on the outcome. Deputies are therefore merely endorsed, not chosen, by the electorate. As individuals, they may perform certain services for their constituents, such as transmitting complaints to the administrative offices, but they are not lawmakers in any real sense. Even in times of crisis, as in Poland and Hungary in 1956, the assemblies did not emerge as exponents of the general will.

Only in Poland, after 1956, did the electoral process take on a greater reality, both in the nominating stage and in the final balloting. In the elections of 1957, said Gomulka, the people must be able to elect and not merely to vote. Although there was no opposition, the smaller parties had a substantial representation, and the nomination of more candidates than seats to be filled gave the voter an opportunity to express his preferences for individuals. In actual fact, there were 717 candidates for 459 seats, and the ruling PUWP party secured only 51 per cent of the seats. There was no evidence of terror or of administrative pressure, although the crisis just passed, and the continuing danger of Poland's position, enabled the communists to secure a sweeping popular endorsement of the common list. The subsequent elections in 1961 and 1965 were somewhat less democratic, with candidates exceeding seats by only 156 and 157 respectively (as compared to 254 in 1957), and a stronger communist ratio allocated.

POLISH ELECTIONS, 1952–65

	NUMBER OF DEPUTIES			
Party	*1952*	*1957*	*1961*	*1965*
PUWP	273	239	255	255
ZSL (United Peasant party)	90	118	117	117
SD (Democratic party)	25	39	39	39
Nonparty	37	63	49	49
(including the Znak circle)		(9)	(5)	(5)

SOURCES: Richard Hiscocks, *Poland: Bridge for the Abyss?* (London, 1963), pp. 283–41, 282–83, and J. Ptakowski, "Parliamentary Elections in Poland," *East Europe*, XIV, 8 (August, 1965), 15–19.

In Yugoslavia, where only one party exists and there is no political opposition, the elections result in an assembly made up largely of communists.[17] In the 1965 federal elections, however, it is noteworthy that there were many more candidates (1,653) than seats to be filled (1,196). The system is also distinguished by the representation of certain social groups and by a unique procedure for nominations and elections. Under successive constitutions, the major nationalities and regions have been given special rights, not only in the federal structure, with its six republics, but also in the form of delegates to the Federal Assembly.[18] Although these federalist features were borrowed from the Soviet Union, the "institutionalizing" of certain other social groups in Yugoslavia has been unique among communist states.[19] Under the 1953 constitution, there existed a Council of Producers, elected indirectly by district producers' councils. As the two major groups, industry, commerce and trade, and agriculture, were represented on the basis of their share in the total social product, there was an overrepresentation of the former in a ratio of between 3 and 4 to 1.[20] Under the 1963 constitution, the Federal Assembly was broadened to include five separate chambers, each with 120 members, and elected indirectly by a different category of the population. In addition to the Federal Chamber representing the population at large and the republics and autonomous provinces, there were four others, each representing specific social groups: the Political-Administrative Chamber, representing the subordinate organs of management and the social-political organizations; and the Chambers of Economy, of Education, and of Social Welfare and Health, each representing the associations in these areas. Most of the work of the Assembly was done by the Federal Chamber acting alone, or in concert with one of the other chambers, but the latter may meet separately to make recommendations, although not to legislate. The Federal Chamber was elected directly by the population in parliamentary elections, with candidates nominated by voters' meetings and selected by the communal assemblies. The four corporate chambers were elected by the communal assemblies, without subsequent popular ratifica-

[17] G. W. Hoffman and F. W. Neal, *Yugoslavia and the New Communism* (New York, 1962), pp. 231, 383, 458–59. See also James C. Lowenstein, "Yugoslavia: Parliamentary Model?" *Problems of Communism*, XIV, 2 (March–April, 1965), 132–35, and R. V. Burks, "Yugoslavia: Has Tito Gone Bourgeois?" *East Europe*, XIV, 8 (August, 1965), 8–10.

[18] Yugoslav federalism and local government will be discussed more fully in Chapter 13.

[19] Djordjević, *op. cit.*, pp. 206–7, 213ff.

[20] Hoffman and Neal, *op. cit.*, pp. 217–18; see also Lowenstein, *op. cit.*

tion; the candidates were nominated by the appropriate organizations in the spheres represented.

THE PARTY AND THE PUBLIC INTEREST

In the absence of an effective representative body, or a public deliberative process, and in the absence also of independent and competing parties or influential pressure groups, it falls to the single or dominant party in the communist countries to fulfill many of these roles, and to perform the crucial task of serving as a broker of the competing group interests. The party is itself a special group, with its leaders and *apparatchiki*, its organization and its ideology, and its own vested interests. Since it already possesses power, it need not concern itself with what is the most important function of parties elsewhere, namely the acquisition of power. Within the party, there are differences of viewpoint expressed by individual leaders, organs, and groups, which sometimes reflect broader social interests and must be reconciled. There is often a hidden struggle for power, a subterranean rivalry over policy and the public interest, sometimes, as we have seen in an earlier chapter, bursting into the open in purge and counterpurge. The victors, in winning and holding power, are free from challenge by competing parties or overt pressure groups, and can themselves manipulate and control the organizations that exist. They may, as in the past, seek to impose their own concepts of correct policy by coercive means, without serious effort at compromise or public satisfaction. In the post-Stalin era, however, with the circle of decision-making widening and public discussion less restricted, the party heads must more and more concern themselves with building a consensus among competing policy groups and the noninstitutionalized associations.[21]

The ultimate result is a somewhat arbitrary definition of the public interest, not necessarily expressing the rational requirements of society as a whole, as suggested by experts and specialists, or the full requirements of doctrinal considerations, as voiced by the ideologues, nor even a happy synthesis of diverse group in-

[21] Brzezinski and Huntington, *op. cit.*, pp. 212ff. There is an interesting discussion in Herbert Marcuse, *Soviet Marxism* (New York, 1958), of the competing special interests in Soviet society, even within the party, and of the role of the "bureaucracy" in representing "the social interest over and above individual interests," and the "real" interest as distinct from the immediate interests of the people (pp. 107–19). The role of the party and the state in reconciling divergent group interests is also discussed by Djordjević and Lakatoš in their articles cited.

terests. It is more than likely a pragmatic compromise, fusing together rational and irrational elements, theoretical and practical considerations, private and group interests, with the party and its current leaders exerting a more than ordinary influence. This is not genuine pluralism, nor pure totalitarianism, but a kind of imperfect monism in which, of the many elements involved, one—the party—is more powerful than all others, but not omnipotent. The final product—public policy—is highly political, reflecting the parallelogram of conflicting forces and interests within the structure of the single party and of the national communist society, and increasingly, of the communist world as a whole.

PART FIVE
IMPLEMENTING DECISIONS

Introduction

No less important than the making of decisions is their enforcement. A government that lacks effective means of securing obedience is a contradiction in terms and is equivalent to anarchy or chaos.

All governments have a wide array of sanctions to secure the acceptance of their policies by their citizens. Broadly speaking, there are two principal categories: persuasion and compulsion. Governments must rely on some combination of both these elements. None can dispense entirely with compulsion, yet none can rely on it alone. Even one that depends mainly on persuasion finds compulsion necessary in imposing its will on a disobedient minority. Each of the two elements supplements and reinforces the other, persuasion rendering compulsion acceptable, and compulsion making persuasion effective.[1]

Just as power is sometimes wrongly identified with compulsion alone, so compulsion is equated with force or violence. In fact, however, we must distinguish two forms of compulsion, one involving coercion, that is, the application of physical constraint or force against the disobedient citizen, the other employing nonviolent forms of control. In some states that lack wide popular support, the enforcement of governmental decisions may depend in large measure on violence or on the threat of its use. Arbitrary recourse to violence may sometimes assume the character of total and unrestricted terror. In extreme cases, as in civil war or revolution, force may be directed against a large segment of the population, perhaps the majority. Even the most democratic and popular of governments must, however, also threaten, and if necessary, employ force in the form of arrest, compulsory trial, imprisonment, and even execution, of lawbreakers.

[1] For an excellent discussion of what he terms "coercive" and "consensual" power, see Carl J. Friedrich, "Political Leadership and the Problem of the Charismatic Power," *Journal of Politics*, XXIII, 1 (February, 1961), 7–8.

Although force always lurks in the background as the final sanction, to be used as a last resort, states normally rely on nonviolent forms of compulsion. All the measures of obligation discussed in preceding chapters—statutes, decrees, ordinances, rules and decisions, even mere commands—are usually enforced without the need for violent sanctions, by the administrative agencies, or to use the traditional term, the "executive arm" of government.

A government of pure and naked coercion or of constant compulsion is less effective, and certainly more costly, than one that convinces its people that its power is "legitimate" and deserves to be respected and obeyed willingly. All governments strive to diminish the need for compulsion and especially for violence, and, through peaceful persuasion, to transfer their "power" into "authority." In varying degrees, every society uses the mass media and other available devices of persuasion to indoctrinate the masses in the superior virtues of its own political system and to mold or manipulate public opinion on specific policies. An important aid is an ideology or a set of political beliefs that legitimizes the system as a whole, and gains voluntary loyalty and obedience.

The distinction between "power" and "authority," however, is smudgy and difficult to determine. Under normal conditions, all systems are characterized by both "legitimate authority" based on consent freely given and "actual power" based on unwilling constraint. In a democracy, the effective participation of many people in decision-making renders more likely the voluntary acceptance of the outcome, and thus obviates the need for ubiquitous terror or widespread propaganda. In a less democratic system, in which decisions are arbitrarily imposed on the population, both propaganda and violence are more necessary. In the most authoritarian state, however, there will always be some voluntary recognition, and sometimes enthusiastic endorsement, of the authority of the rulers and of their edicts, sometimes by a substantial majority.

Eastern European governments differ from other states not in an exclusive dependence on compulsion or violence, but rather in the particular admixture of compulsion and persuasion, of violent and nonviolent forms of compulsion, an admixture which varies from period to period and from country to country. In general, communist governments employ methods for the enforcement of decisions essentially similar in form to those of other governments, although often radically differing in content and in relative importance. In the first place, there is an elaborate mechanism of public administration, headed by the cabinet or Council of Ministers, and supplemented by the party apparatus and its own hierarchy (Chapter 12). This system also includes the institutions operating at lower levels and in lesser areas of jurisdiction, such as district, region, city or town, and where they exist, provinces or republics, as in Yugoslavia (Chapter 13). In the third place, there is a network of propaganda for the manipulation of public opinion, directed by the party and its apparatus and assisted by government agencies and by nonpublic organs of communication, such as the press (Chapter 14). Finally, there is a structure of courts, and police and armed forces, designed to constrain forcibly the citizens' behavior, either with justice or through terror, the balance between the two varying at different times (Chapter 15).

12: Organizing Obedience

No government can dispense with public administration. In the modern state especially, a crucial position is occupied by "officials working in offices," whose task is to carry out the policies decided by those in power.[1] Receiving instructions from above and giving orders to those below, the administrators or civil servants constitute a hierarchy of command, or, in Max Weber's expressive words, a system of "imperative coordination." Normally operating within a framework of legal norms, the administrators' function is to apply these abstract rules to particular cases, and to compel the citizens to obey them. Although ostensibly purely "administrative," the bureaucracy in any state enjoys a "power position" not adequately expressed by that term. In some countries, it has become the "master" rather than the "servant" of politics; in all, it has become the maker of policy, as well as its executor.

BUREAUCRACY IN POLITICS

In the communist countries of Eastern Europe, the administrative machinery has assumed unparalleled authority. Grafted upon long traditions of executive absolutism, administration has become a leviathan dominating the entire body politic. Critics, from Trotsky to Djilas, have characterized it as a state bureaucracy controlling and exploiting the people. Others have recently described communism as an "organizational" or "administered" society, in which the entire range of community life is coordinated by a unique party-centered system of command from above.[2] As in other states, a significant part is played by the governmental administration proper, including the Council of Ministers and the individual departments of government, but this is paralleled, in an unusual fashion, by the party, which is itself an "integral part of the administration" and indeed more important than the state in providing "overall coordination at various levels

[1] On the role of modern bureaucracy, see Max Weber, "The Theory of Social and Economic Organization," in Roy C. Macridis and Bernard E. Brown (eds.), *Comparative Politics: Notes and Readings* (Homewood, Ill., 1961), p. 386. See also excerpts from the same work in S. M. Miller (ed.), *Max Weber* (New York, 1963), pp. 59ff., and H. H. Gerth and C. Wright Mills, *From Max Weber: Essays in Sociology* (New York, 1958), pp. 196ff.

[2] T. H. Rigby, "Traditional, Market, and Organizational Societies and the USSR," and Allen Kassof, "The Administered Society: Totalitarianism Without Terror," both in *World Politics*, XVI, 4 (July, 1964), 539–57; 558–75.

to all other territorially based organizations."[3] The customary hierarchical character of public administration is thus distorted by the party's outside interference and control, which generate tensions and conflicts peculiar to the communist form of government.[4]

In all political systems, the line between politics and administration is not as sharply defined as theoretical analysis would indicate, and is drawn differently in each system. Within the executive sphere there is always mutual interaction and persistent tension between the political leaders and the career administrators, or bureaucrats. Top-ranking executives, for example, British cabinet members, are more "political" than "administrative," and share in the making of fundamental policy. Civil servants of middle and even lower rank, too, although basically serving as specialists, exert a subtle and imponderable influence on the making and the execution of policy, as they fulfill their functions of planning, organizing, and staffing the work of their department or bureau; coordinating its various segments; providing the information and submitting the advice needed by superior officers; preparing budgets and policy drafts; and so on. Only at the lowest levels of any bureaucratic hierarchy are duties purely administrative.

THE CABINETS AND MINISTERS

In communist East Europe, the Council of Ministers is defined as the chief executive and administrative branch of government. Except in Yugoslavia, the cabinet is more or less uniform in composition, including a chairman (sometimes termed a Prime Minister), several deputy chairmen (or deputy premiers), a varying number of ministers heading individual departments, and a lesser number of chairmen of so-called commissions or committees, such as the planning agency. Due to the Council's size and the overriding authority of the top party organs, political-executive leadership, as we have seen, is exercised not by the Council as a whole, but rather by its chairman and the deputy chairmen, who together constitute its Presidium. All derive their power mainly from their status in the party.

As in other countries, individual departments develop their own vested interests and may conflict with each other in current

[3] Rigby, *op. cit.*, pp. 550–53.

[4] Carl Beck, "Party Control and Bureaucratization in Czechoslovakia," *Journal of Politics*, XXIII, 2 (May, 1961), 279–94.

administration. The Prime Minister is principally responsible for eliminating or reducing such interdepartmental frictions. In the words of a Czech spokesman, his is "the most important co-ordinating office, guaranteeing the harmonious cooperation of the ministries."[5] The members of the Presidium, who do not usually hold special departmental portfolios, are responsible for coordinating and controlling the activity of several ministries within certain broad spheres of governmental action. The attainment of integration is facilitated by the all-pervasive system of party control, to be described later, but still leaves much to be desired.[6]

Although the Council of Ministers is everywhere the chief administrative agency, in a few states it shares the executive power with a president. In Czechoslovakia, for instance, this office has been kept from precommunist days, and has remained the pinnacle of executive leadership.[7] The role of the Prime Minister is thus reduced in importance. The Czechoslovak President's powers under the constitution are far-reaching, including the appointment of the chairman and other members of the government, and other high officials, and the command of the armed forces. On the whole, however, the more ordinary tasks of administration are left to the cabinet and the ministers. The Yugoslav President plays a similar role. Until 1962, he had the constitutionally assigned task of presiding over the Federal Executive Council, and there was no Prime Minister. Elsewhere in Eastern Europe, the collective presidency—the assembly's Presidium or State Council—performs some administrative functions, normally exercised by heads of states (conferring decorations, granting pardons, receiving diplomats, and so on). As it lacks a large staff and is not engaged in day-to-day administration, it cannot compete with the massive bureaucracy of the Council of Ministers.[8]

Although most ministers are communists, they are usually not members of the party's Presidium, or sometimes even of the Central Committee, and do not therefore belong to the inner circle of policymakers. They are "routine administrators,"[9] not political executives, and run their individual departments within

[5] *Rudé právo,* March 28, 1952, cited in H. Gordon Skilling, "Czechoslovakia: Government in Communist Hands," *Journal of Politics,* XVII, 3 (August, 1955), 429.

[6] Ernst Richert, *Macht ohne Mandat* (2d ed.; Köln and Opladen, 1963), pp. 162–65.

[7] See E. Taborsky, *Communism in Czechoslovakia, 1948–1960* (Princeton, 1961), pp. 187–94, and Skilling, *op. cit.,* pp. 427–28.

[8] See pp. 116–17, 120–21.

[9] Taborsky, *op. cit.,* p. 200.

the framework of decisions made by others. Many of them lack the technical competence of career officials, and are appointed, like British or American cabinet members, as reliable spokesmen of official policy. Others are named because of specialized knowledge or experience, and are flanked by a deputy minister of a more political character. Below the ministerial level, the heads of divisions and bureaus and other officials of higher rank are normally appointed on the basis of expertness in a given sphere, although political loyalty is, needless to say, a *sine qua non.* In the early years of communist rule, wholesale dismissal of "bourgeois" officials and their replacement by loyal party cadres, who were often without skill or experience, was the rule. In later years, efforts have been made to train personnel combining political reliability and specific competence, but the former remains a predominant consideration. Since the death of Stalin, the appointment of nonparty specialists to posts other than the highest has become more common, notably in Hungary, where this practice has been adopted as a central principle of governance.

In Yugoslavia, a deliberate effort was made in the 1953 constitution to divide the executive function into the "political-executive," involving "political action of a creative or directive nature," and the "technical executive," consisting of day-to-day administration.[10] By separating these two elements, and subordinating the political-executive function to the control of the assembly, it was hoped to prevent the "bureaucratic authority" from dominating society, as it had done during the so-called "administrative period" after 1945. This principle was embodied in two organs: (a) a Federal Executive Council, whose members were relieved of all departmental administrative duties, and (b) the five state secretariats—National Defense, Foreign Affairs, Finance, Trade, and Internal Affairs—which were really departments under another name, but not headed by ministers. This meant, wrote Djordjević, that the Federal Executive was no longer a "government in the traditional sense, or a ministerial system," and that the Federal Executive Council was "neither a central administration nor a controlling administrative organ." In fact, as

[10] See J. Djordjević on Yugoslavia in "The Role of the Executive in the Modern State," *International Social Science Bulletin,* X, 2 (1958), 258–69. See also G. W. Hoffman and F. W. Neal, *Yugoslavia and the New Communism* (New York, 1962), pp. 218–23. It is also argued by the Yugoslavs that the avoidance of state bureaucratism was accomplished by decentralization, which has amounted to a gradual "withering away" of state administration (*Ibid.,* pp. 163–70, 211–13). See also Chapter 13 below.

he admits, a "functional and personal symbiosis" occurred, as almost all the state secretaries became members of the Federal Executive Council, and were in any case responsible to it, and the Council itself had twelve other secretariats directly under it.[11] The difficulty of separating the two aspects of the executive was thus demonstrated, and perhaps explains why it was omitted in the 1963 constitution. The Federal Executive Council at present consists of all the secretaries responsible for federal administrative organs, as well as the presidents of the executive councils of the republics. It presumably remains, as in the past, "one of the main levers of the political and administrative system."

THE DEPARTMENTS

In other communist countries, the Council of Ministers has more closely approximated that of the USSR. Like its prototype, it has included two principal types of department. One has consisted of the traditional ministries, such as foreign affairs, national defense, foreign and domestic trade, education and culture, justice, and internal affairs. Although their functions resembled their counterparts in noncommunist states, their methods and some of their purposes have differed substantially. More distinctively communist have been the ministries in the second category, those concerned with the detailed execution of the economic plans. As in the USSR, and often explicitly following Soviet examples, there has been a constant flux in the roster of these ministries, as new departments were created and old ones abolished, divided, and combined, with bewildering rapidity. The size of the cabinet has increased steadily, especially in the number of the economic ministries, as industry has grown, and its individual sectors have been placed under separate departments. There has also been a tendency to establish government commissions for certain areas, such as statistics and control, science and technology, art and culture, construction, or agriculture. By the time of Stalin's death, most of the cabinets of Eastern Europe, with the exception of less-industrialized countries such as Albania and Bulgaria, had reached dimensions comparable to their Soviet model, numbering from 30 to 40 ministries and commissions.[12] Since then, the num-

[11] For legislation and organization, general economic affairs, industry, agriculture and forestry, communications, labor, education and culture, public health, social affairs, legal affairs, information, and general administration.

[12] See Skilling, *op. cit.*, p. 431, for the evolution of the Czechoslovak cabinet; for the Polish, see the chart on the facing page.

Evolution of the Council of Ministers, Poland, 1956–64

1956	*1964*
Prime Minister	Prime Minister
First Deputy Prime Ministers (2)	Deputy Prime Ministers (6)
Deputy Prime Ministers (6)	
Agricultural Food Industry Meat and Dairy Industry Purchasing	Food Industry and Purchasing
Agriculture	Agriculture
Automobile and Tractor Industry Machine Industry Foundry	Heavy Industry
Building Materials Industrial Building	Building Industry
Chemical Industry	Chemical Industry
Communal Economy*	
Communications	Communications
Culture and Art	Culture and Art
Defense	Defense
Domestic Trade	Home Trade
Education	Education
Energy Mining	Coal Mining and Power
Finance	Finance
Foreign Affairs	Foreign Affairs
Foreign Trade	Foreign Trade
Forestry	Forestry
Health Labor and Social Insurance	Health and Social Welfare
Higher Education	Higher Education
Interior	Interior
Justice	Justice
Light Industries Small Industries and Handicrafts Wood and Paper Industry	Light Industry
Shipping	Shipping
State Control*	
State Farms*	
Town and Country Planning*	
Public Security Affairs (Committee)*	
Railroads Road Transport and Aviation	Transport

* Abolished by 1964.

ber of departments has been reduced by amalgamation, but the Soviet abolition of many central ministries in the 1957 reorganization has not been imitated, except in Bulgaria.

The cabinet has thus become a kind of general board of directors for the management of the entire economy.[13] Except for some of the traditional ministries, its departments serve as the "central executive instances" of the planning system.[14] Most of them control directly a sector of industry or trade through the administrative operation of state enterprises. Others, such as agriculture, health and social welfare, and domestic and foreign trade, are also mainly engaged in carrying out the provisions of the plan, although they function, except for foreign trade, through the medium of the organs of local government. The tasks of most ministries have thus ceased to be "political" or "parliamentary" in the traditional sense, and have become "organizational." They are, in the words of a Czech leader, centers to "ensure . . . the coordinated and smooth functioning of . . . organs and organizations and the planned, harmonious and disciplined fulfillment of political and social tasks, laid down in laws and plans."[15]

Beneath the pinnacles of president, cabinet, and ministers, communist bureaucracy has many features common to public administration generally. Authority is distributed among a number of separate departments, and within these, among bureaus or divisions, each having its own sphere of competence. As in an army, commands come from above, without pretense of control from below. Each department is headed by a single minister, who enjoys exclusive responsibility within it. Where collegial bodies made up of the highest officials exist, they are merely advisory and do not negate the rule of "one-man management." Each department is organized on a hierarchical principle, with several levels of authority arranged in pyramidal form, with each official responsible to his superior, and all ultimately subject to the minister. Some are "staff" agencies, without operational duties, advisory to the minister in certain general areas; others are "line" agencies, working within partial sectors of the department's jurisdiction; still others are auxiliary or service agencies. The host of bureaucrats who man the departments are appointed to their posts, and promoted and transferred, by their superiors and may

[13] *Ibid.*, pp. 429–34.

[14] Richert, *op. cit.*, p. 151.

[15] Cited in H. Gordon Skilling, "The Czechoslovak Constitution of 1960 and the Transition to Communism," *Journal of Politics*, XXIV, 1 (February, 1962), 154.

be demoted or dismissed by them. They are ostensibly full-time "career" officers, selected on the grounds of technical competence or training, and paid a fixed salary according to rank and seniority.

PARTY CONTROL

The real uniqueness of communist administration is, however, the product of the "leading role" of the party. Formally outside of, and separate from, the state structure, the party arrogates to itself full power to intervene directly in all matters of public administration.[16] In communist theory, there is a sharp separation of functions between the party as the policy-making body and the government as the formal agency of administration. The party is not supposed to perform any operative functions. Paradoxically, however, it is entitled to "supervise" the government administration in order to ensure that policy is correctly implemented. "Control," in the peculiarly European sense of that word, namely "checking up," is one of the most characteristic aspects of communist government. Under the party statutes, for instance, the Central Committee is empowered to "direct and control the activity of administrative organs," and the same right is assigned to party committees at all levels. Of course, all high officials are communists and are required to carry out instructions in their sphere of activity. "Control," however, gives the party another way of "checking up" on them. The party organizations within individual ministries also have extensive rights to watch over the work of their departments. The line between "supervision" and operation is therefore smudged, if not erased, and the government is often reduced to a secondary and instrumental agency. In Stalinist times, the party tended to usurp its functions entirely.[17]

The functions of control are performed by the entire party, including its organs at every level and within each area, and its individual members. The central apparatus, however, plays a key role. Its sections, which to a considerable extent parallel and duplicate the government departments, are "the Party's workhorses for implementing decisions."[18] On the surface their task

[16] Beck, *op. cit.*, pp. 286–87, 291–93.

[17] See complaints to that effect by Nagy in F. A. Váli, *Rift and Revolt in Hungary* (Cambridge, 1961), p. 109, and by Gomulka in Richard F. Staar, *Poland, 1944–1962* (New Orleans, 1962), pp. 153–54, 195–96.

[18] *Ibid.*, p. 192. The departments of the central apparatus of the Polish Communist party in 1962 were: Administration; Agriculture; Culture;

is to guarantee that the decisions of the party are carried out by *its own* organizations. The important "organization department," for instance, has the duty of "implementation and control over the fulfillment of Central Committee resolutions."[19] In view of the dominant role of the party both in making public policy and checking on its execution, the apparatus constitutes a second, but not at all secondary, instrument for enforcing decisions of both government *and* party. Each minister, it is said, is responsible to the relevant branch of the apparatus.[20] All important government decisions are transferred to the appropriate department of the secretariat, and through it to the corresponding party organ in province, region, district, or city.

A principal channel of party control is the "cadre" section at every level. All matters of personnel, although nominally in the hands of the superior officials and a special office in each government department, are subject to the overriding authority of these party agencies. The ministers themselves are appointed by the party, through the central "cadre" office. The tenure of all officials is conditional upon the approval of the cadre section within whose *nomenklatura* (list of offices under its jurisdiction) their positions fall. Questions of loyalty and security play some part in public administration throughout the world, but in communist states, such considerations frequently overrule professional qualifications in appointments and dismissals, even in normal times, and in periods of crisis justify widespread purges of civil servants. The permanent "career" of an administrator is thus threatened by the risk of discharge or transfer for political reasons. This system is designed, no doubt, to give the party the opportunity to use experts without being dominated by them. It leads, however, to

---

Economic; Foreign; General; Military; Organization; Propaganda and Agitation; and Science and Education. In addition, there were sixteen commissions: Construction; Cooperative; Local Industry and Handicrafts; Education; Employment and Wages; Heavy Industry; Justice; Light Industry; Market Supplies; National Affairs; Publishing; People's Councils; Social; Sports and Tourism; Transport; Workers' Councils; and Youth. There were also several bureaus: cadres, the press, letters and inspection, and so on. See Richard F. Staar, "The Central Apparatus of Poland's Communist Party," *Journal of Central European Affairs*, XX, 3 (October, 1962), 337–48. Cf. the departments of the Polish cabinet (see chart, p. 000). For the SED apparatus, see Carola Stern, *Porträt einer bolschewistischen Partei, Entwicklung, Funktion, und Situation der SED* (Köln, 1957), pp. 339–46.

[19] Staar, *Poland, 1944–1962*, p. 193.

[20] Beck, *op. cit.*, p. 287.

a constant conflict between technical and ideological considerations, and distorts the supposedly rational character of the administrative process.[21]

OTHER CHECKS ON BUREAUCRACY

Bureaucracy as a malignant growth, escaping popular control, usurping democratic processes, and stifling the initiative of citizens and administrators alike, has been a target for criticism in most parts of the world. In democracies, the power of the bureaucrats is checked in some degree by legal restraints, by an alert press and public opinion, and by vigorous parliamentary opposition or congressional investigation. Legal and parliamentary controls have not been effective in communist countries. In none except Yugoslavia has there been a constitutional or administrative court with the power to curb illegal actions of bureaucrats.[22] The Presidium of the assembly may usually nullify actions taken by the Council of Ministers or other administrative agencies, but has seldom if ever availed itself of this power. The cabinet, it is true, is formed by vote of the assembly and is responsible to it. Appointment, however, is a purely formal ratification of ministers already secretly selected by the top party bosses. Responsibility is similar to that of a British cabinet possessing a safe majority, with the difference that there is no opposition to question policy and not the remotest possibility of an adverse vote. The right of interpellation enjoyed by members is not one that need embarrass or frighten ministers, who rest secure in their positions as long as the party leadership retains confidence in them. Debate in the assembly gives some opportunity for exposing bureaucratic abuses and failures to implement party decisions, but in the absence of financial or other sanctions, is not likely to be effective. Since the death of Stalin, there has been an effort to stimulate the assemblies to engage in critical discussion of administrative actions, and to supplement this, on the Soviet model, with so-called organs of "people's control," semi-official bodies at all levels, made up of activists from various associations and public agencies, and supervised by a central body. The press is also expected to serve as a kind of watchdog of the public interest, censuring administrative abuses.[23]

[21] Beck, *op. cit.*, pp. 291–94; Paul E. Zinner, *Revolution in Hungary* (New York, 1962), p. 155; Taborsky, *op. cit.*, pp. 218–20, 223–29.

[22] See p. 154.

[23] See Chapter 14.

Communist states, in their efforts to curb excessive bureaucracy, have tended to rely mainly on checks from above, such as the party's own agencies of control already described, and its disciplinary and supervisory bodies, the Control Commission and the Auditing Commission. In addition, a Ministry of State Control is normally created and empowered to exercise surveillance over the entire administrative machinery and personnel. There has been a plethora of other "controls," such as those wielded by the state agencies of finance, planning, and the procuracy, police, and public security.[24] This tangle of interlocking controls has only compounded the problem of bureaucracy, and has placed the greatest emphasis not on the protection of the individual and his rights *vis-à-vis* the state administration, but rather on the enforcement of the commands of party and government on officials and citizens.[25] Only in Yugoslavia may the individual himself protest an administrative action and sue for damages in the courts.[26]

Communist administration has therefore developed its own peculiar brand of bureaucratic politics, in which the normal operation of an administrative mechanism has been distorted by an all-pervasive system of party regulation. Yet the resulting system is not as monistic as is usually assumed. The network of controls, devised to guarantee the effectuation of the party's will and to prevent the emergence of autonomous centers of power, has only succeeded in creating new countervailing forces at every level. Cutting across the formal lines of responsibility, the "multiple hierarchies" of control and administration check and balance each other in every sphere. Behind the totalitarian facade, as Fainsod writes of the Soviet Union, there takes place a "struggle for preferential advantage" by the various bureaucratic groups, a struggle not totally unlike that within any administrative system but taking on its own dimensions and forms within the communist framework.[27]

[24] For discussion of the procuracy and the courts, see Chapter 15 below.

[25] Taborsky, *op. cit.*, pp. 208–13; Richert, *op. cit.*, pp. 169, 249–50.

[26] Hoffman and Neal, *op. cit.*, p. 388. The 1965 Rumanian constitution contains a similar provision.

[27] Merle Fainsod, *How Russia Is Ruled* (2d ed.; Cambridge, 1963), pp. 386–88, 417–20.

Subordinate Governments

In all states, the burden of governing is too great to be borne exclusively by a central government and is thus shared by various subordinate agencies within territorially defined areas. Powers are divided between a principal authority, which acts in the state as a whole and within a broad jurisdiction, and local or regional authorities, which enjoy a lesser competence within their narrower domain. "Government" is therefore carried on by many "governments," thousands in number. If the state is continental in size or heterogeneous in national or other respects, authority is usually shared on a "federal" basis by a few large entities—states, provinces or republics—enjoying wide powers that cannot be removed or diminished by the central government, and that are exercised independently to a large degree. Below the level of the province or republic in a federation, or of the central government in a unitary state, are the organs of local government, with which only the tiniest of national systems can dispense. These are clearly "subordinate governments," deriving their authority from the higher body, and subject to the latter in employing it.

FEDERALISM IN YUGOSLAVIA

Apart from Yugoslavia, none of the communist states of Eastern Europe is large enough in territory or population, or sufficiently diverse ethnically or economically, to require a federal system. Neither Czechoslovakia, with its separate Czech and Slovak nations, nor Rumania, with its substantial Magyar minority, have resorted to federalism.[1] Yugoslavia, however, chose, from the beginning of communist rule, a federal structure as a means of reconciling the requirements of state unity and of ethnic and historic diversity. Of its six "people's republics," at present called "socialist republics," four were territories inhabited by different nationalities: Serbia, Croatia, Slovenia, and Macedonia. Two others, Montenegro and Bosnia-Herzegovina, although peopled by Serbs, and Serbs and Croatians, respectively, had had their own historic and cultural experiences as separate entities for cen-

[1] The German Democratic Republic, originally formed as a kind of federation of *Länder* or provinces, retained these federal forms even in the constitution as amended in 1958, but the five *Länder* had long since been replaced in actuality by 14 regions (*Bezirke*) as organs of local authority (Ernst Richert, *Macht Ohne Mandat* [2d ed.; Köln and Opladen, 1963], pp. 180–81).

turies. Moreover, the assignment of Bosnia-Herzegovina to either Serbia or Croatia would have resulted in a serious disproportion among the constituent parts. The creation of Macedonia, which had formed part of prewar Serbia, was based on the desire to foster a distinctive Macedonian nationality. Within the Serbian republic, two special entities, not considered federal in character, were also created—the Autonomous Province of Vojvodina, an area of great national mixture, including Magyars, Rumanians, Slovaks, and Germans, as well as Serbs, and the Autonomous Kosovo-Metohija Region (Kosmet), with a Shiptar or Albanian majority.

In the earliest (1946) constitution, Yugoslavia's system was deliberately modeled on that of the Soviet Union.[2] The republics, exercising the right of national self-determination, were said to have opted voluntarily to live together in a federative state. Like the Soviet republics, they were regarded as "sovereign," their sovereignty limited only by the rights assigned by the constitution to the federation as a whole, the residual powers remaining with the parts. They did not, however, explicitly have the right to secede, as in the Soviet case. Each had its own constitution, setting forth, "in conformity with the Federal Constitution," its rights and duties, and its own representative assembly and administering and governing organs. No territorial changes were to be made without the consent of the republic concerned. The individual republics were equally represented in a Council of Nationalities, one of two houses in the federal assembly.

There is little doubt that during most of the lifetime of this constitution the facade of Yugoslav federalism concealed the reality of a highly centralized bureaucratic system. The distribution of powers was extremely lop-sided, with a wide array of important functions assigned to the federal government. The modest residual competence of the republics hardly constituted a substantial degree of sovereignty. Some of the designated powers were to be exercised exclusively by the federation, and some concurrently with the republics, the federation enacting "basic legislation." Amendment of the constitution was solely within the jurisdiction of the central organs. Federal law was supreme and took precedence over republican legislation. All republican law had to conform with federal law, even when adopted within the area of republican competence. Borrowed from the Soviet system was the triune form of administration, with some central minis-

[2] See Joseph Frankel, "Federalism in Yugoslavia," *The American Political Science Review*, XLIX, 2 (June, 1955), 416–30.

tries exclusively "federal," others "federal-republican," with corresponding offices in each republic, and other departments exclusively "republican" in character. The Federal Executive Council and the Assembly's Presidium had the constitutional right to suspend or cancel actions of republican governments. These features, together with the single federal budget and the national plan, assured unified and centralized treatment of most problems, as did the all-pervading influence of the Communist party. The republican organs were thus rendered hardly distinguishable from the lesser organs of local authority, except in the size of their territorial jurisdiction.

From 1950 on, Yugoslavia moved toward increased decentralization, but mainly through the elevation of the self-governing "communes" and other local organs, thereby undercutting in some degree the authority of the six republics. Although the latter were retained in the constitution of 1953 embodying the new system, they lost much of the formal status they previously held.[3] The republics were no longer said to exercise "sovereignty" or to possess the residual powers of government. The lion's share of legislative power remained with the federal organs, which retained a sphere of exclusive jurisdiction and were empowered to enact fundamental or general legislation as a framework for action by the republics. The triune system of administration was abolished, and the separation of the executive from the administrative at the center was duplicated on the republican level.[4] The republican Executive Council and the state secretariats were responsible for enforcing both federal and republican laws and decrees, and became more than ever subordinate administrative agencies. Even the representation of the republics in the Council of Nationalities was reduced in significance, as this body was merged with the Federal Council and was entitled to meet separately only to discuss constitutional amendments and certain other matters affecting the position of the republics and the nationalities. These rights were purely formal and had at first little real effect. Paradoxically, however, the republics gradually took on more of the substance of power as a result of the weakening of the centralism of the party. Communist leaders in each of the republics, who themselves held the posts of

[3] *Ibid.*

[4] The state secretariats included Internal Affairs, Economic Affairs, Justice, Budgetary Affairs, and State Administration. There were, in addition, Councils for Culture and Education, and for Public Health and Social Policy.

presidents of the assemblies, often identified themselves with the interests, especially economic, of their regions. Frequent clashes occurred between the more developed republics, such as Croatia and Slovenia, and the less-developed, Macedonia, Montenegro, Bosnia-Herzegovina, and even Serbia, necessitating reminders from Tito of the priority of the all-national interests of Yugoslavia.[5]

The latest constitution (1963) has retained the republics and the general features of a federal system. There is still a Chamber of Nationalities within the Federal Chamber, with a position similar to that defined by the 1953 constitution. It is difficult to assess the actual status of the republics, as their powers have in some respects been broadened, for instance, in regaining the residual powers, but in others, narrowed.[6] The most distinctive change has been the establishment of a Constitutional Court for Yugoslavia, together with similar courts in the republics. In previous constitutions, the interpretation of laws and decisions on constitutionality has been left to institutions of a political character, the Presidium of the Assembly (1946) and the Assembly's Commission for the Interpretation of Laws (1953). In 1963, for the first time in any communist country, these functions were assigned to a purely legal body, which received the power to interpret the constitution and to declare invalid either federal or republican laws. It seems unlikely, however, that this judicial organ will emerge as a powerful arm of government, as in some democratic federal systems, counterbalancing the representative and executive arms and affecting the distribution of powers and even the content of policy-making.[7]

Federal systems everywhere are compromises between the demands of unity and diversity, and are bound to manifest continuing tension between centrifugal and centripetal forces. The division of power is seldom precise, almost always ambiguous,

[5] Tito's speech in Split, May 6, 1962, and *Borba*, May 7, 1962. See also G. W. Hoffman and F. W. Neal, *Yugoslavia and the New Communism* (New York, 1962), pp. 493–97.

[6] See the paper by Fred W. Neal, "The Republics in Yugoslavia," delivered at the American Political Science Association meeting in September, 1964 (unpublished).

[7] The Federal Court has, however, struck down actions by a federal secretariat and by communal assemblies. See R. V. Burks, "Yugoslavia: Has Tito Gone Bourgeois?" *East Europe*, XIV, 8, (August, 1965), 10–11. The 1963 constitution also provided, in case of disagreement between the Federal Council and the Council of Nationalities on constitutional matters, for various complicated procedures, such as a joint commission, periods of delay, a dissolution of the Federal Council, and even a referendum.

and normally involves an intermingling of federal and provincial action. Yugoslavia is no exception. The ethnic diversity of the country and wide differences in historic background and economic level make the federal system necessary. The republics are likely to continue to serve as channels for expressing national and regional interests and to exercise a degree of independence, especially as long as the regional party leaders make their cause their own. At the same time, the politics of socialism requires a considerable degree of centralism, in view of the wide competence of the state in the economic and social fields. Decentralization on the Yugoslav model seems to benefit the local organs and industrial management more than the republics. As in all federal systems, the balance of power is likely to shift continually in response to secular changes in society. In Yugoslavia, such changes are less likely to occur through judicial decisions than through a political process reflecting the pressures of the federal and the republican governments and the single party and its component parts.

DECLINE OF SLOVAK AUTONOMY

Czechoslovakia was restored after the war as a state of two nations, Czechs and Slovaks, declared to be equal in rights. The Slovaks, who had enjoyed only the most modest home rule before 1939, and thereafter had become "independent," under Nazi protection, were given a special position in a system which was neither federal nor autonomous, but represented a peculiar form of "dualism." Under the 1948 constitution, special organs were created for Slovakia—the Slovak National Council and the Board of Commissioners—but none for other parts of the republic.[8]

Slovakia was not in any sense considered to be sovereign, nor was it termed a republic or given a constitution of its own. There was no provision for special representation of Slovaks at the center, other than by the normal process of election to the assembly or appointment to the cabinet. Moreover, the overwhelming share of authority was assigned to the government in Prague, which possessed also substantial controls over the operations of the regional Slovak organs. Even this modest degree of home rule was whittled away by later constitutional amendments

[8] See H. Gordon Skilling, "The Czechoslovak Constitutional System: The Soviet Impact," *Political Science Quarterly*, LXVII, 2 (June, 1952), 213–16, and his "Czechoslovakia: Government in Communist Hands," *Journal of Politics*, XVII, 3 (August, 1955), 439–42.

and changes in actual practice. From the beginning, the Slovak National Council was almost a cipher in terms of legislative activity. As the central cabinet increased in size and responsibility, the Board of Commissioners declined and became a mere tool for implementing Czechoslovak laws and decrees in so far as this was not done by Prague through its own local offices. The Communist party was highly centralized and unified, and the Slovak section had little or no influence over policy. After 1950, a vicious campaign against so-called bourgeois nationalism led to the removal of Slovak communists identified with a more nationalist viewpoint, and to their replacement by persons of strongly centralist outlook. These not only held the leadership positions in the Slovak party but also represented it in the Czechoslovak organs of party and state.

By 1956, Czechoslovakia had become a highly centralized state, and Slovak home rule reduced almost to nil. In the post-1956 climate, some gestures were made to broaden the authority of the Slovak bodies. Increasing emphasis was laid, however, on the necessity of integrating Slovakia within a unified economy, and even the bare forms of Slovak autonomy were still the object of suspicion by the regime. The constitution adopted in 1960 further weakened the position of Slovakia.[9] There was no expansion of its legislative functions and administratively there was a decline in its position. The Board of Commissioners was abolished and replaced with a complicated and ambiguous administrative system, based on commissions of the National Council, and with trustees responsible for individual departments. Although the representation of Slovakia in the Prague cabinet was formally strengthened, this did not add appreciably to its actual ability to influence decisions. Meanwhile, the transfer of some authority to the organs of local government, the national committees, and in particular to three regional committees in Slovakia undermined the position of the all-Slovak organs. The removal after 1963 of some of the most pronounced centralist and Stalinist Slovak leaders, and the appointment of a Slovak as Prime Minister of Czechoslovakia, may eventually lead to a significant upgrading of Slovakia. In 1964, steps were taken to try to make the sessions of the National Council more meaningful.

[9] See H. Gordon Skilling, "The Czechoslovak Constitution of 1960 and the Transition to Communism," *Journal of Politics*, XXIV, 1 (February, 1962), 156–59, cited above; E. Taborsky, *Communism in Czechoslovakia, 1948–1960* (Princeton, 1961), chap. XIV; Pavel Korbel, "Prague and the Slovaks," *East Europe*, XII, 3 (March, 1963), 6–12.

NATIONAL REGIONS

Apart from Czechoslovakia and Yugoslavia, Rumania is the only other communist government that makes special provision for a large national minority. Under the 1952 constitution, a Magyar Autonomous Region was established in an area inhabited predominantly by Magyars and Szeklers, with its capital at Tîrgu-Mureş. Although this region had its own organs of government, its status was hardly different, except in form and in name and in the use of the Hungarian language, from the other regions into which Rumania was divided. Moreover, in the administrative reorganization of 1960, some counties were added and others removed, so as to reduce its Magyar composition, and it was renamed the Mureş-Magyar Autonomous Region. Certain other zones with a large Hungarian population, such as the Cluj area, were not treated differently from other administrative entities. In a somewhat similar way, the autonomous provinces in Yugoslavia, the Vojvodina and the Kosmet, differ from other areas of local government only in that they are considerably larger territorially, and are represented in the Chamber of Nationalities.[10] None of these regions enjoys, even in form, a status comparable to the autonomous republics of the USSR.

LOCAL ORGANS

The pattern of local government is strikingly similar in all the communist states of Eastern Europe and is modeled closely on the system of "local soviets" in the USSR.[11] Described in the constitutions as "local organs of state power," the "people's councils," as they are usually called (in Czechoslovakia, "national committees"), have a wide competence in almost all spheres, except in foreign affairs, defense, and public security, and play a crucial role in supervising the whole realm of economic, social, and cultural life. At first functioning within prewar geographical divisions, they were eventually reorganized in a more or less

[10] Under the earlier constitutions, the province of Vojvodina had six representatives, the Kosmet region, four. In 1963, the two units were both called autonomous provinces and given five seats each.

[11] See Skilling's three articles already cited, and R. A. Jones, "Polish Local Government Reorganized on Soviet Model," *American Slavic and East European Review*, X, 1 (February, 1951), 56–68. See also Taborsky, *op. cit.*, chap. XIII, and Richert, *op. cit.*, chap. 7.

uniform four-tier system, including regions, cities, districts, and villages or rural communes.[12] There have often been later alterations in the size and number of the regions and districts. The cities, depending on size, are subordinated to district, region, or central government, and are generally subdivided into boroughs, which have their own councils. After years of delay, elections were held for the local councils, but because the procedure was similar to that of the national assemblies, the composition of the councils was easily controlled by the ruling parties. Communists were usually in a minority, especially at the lower levels, but had no trouble in effecting leadership over loyal and obedient non-communists.[13]

The plenary sessions of the people's councils, although infrequent and brief, provide a forum for public criticism within the limits permitted by the party, and are without genuine opposition. The local organs have in a sense become supplementary "mass organizations," involving the participation of large numbers of people, either as elected deputies or as activists or specialists associated with the councils through the latter's permanent commissions, or through other committees in school, street, apartment house, and the like.[14] Although this can hardly be regarded as authentic democratic participation, and the deputies are not genuine representatives of the popular will or of group interests, these organs deal with matters of direct concern to the population and may be more responsive to local wishes than is the more remote central government.

The real power of administration rests, however, with the so-called "executive and administrative organs," rather than the broader plenary bodies. The executive committee, including a chairman, several deputy chairmen, and at least some of the heads of local departments, is, like the central cabinet, the real embodiment of political authority at its own level. Working under it are the offices and hired employees of the local administration. The committee as a whole and its members are in theory accountable to the plenary bodies that elect them. In fact, they owe their

[12] In March, 1959, Bulgaria experimented with a two-tier system, with administrative units in the *okrug* (or county), and town and village commune.

[13] After the 1958 elections in Poland, only 38 per cent of the people's councillors belonged to the PUWP (Richard Hiscocks, *Poland: Bridge for the Abyss?* [London, 1963], p. 276).

[14] In Poland, over 100,000 persons were members of people's councils in 1953, and another 140,000 associated with commissions and the like. By 1955, the former had doubled.

position to the next higher administrative authority and can be removed by it. The bureaucratic element clearly predominates over the representative element.[15]

Governments at the local level must everywhere work within a framework of policy over which they have no control, and differ only in the degree to which they have, as in the British or American systems, a reasonable latitude of autonomous action in their own spheres. In communist countries, following the tradition of continental Europe, local governments are strictly subordinated, through a hierarchy of command, to the central government, usually to the cabinet as a whole (occasionally to the Ministry of the Interior), sometimes to the Presidium or State Council. According to the principle of democratic centralism, their responsibility is a dual one—upward to the next higher administrative link and downward to the plenary body at their own level. In fact, as in the Soviet Union, the upper restraint has far outweighed the lower. Not only was the entire executive committee of, say, a district responsible to the regional committee, and that in turn to the central government, but each individual department was responsible to the corresponding regional department and to the appropriate ministry. The higher authority in each case had the explicit power to suspend or annul actions taken by subordinate organs; the latter were expected in all their activities to conform to policies laid down from above. As has been said of the Polish system, the local organs were thus "a part of the chain of command of the Government" and amounted to little more than "field offices of individual ministries in a highly centralized governmental system."[16] They were hardly to be distinguished from the local bureaus that some ministries created for the implementation of their directives.

Since 1956, there has been a persistent effort to make local government more genuinely autonomous and democratic. Most countries extended the competence of local authorities by transferring responsibility from higher to lower levels. In some states, the management of certain industries was shifted, on the Soviet model, from central ministerial direction to local control. The trend has been erratic, however, and in some cases abruptly reversed. A substantial decentralization was introduced, for instance, in Czechoslovakia in 1958, and Bulgaria in 1959, but was

[15] Taborsky, *op. cit.*, pp. 323–24.

[16] V. Gsovski and K. Grzybowski (eds.), *Government, Law and Courts in the Soviet Union and East Europe* (2 vols.; London and The Hague, 1959), I, 349.

abandoned a few years later in favor of closer supervision of the national committees by central organs.

The local system is a miniature of the national government, with the same subordination of the representative to the bureaucratic element, and of both to the party, whose importance indeed cannot be overemphasized.[17] At every level of administration—region, district, city, and village—the party organization is under the aegis of the next higher body, and ultimately of the Central Committee apparatus, and must see to it that the people's councils within its area of jurisdiction are carrying out the will of the party and the directives of the government. As at the center, there is the same regulation of administrative and political personnel through the cadres' jurisdiction, with confirmation of appointments by the next higher level usually required. There is the same effort to mobilize the activists, as trade unionists, peasants, writers, or housewives, by means of a myriad of committees and mass organizations and the leadership of communists within each. The party organization at each level must also take steps to stimulate and guide the activities of the lower party organs, and has a staff of "instructors" constantly supervising their work.

THE YUGOSLAV COMMUNE

As so often is the case, Yugoslavia is an exception to the general rule. Until 1950, its system of local government was much the same as elsewhere in Eastern Europe. The trend to decentralization, beginning in that year and steadily gathering strength, made the Yugoslav system unique in the communist world. In their own belief, far-reaching decentralization has ended the earlier bureaucratic system, established a new form of socialist democracy, and begun the long slow transition toward the withering away of the state. Since 1953, there have been two tiers of local government, the district or *serez* (except in Montenegro), 40 in all, and the commune or *opština*, 581 in number. The latter was the key unit of local authority and enjoyed, under the 1953 constitution, all powers of government except those assigned to the federation and the republics. Although somewhat modified by the 1963 constitution, its powers remain very broad. The commune occupies a crucial position in the regulation of economic life, possessing a close relationship with the workers' councils in industrial enterprises, wide authority to draft the plans for its territory, and

[17] See chapters 6 and 9 above, and Richard F. Staar, *Poland, 1944–1962* (New Orleans, 1962), chap. 11.

considerable financial autonomy. Its organs are the only ones directly elected by the people, and have the right to select deputies to the federal, republican, and district assemblies.

The internal organization of the commune and its relationship with the people render it a quite distinctive form of local government. Since 1952, the assembly has been bicameral, with, at present, a communal chamber representing citizens as citizens, and a chamber of the working communities, representing citizens as working people. Unlike people's councils elsewhere, the commune has no executive and administrative committee, but is under the general control of several so-called "citizens' councils." These are advisory bodies, each of which consists mainly of private citizens and is entitled to supervise the work of one or two administrative departments. Within each commune, there are, in addition, several voters' meetings, which hold sessions at least every two months, and which have the right, not only to nominate candidates for the communal and higher assemblies, but also to discuss the work of the commune and make recommendations to it. Then there are the so-called "public boards," made up of private citizens and employees, and empowered, under the supervision of the commune, to run hospitals, libraries, schools, radio stations, some newspapers, and apartment houses, and to manage the social insurance system. There are also consumers' councils, neighborhood councils, and other forms of citizen activity, as well as the workers' councils in industry. All these many forms of "social management," as it is termed, constitute a kind of approach to direct democracy. It is true, of course, that the great majority of the members of the local assemblies and the citizens' councils (although *not* of the organs of social management) are communists, but the inclusion of many noncommunists and the decentralized character of the party itself make the method of party control substantially different from that elsewhere. Moreover, in the 1965 election, there were roughly twice as many candidates as seats to be filled. Even if this does not constitute democracy in the Western sense, it assures a wider popular participation than in other communist states.[18] The commune may, in the opinion of some, ultimately replace the republics entirely as the most efficient means of assuring the defense of local, regional, and national interests.[19]

[18] For a fuller discussion, see Hoffman and Neal, *op. cit.*, pp. 223ff., and Jack C. Fisher, "The Yugoslav Commune," *World Politics*, XVI, 3 (April, 1964), 418–41. See also Burks, *op. cit.*, p. 10.

[19] Fisher, *op. cit.*, pp. 439–41.

14: Shaping Public Opinion

Communist government is often thought of purely in terms of coercion, and the role of persuasion is ignored or minimized. Yet like the Soviet system, other communist regimes, in accordance with Lenin's dictum, have sought a balance between coercion and persuasion, with the balance varying from time to time, and from country to country.[1] Indeed, the "political pedagogical" function of the state has necessarily assumed great importance where a minority rules over an unwilling majority, and where the latter are expected to subordinate their individual interests to a social interest as defined by the party.[2] At least in theory, communist leaders have seen the advantages of lessening the need for force and terror and of inculcating discipline through mass persuasion. They have hoped thereby to develop a "socialist consciousness" among the masses and to bring about an identity between their own ideological conceptions and the feelings and actions of their supporters and the population in general.[3]

A black and white analysis would suggest that in democracies public opinion determines government policy, whereas under communism, the government dictates public opinion. In fact, of course, democratic leaders, although responsive in some degree to the popular will, also seek to direct it. The rise of public relations in politics has created fears of the emergence of a "brave new world" in which the aim of government is "making people like their unescapable social destiny."[4] Communist control of opinion far exceeds the democracies in this respect, in the elaborate apparatus employed, in the systematic character of indoctrination, and above all, in the largely one-directional flow of communications from leadership to the masses. Whether there is a reverse effect of popular attitudes on the government and its

[1] For this and the following, see the excellent book by Alex Inkeles, *Public Opinion in Soviet Russia: A Study in Mass Persuasion* (Cambridge, 1950), esp. pp. 3–5. Less satisfactory studies of this subject in its Eastern European forms are Vladimir Reisky de Dubnic, *Communist Propaganda Methods: A Case Study on Czechoslovakia* (New York, 1960), and Antonin Buzek, *How the Communist Press Works* (London, 1964).

[2] Ernst Richert, *Macht ohne Mandat* (2d ed.; Köln and Opladen, 1963), pp. 169–72, 233. See also E. Richert, with Carola Stern and Peter Dietrich, *Agitation und Propaganda: Das System der publizistischen Massenführung in der Sowjetzone* (Berlin and Frankfurt a/M., 1958).

[3] Richert, *Agitation und Propaganda*, pp. ix, 4ff.

[4] Aldous Huxley, *Brave New World* (London, 1964), pp. 12, 195.

policies, especially since Stalin, is a question to be discussed at the end of this chapter.

In the modern world, public opinion is the product, not merely of the rational and free thought of individuals, but much more, of powerful media of communication, both private and governmental, and of the subtle pressure of community patterns of behavior and thought. In no country is there an entirely "free market of ideas." The environment is always "weighted," to use Harold Laski's term, with some persons and institutions stronger than others in the area of communications, and with the masses tending to conform to the line of the opinion leaders.[5] Unpopular or heretical ideas are difficult to express even in the freest of societies. In communist countries, the market place of ideas is dominated by a single viewpoint dispensed by all-pervasive means of communication under unified control. The rights of free speech and of free opinion, enshrined in the constitutions, are negated by this official system, which has almost a complete monopoly of the mass media and permits little or no rivalry from competing voices.[6] The propaganda is ideological and partisan in content, based on the doctrine of Marxism-Leninism and its current embodiment in the party line. In these circumstances, it is extremely difficult for the citizen to inform himself objectively about events, or to resist the opinions imposed upon him. The distinction between persuasion and coercion is in a sense obliterated, since persuasion involves a kind of "psychological compulsion," with severe penalties for any breach of the totality of control, or for the expression of dissident thoughts.[7]

AGITATION AND PROPAGANDA

In communist terminology, the task of molding the thinking and of guiding the actions of the people falls into two catgeories: "propaganda" and "agitation."[8] The distinction between them drawn by Lenin before the revolution is still maintained in theory, although in practice the separation is no longer so sharp. In essence, propaganda involves the presentation of many ideas to a few, and appeals more to the intellect than the emotions. It

[5] Harold J. Laski, *The American Democracy* (New York, 1948), p. 617.

[6] See Chapter 11 on propaganda, in Carl J. Friedrich and Z. K. Brzezinski, *Totalitarian Dictatorship and Autocracy* (Cambridge, 1956).

[7] Richert, *Agitation und Propaganda*, pp. 8–9.

[8] See Inkeles, *op. cit.*, chap. 2 *et seq.*, and Buzek, *op. cit.*, pp. 22ff.

comes closer to what we in the West would call "indoctrination," and involves the systematic teaching of Marxism-Leninism and its contemporary application in party policy. The target of propaganda in this sense is not the masses, but the leaders, that is, party functionaries and activists. Communist ideology, as will be seen in a later chapter, serves the extremely vital functions of legitimizing the communist system and all its actions, and thus winning the loyalty of the people. Propaganda is therefore indispensable as a means of extending the cadres' knowledge of theory, of deepening their convictions, and of training the propagandists of the future. It is carried on through an intensive program of "schooling," and in newspapers and other publications of an ideological character. In a broader sense, however, it permeates the whole realm of cultural and scholarly activity, including education and the creative arts.[9]

"Agitation," on the other hand, involves the expounding of a few ideas to many, and appeals more to the sentiments and feelings of the masses. Close to what would be called propaganda in the West, its purpose is to convince the people of the correctness of individual acts of official policy, and to get them to take the actions necessary for their implementation. The mass media, especially the press and the radio, are used, but great reliance is placed on special types of agitation, involving face-to-face oral persuasion. Although the party as a whole and each member are expected to contribute their share, specially designated "agitators" are assigned a major responsibility and perform a function unknown in other societies.[10]

The complex machinery by which this dual job of propaganda and agitation is performed is a curious medley of party, government, and unofficial agencies, with the party, of course, the decisive unifying force. In the words of *Nová mysl*, the Czechoslovak theoretical organ, "The guidance of political propaganda and agitation is the business of the Party and nobody else."[11] The distinction usually drawn between the "directing" duty of the party, and the "operating" function of the government proper, is not so clearcut in the field of opinion-formation. Although many tasks are left to the organs of the state (for instance, the Ministry of Culture), or to nonparty associations (for example, the newspapers), the party itself conducts extremely important activities of a propagandist or agitational nature. This is regarded as the responsibility of the party in its entirety, and not limited to any

[9] See Chapter 17.

[10] Reisky de Dubnic, *op. cit.*, pp. 38ff.

[11] No. 3, March, 1954, p. 334.

specific organ or branch. The First Secretary occupies a crucial position in the leadership of public opinion, expounding the current doctrine and party line in his speeches and articles. He is assisted by his closest colleagues at the center, and the leaders at every level. An important part is played by the sessions of congresses, central committees, and district and regional conferences. The party organizations in the cities, regions, and districts have the particular job of supervising the schooling within their area; the basic organizations have a special role in the conduct of day-to-day agitation. The individual member, as the rules make clear, must "consistently defend the policy of the party, explain it to the broad masses and win them for its implementation," and must "master Marxism-Leninism, raise his ideological level, and actively contribute to the education of man in a communist society."[12] An elite of thousands of professional propagandists and tens of thousands of semiprofessional or amateur agitators is thus available to work for the party, the state, and the mass associations.

Serving the cause of both propaganda and agitation are the publications of the party, in particular its daily newspaper, issued by the Central Committee, and other regional and local organs. In addition, each communist party has a monthly theoretical

Country	*Daily newspaper*	*Theoretical organ*
Albania	*Zeri i popullit* (People's Voice)	*Rruge e Partisë* (Party Path)
Bulgaria	*Rabotnicheskoe delo* (Workers' Cause)	*Novo vreme* (New Times)
Czechoslovakia	*Rudé právo* (Red Justice) (in Czech and Slovak) *Pravda* (Truth) (in Slovak)	*Nová mysl* (New Thought)
East Germany	*Neues Deutschland* (New Germany)	*Einheit* (Unity)
Hungary	*Népszabadság* (People's Freedom)	*Társadalmi Szemle* (Social Review)
Poland	*Trybuna ludu* (People's Tribune)	*Nowe drogi* (New Ways)
Rumania	*Scinteia* (The Spark)	*Lupta de clasa* (Class Struggle)
Yugoslavia	*Komunist* (weekly) *Borba* (Fight) (daily organ of the Socialist Alliance)	*Naša stvarnost* (Our Reality)

[12] Paragraph 1 of the 1962 rules of the CPC.

journal and a magazine concerned with organization and agitation.

The directing link in this massive system of persuasion and indoctrination is a special branch of the central apparatus known as the Department of Agitation and Propaganda (Agitprop). The extent of its jurisdiction is indicated by its sections, usually including offices for party and mass propaganda, agitation, culture, press, radio and television, schools, publishing, the arts, films, and sport. If it does not itself conduct these operations, Agitprop exercises the ultimate authority over the agencies that do, such as the broadcasting system or the newspapers. At the center, the department serves as a right arm of the leadership, advising on theory and policy and managing the major journals and institutions in this field. It oversees the work of the lower party organs through agitprop sections in the cities, regions, and districts, and corresponding committees in the basic organizations.

Ideological indoctrination is important, not only in facilitating the selection of cadres for important positions, but in strengthening their "sense of mission" and in creating a disciplined manner of thinking and behavior.[13] The party has its own system of schools in the regions and districts, and a university for the country as a whole. Promising cadres in the party and other organizations, such as the trade unions, are assigned to one of these institutions for varying periods of residence, and undergo detailed training, not only in Marxism-Leninism, but also in practical questions of industrial and agricultural leadership. In addition, the entire membership is expected to "go to school," either in evening classes or through independent study, following a general program prepared by Agitprop. An army of "propagandists" or instructors is, of course, required for this undertaking, usually under the guidance of local study and consultation centers. The party issues reading materials specially prepared for this purpose, as well as many other publications, such as the collected works of the leader or former leader (for example, Gottwald's *Spisy*); the works of Marx and Lenin, and of Soviet leaders; the proceedings of congresses and central committees; a history of the party; and translations of major Soviet works on Marxism-Leninism.

A multipronged system of agitation seeks to exert a direct and continuing impact on the noncommunist masses, "explaining" the party line on concrete matters and "instructing" them on the

[13] See especially Richert, *Agitation und Propaganda*, pp. 269–81.

actions to be taken to achieve the goals. It includes various written forms, such as factory and village newspapers, wall newspapers, posters and billboards, pamphlets and brochures, but above all, "oral agitation," that is, direct personal contact by specially designated agitators in the factory, in the village, and even in the home or apartment. The purpose is often to secure pledges of action, such as "volunteer" work by the individual, or factory resolutions on increasing production. Although on the surface these are measures of persuasion, an important element of "compulsion" is involved, since the individual is often obliged to yield against his will to the pressure of the agitator.[14]

Space forbids more than a brief mention of the role of government, and of nongovernmental, nonparty associations, in agitation and propaganda. The functions of the former are sometimes operational, as in the administration of the broadcasting system, or the film industry, and sometimes supervisory, as in the case of the press. These and many other tasks are normally carried out through a Ministry of Culture, with wide authority over all mass media, supplemented often by separate departments in such fields as education. Needless to say, the work of the government is strictly controlled by the party through the general direction of Agitprop, through cadre control of all officials, editors, broadcasting executives, and the like, and through party members within the entire communications network.

Nonparty organizations, such as the national fronts and their constituent mass associations (trade unions, youth groups, women's leagues), duplicate almost all the activities of the party in both propaganda and agitation. Where other parties exist, as in Czechoslovakia and Poland, similar functions are performed, including the publishing of their own newspapers and even the schooling of members. Professional associations, such as the Union of Writers or of Journalists, through their organs and their periodic meetings, play a vital part in indoctrinating and controlling their members and stimulating their actions in the desired direction. Special purposes are served by the Soviet Friendship Association, which publicizes Soviet achievements and organizes the study of the Russian language, and the Society for the Dissemination of Political and Scientific Knowledge, which fights against religion and bourgeois ideas, and propagates the "scientific world outlook."[15]

[14] *Ibid.*, pp. 185–222.
[15] Reisky de Dubnic, *op. cit.*, pp. 64ff. and 99ff.

THE NEWSPAPERS

The press deserves special attention for its unique task of manipulating and controlling opinion. The concept of newspapers and journals as organs of competing social forces and conflicting viewpoints, contributing through free discussion and objective reporting to the creation of a public opinion, is rejected. Rather, the press is quite openly described as "a political instrument of the Communist party."[16] In propaganda, it must purvey expositions and commentary on Marxism-Leninism and the major lines of party policy; in agitation, it must present the party's wishes on day-to-day issues. This must be done by the communist newspapers, but also by those of the National Front, the mass associations, or other parties, where they exist; by those published in regions and cities, in factories and villages, and the more specialized papers for agriculture, teachers, writers, and the armed forces; as well as by the central organs published in the capital. All fall under the general control of Agitprop and its press department. Unlike the Soviet Union, the governments in Eastern Europe do not have their own daily newspapers corresponding to *Izvestia.* All newspapers, however, come under the direct supervision of the government, receive the bulk of their information from an official news agency, such as Četeka in Czechoslovakia, and are guided by instructions from a press office. With party control superimposed on government regulation, the press, whatever its ostensible affiliation, is completely unified in outlook. Its task is not to reflect diverse currents of opinion but to "create a correct public opinion for every question."[17] Like other mass media, the papers are not designed to provide objective information on the news of the day, but to provide the correct party-endorsed views on all issues.[18] The journalists are "soldiers on the ideological front,"[19] whose job is to educate, indoctrinate, and agitate.

The press also has an "operative function" that approximates it to a mass association or an administrative agency.[20] Lenin, in a famous pre-revolutionary slogan, spoke of it as being a "collective propagandist," a "collective agitator," and a "collective

[16] See Adolf Hradecky in *Nová mysl,* No. 9, September, 1964.
[17] Richert, *Agitation und Propaganda,* p. 79.
[18] See Buzek, *op. cit.,* esp. pp. 55–64.
[19] E. Gierek, in *Prasa Polska,* November, 1964.
[20] Richert, *Agitation und Propaganda,* pp. 139–40.

organizer." In the greatly changed conditions of communist rule, the press is expected to assist the party and government in securing from the people, not merely outward assent to public policy, but the concrete action necessary to implement it. This has been called the "critical and controlling function" of the newspaper.[21] In the absence of elections or effective parliamentary control over the executive, the press draws attention to deficiencies as well as achievements in fulfilling the party line, and urges the necessary corrective actions. This it does through its news columns and also through carefully selected letters from readers, and through nonprofessional local contributors known as worker and peasant correspondents. Criticism, of course, must fall within strictly defined limits; it must be "party criticism," designed to remove failings and not to question policy itself.[22]

PUBLIC OPINION AND POLICY

The question may now be raised as to whether there is any sense in which public opinion exerts an influence on policy. Nowhere in the world does public opinion greatly affect the day-to-day actions of government, but it is never entirely absent as a limiting factor and as a positive force in the long run. In democracies, there are many "public opinions," inchoate, often contradictory, and with a varying ability to make themselves known and to have an effect. In communist countries, the massive dimension of the propaganda effort implies that there is a need to change the actual opinions of the public, and to break down resistance to official policies. In spite of the all-pervasive propaganda, as Milovan Djilas pointed out, men continue to think—and differently from the prescribed manner.[23] Diverse attitudes on public issues reflect differences of family, region, nationality, class, profession, religion, and level of education. Although these views may not be publicly expressed, they can be transmitted by word of mouth or in Aesopian language. The approach to total control of communication was a gradual one in most East European countries, and has never been complete. Conflicting information and ideas have been received in varying degrees from tourists, foreign broadcasts, communist newspapers from other countries, in classical literature, and even in the writings of Marx or Lenin. The German Democratic Republic in particular was open to powerful

[21] Buzek, *op. cit.*, pp. 52ff.
[22] Hradecky, *op. cit.*
[23] *The New Class* (New York, 1957), p. 133.

influences from abroad. Above all, domestic institutions such as the family or religion counteracted official propaganda and agitation.

Since the death of Stalin, the relationship of public opinion and power has shifted noticeably. With the reduction of the role of coercion, persuasion has taken on increased importance, and has had to be modified in form and substance. Although the function and structure of the opinion-forming system has not essentially changed, there has been a conscious effort to remove some of the most obvious defects of the past.[24] In particular, the regimes have sought to make the press and other media somewhat less distorted mirrors of reality, and to encourage a greater degree of authentic discussion. Restrictions on access to other sources of information have been lessened, notably through wider freedom to travel, cultural exchange with the West, the almost complete elimination of jamming of foreign broadcasts, and a limited sale of foreign newspapers. The media of communications have not, however, ceased to be partisan and ideological, and still serve as instruments designed to "form, enlighten, mobilize, and organize public opinion."[25]

The post-Stalin change of climate has led to a phenomenon not planned, or welcomed, by the regimes, that is, the emergence of an embryonic public opinion outside the officially defined framework. The journalists themselves, and writers generally, in one country after another have urged more objective reporting and freer discussion of public issues, and sometimes in defiance of party directives, have expressed their own distinctive viewpoints. This was notably true in Poland and Hungary during the thaw after 1955. Although this tendency was suppressed in Hungary in October, 1956, and subjected to increasing restrictions in Poland, it has reappeared in more conformist countries, such as Bulgaria, East Germany, Rumania, and Czechoslovakia. In Yugoslavia, ever since 1950, there has been somewhat more freedom for the press, although it expands and declines with changing circumstances.[26] In Czechoslovakia, in 1963 and after, writers and journalists indulged in frank and open venting of opinions, and even criticism of official policies. Sharpest expression was given

[24] See Buzek, *op. cit.*, chap. 7 and pp. 176–83; Richert, *Agitation und Propaganda*, pp. 165–82.

[25] Z. Komocsin, "The Ideological Guiding Principles and the Press," *Társadalmi Szemle*, July, 1965.

[26] G. W. Hoffman and F. W. Neal, *Yugoslavia and the New Communism* (New York, 1962), pp. 399, 411–13; Buzek, *op. cit.*, p. 110.

by a Slovak professor of journalism, Miro Hysko, in a celebrated speech in May, 1963, in which he bitterly assailed the government's slowness in de-Stalinization, and claimed the right of journalists to "respect only directives which are in no conflict with the fundamental principles of socialist morality," as interpreted by them.[27] The regime responded by declaring that journalists and newspapers were obliged to confine their criticism within the limits set by the party, and were not entitled to an independent voice of their own. In spite of continuing pressure, a number of the newspapers stood their ground in a manner unheard of in the past. That the situation is sometimes duplicated in other countries is indicated by the speech of Arthur Starewicz, head of the Polish party's press department, in which he lamented the existence of "false views" that the press should be independent and that its mission should consist, "not in the shaping of public opinion, but in 'reflecting it' and in exerting pressure on the government."[28]

It is evident from such examples that public opinion, or the opinions of certain groups or persons, have sometimes escaped from the all-embracing thrall of official propaganda. In the case of Czechoslovakia, this had a noticeable effect on government actions; in other cases, it may have set limits to the enactment of official decisions, and still more, to their effective implementation. In a more discreet and accepted manner, the views of specialized groups are brought to bear on the making of policy, as explained earlier (chapters 10 and 11). Even the governments have given greater attention to sounding out public opinion, using the press and journalists as "sensitive antennae" for this purpose,[29] and resorting to the technique of polling. Within the strict limits of official propaganda, therefore, public opinion has occasionally emerged as a factor, and a two-way relationship between people and government has sometimes developed.

[27] *Pravda* (Slovak), June 3, 1963. For a full discussion, see H. Gordon Skilling, *Communism National and International* (Toronto, 1964), esp. chap. 7.

[28] July, 1963, cited by Buzek, *op. cit.*, pp. 256–57.

[29] E. Gierek, in *Prasa Polska*, November, 1964.

15: Force and Legality

According to Lenin, every political system was a dictatorship of a ruling class, imposing its will on the oppressed classes. As he said at the end of 1918, a dictatorship was "power based directly upon force and unrestricted by any laws."[1] This view stressed the compulsive aspects of political authority, and in particular, the state's instruments of violence, such as the police, the army, courts, and prisons. Democratic theory, in contrast, although recognizing the role of coercion in any political system, advocates the regulation of its use by legal procedures and limitations. In the Soviet Union, after an initial period during which law was discredited, it came into its own again in the form of "socialist legality." Although this term to some degree implied the regularity and certainty of legal processes, under Stalin it was identified with the strictest enforcement of government and party orders, with a minimum of regard or protection for the legal rights of the individual. Indeed, by the thirties, socialist legality had come to be synonymous with terror.

BALANCE OF LAW AND TERROR

Nonetheless, the Soviet Union was a curiously dual system, with law and terror in uneasy coexistence.[2] Both involved coercion or the use of force, but in the first, it was, in some degreee, ordered and just, and in the latter, unregulated and arbitrary. Laws, as well as imposing obligations and providing penalties for their breach, proclaimed rights and established procedures for their protection. Terror—the unrestrained employment of violence—was almost exclusively a system of punishment, sometimes for undefined "crimes" and potential offenders, and totally neglected any safeguards for the individual.[3] Paradoxically, both forms of coercion contained elements of persuasion, or dissuasion, since the threat of force induced citizens to obey the commands of authority. With the death of Stalin, the balance of terror and justice, once

[1] V. I. Lenin, *The Proletarian Revolution and the Renegade Kautsky*, in *Selected Works* (New York, 1943), VII, 123. See also V. I. Lenin, *State and Revolution* (New York, 1932), pp. 10–11.

[2] See Harold J. Berman, *Justice in the U.S.S.R.* (rev. ed.; New York, 1963), pp. 7–9. Cf. Merle Fainsod, *How Russia Is Ruled* (2d ed.; Cambridge, 1963), pp. 421, 462.

[3] See Jerzy G. Gliksman, "Social Prophylaxis as a Form of Soviet Terror," in Carl J. Friedrich (ed.), *Totalitarianism* (New York, 1954), pp. 60–74.

tipped decisively in favor of the former, shifted substantially. Persuasion and other methods of compulsion were given preference, and terror was increasingly regarded as a last resort. A new version of socialist legality evolved, which placed more emphasis on the limits on the use of coercive power.

The unique Soviet system of terror-cum-legality was imposed, in its Stalinist extreme, on Eastern Europe.[4] Where communism was not fully entrenched, it was employed at first as a weapon for attaining complete power and eliminating all opposition forces. By 1948, each of the communist countries had established an "all-pervasive apparatus of institutionalized terror"[5] whose main purpose was the maintenance of the political system and the enforcement of the party's will on the population. Negative sanctions predominated overwhelmingly over positive ones. As the Czech leader, Novotný, later lamented, "brute force" was the only feature of the dictatorship of the proletariat.[6] For a time, repression was successful in securing obedience and protecting the stability of the regimes, but in the long run might have proved fatal.[7] After the onset of de-Stalinization in the Soviet Union, other communist states, conscious of the danger of continued reliance on terror, began the difficult and delicate operation of shifting the balance in the direction of justice or legality.

During the period of communist rule, there have been three major elements of coercive enforcement: (1) the police and security system, (2) the armed forces and various paramilitary organizations, and (3) the courts and prosecutor. The chief difference between the periods before and after Stalin lay in the degree of importance of the three main elements, as well as the way in which each functioned. All of these components have had essentially the same general purpose: to protect the social and political order, and to compel the implementation of the edicts of the rulers. All have, of course, been tightly unified by

[4] See V. Gsovski and K. Grzybowski (eds.), *Government, Law and Courts in the Soviet Union and Eastern Europe* (2 vols.; London and The Hague, 1959), for detailed descriptions of each country's system of law and security, mainly before 1956. The chapter on Poland is especially good. See also H. Gordon Skilling, "The Soviet Impact on the Czechoslovak Legal Revolution," *Soviet Studies*, VI, 4 (April, 1955), 361–81.

[5] E. Helmreich (ed.), *Hungary* (New York, 1957), pp. 132–33.

[6] April 10, 1956, as quoted in V. Reisky de Dubnic, *Communist Propaganda Methods: A Case Study on Czechoslovakia* (London, 1964), p. 10.

[7] Cf. Paul E. Zinner, *Revolution in Hungary* (New York and London, 1962), pp. 127–28; F. A. Váli, *Rift and Revolt in Hungary* (Cambridge, 1961), p. 65.

the party's direction, but also by an interlocking of functions and activities. The security police, for instance, played a significant part in the judicial system, and the army supplemented the security forces in counteracting domestic subversion or suppressing revolt. All of them, especially under Stalin, permeated, as we have noted, the "noncoercive" processes of enforcement, lending support to their efficacy by the omnipresent Damocles' sword of coercion.

THE POLICE

During the Stalin period, the police and security system outranked the others as the chief buttress of communist power. The Ministry of the Interior was usually the focal point of the apparatus, although at times its powers were shared with a separate Ministry of Public Security. These departments controlled not only the ordinary police but also various types of militia, such as factory guards, frontier police, and special combat troops, which constituted a kind of domestic army and played an important part in suppressing the revolts in Pilsen and Poznań. They also had jurisdiction over the political prisons and the special labor camps. At the height of Stalinism, the Ministry of the Interior and its subordinate agencies had extensive powers of "administrative justice," empowering them to arrest and imprison persons without trial. It wielded great influence even in the normal processes of "justice," as it had the major responsibility for investigating suspects before the trial, and preparing the case for ultimate formal disposition by the courts.

The core of the system was the dreaded secret or security police, the wide scope of which in the conduct of terror is well illustrated by the Hungarian case.[8] The seventeen departments of the AVH included those dealing with the elimination of internal political opposition; the conduct of special investigations; the arrests and interrogations of prisoners; espionage and counterespionage; surveillance of foreigners; supervision of religious affairs, youth organizations, the army, and government ministries; the keeping of secret files; the maintenance of labor discipline; the checking of party members; and the protection of leading party and government personnel.

All the communist states, including Yugoslavia until 1949, were "police states." Terror was "the hallmark of power," and was usually regarded as the indispensable ingredient of totali-

[8] Váli, *op. cit.*, p. 59.

tarianism.[9] Power was ultimately vested, it has been said, in the person who could order the arrest of another and have it carried out.[10] The security system became "a law unto itself," a "state within a state." The men who held the reins, such as, for example, Lászlo Rajk, the Minister of Interior, or Gábor Peter, head of the Security Police, in Hungary, were shadowy figures of immense authority. Yet even they were not invulnerable. The system of repression was subordinated to the party, and in particular to the security department in the central committee apparatus.[11] More decisively, ultimate authority rested with the party's topmost leader, and beyond him, with the Soviet security police and its emissaries. Frequently the very person who apparently dominated the security system, such as Rajk, fell victim to the monster he had himself nurtured.

THE ARMED FORCES

The second element of repression—the armed forces, both Soviet and national—were not employed from day to day as were the security forces, but stood ready for use in case of a threat to the existence of the regime. Although ostensibly concerned mainly with the defense of the country, they performed a hardly less important function of preserving domestic order by their mere existence, and of suppressing local disorders or armed uprisings if they occurred. The role of the Red Army in putting down the revolt in East Berlin in 1953, and in Budapest in 1956, is too well known to require more than this mention. During the latter crisis, movements of Russian troops in Poland and Rumania were designed to ward off a repetition of the Hungarian events. Soviet troops had never been on the territory of Albania, and were withdrawn, at an early stage of communist rule, from Czechoslovakia, Bulgaria, and Yugoslavia.

National armed forces were created in each of the communist countries, including East Germany, where the *Volkspolizei* was eventually transformed into the People's Army. Prior to 1956, all of these could be considered as components of the Soviet armed forces.[12] Despite the fact that they were under the direction

[9] Carl J. Friedrich and Z. K. Brzezinski, *Totalitarian Dictatorship and Autocracy* (Cambridge, 1956), pp. 10, 132, 138. Cf. Váli, *op. cit.*, p. 64.

[10] Zinner, *op. cit.*, pp. 145–46.

[11] In the SED, department "S" supervised *inter alia* the army, *Volkspolizei*, and state security.

[12] See Váli, *op. cit.*, chap. 6; Richard F. Staar, *Poland, 1944–1962* (New Orleans, 1962), chap. 8.

of a Ministry of National Defense in each country, the armies were in fact integral parts of the unified defense system of the entire East European bloc and were modeled on the Soviet in every respect, including equipment and even uniforms and decorations. Each was also directly subordinated to Moscow's control by the presence not only of military advisers from the USSR but of officers of Soviet citizenship. An extreme case was that of Rokossovsky, a Soviet marshal of Polish origin, who was head of the Polish armed forces as Minister of Defense, and even a member of the Politburo. Many of the native officers had served in the Red Army during the war or had been trained in Russia. Noncommunist career officers, and even communist cadres, appointed without military training or with experience in guerrilla warfare, were gradually replaced by a younger generation of newly-trained officers.[13] Only in Yugoslavia was there a well-organized communist army, formed prior to the establishment of communist rule, and staffed by veterans of partisan action, and hence capable in 1948 of escaping from Soviet domination.

In no instance has there been evidence of the military elite emerging as an independent political force. The armed forces, like all other institutions, were subjected to party regulation through the Main Political Administration, under a Deputy Minister in the Department of National Defense. In addition, the minister was usually a top-ranking communist leader, often without military training.

THE COURTS AND PROSECUTORS

Before 1953, the legal element of enforcement, represented by the courts and the prosecutor, was a subordinate one, and was itself pervaded through and through by terror. The rights of citizens were profusely proclaimed in all the constitutions, but were in fact honored more in the breach than in observance. The major aim of socialist legality was the defense of the state, the protection of the existing social system, the safeguarding of public property, and only incidentally and exceptionally, the safeguarding of individual rights. The courts were openly described as "instruments of class justice," which in fact under prevailing conditions signified "party repression." As a Yugoslav statute put it in 1949, "Courts are agencies of the government which apply government coercion for the benefit of the ruling class."[14] The Soviet concept of crime

[13] A study of the military elites in Eastern Europe is available in Ithiel de Sola Pool, *Satellite Generals* (Stanford, 1955).

[14] Gsovski and Grzybowski, *op. cit.*, I, 804.

as "a socially dangerous act" permeated the criminal code. Procedural rules, such as the right to counsel, set forth in statutes on the judicial system, were not seriously enforced, especially in political trials. Confessions, secured by torture during the investigations, often served as sufficient evidence of guilt. Judges, although supposedly independent, were actually obliged to apply their party's interpretation of existing laws.[15] Professional judges were supplemented by lay judges, or people's assessors, as in the Soviet system. The lawyers were organized in collectives, and were expected to put the social interest above that of their client.[16] Above all, the role of the security police in pretrial investigations and of the prosecution in the trial proceedings predetermined the outcome.

The office of Attorney General or Public Prosecutor was eventually established, in direct imitation of the Soviet system, in all communist countries, including Yugoslavia. A leading figure in the central administration, the Public Prosecutor was in charge of a streamlined hierarchy of prosecutors at lower levels, all exempt from local control. The concentration of power in this apparatus was enormous, embracing not merely a part in pretrial investigations, the prosecution of all criminal cases, and participation in civil cases, when necessary, but also the supervision of the whole realm of law enforcement, both against individuals and officials and institutions. He was, in Soviet terms, the watchdog of socialist legality, checking on both the executive and the judiciary. He had the right, along with the Chairman of the Supreme Court, to re-open judicial cases for retrial, and to examine and protest actions taken at any point in the whole of public administration. In theory, he was regarded as a protector of the rights of the individual against illegal arrest or investigation, arbitrary administrative action, and unlawful judicial decisions. In fact, however, in the climate of the times, he served simply as an added weapon of the regime for the rigid and terroristic enforcement of its own concept of "legality."

DECLINE OF TERROR

As noted, the system of sanctions underwent stringent criticism and in some cases substantial reform after 1953. The main impulse for change came from the USSR, in particular from Khrushchev's assault on Stalinism and the subsequent amendments

[15] See *ibid.*, I, 665, on Bulgaria.

[16] E. Taborsky, *Communism in Czechoslovakia, 1948–1960* (Princeton, 1961), pp. 293–94.

of the Soviet legal system. These in turn released strong pressures for reform in Eastern Europe, especially in Poland and Hungary, as increasing condemnation of the earlier terror was voiced, and its replacement by legality was demanded. The course, however, was a zigzag one, with occasional reversals of direction and great variation in pace.

In Albania and East Germany, the Stalinist balance of terror and legality has remained largely untouched to the present. In Rumania and Bulgaria, reforms were superficial and have not altered seriously the foundations of the earlier system. Even in these states, however, with the exception of Albania, amnesties have been proclaimed and subtle changes in the climate of law and order have occurred. In Czechoslovakia, changes after 1956 were slight and were soon reversed. The situation was hardly affected by the adoption of the new constitution in 1960. In Hungary, the defeat of the revolution led to a complete *volte-face* under Kádár and the return to extreme repression, culminating in the execution of Nagy and the restoration of many of the old methods, although in somewhat more subtle form.[17] In Poland, although the framework of the old system was retained, there were extensive innovations in practice and especially in the spirit of its operation.[18] Yugoslavia, where terror had been dominant prior to 1949, anticipated the changes that were to come later in other communist states.[19] Modifications began to be made in 1951, but were timid, and retrogressive steps were taken later. As the case of Djilas demonstrated (see p. 94), repression, although reduced in importance, continued to be used if deemed necessary.

Reforms affected each of the three elements of coercive enforcement, and were usually modeled on the measures taken in the Soviet Union, although with significant variations.[20] In most cases, there was a decline in the role of the security system, with an end to administrative procedures for imprisonment and execution. In almost all countries, high security officials were blamed for the terror, removed from office, and often punished for their crimes. The secret police, under new leadership, was downgraded,

[17] Váli, *op. cit.*, chaps. 26 and 28.

[18] Gsovski and Grzybowski, *op. cit.*, I, 780–88.

[19] *Ibid.*, pp. 823–36; G. W. Hoffman and F. W. Neal, *Yugoslavia and the New Communism* (New York, 1962), chaps. 6 and 19.

[20] For the Soviet Union, see Berman, *op. cit.*, esp. chap. 2, and a special issue of *Problems of Communism*, XIV, 2 (March–April 1965), on "Law and Legality in the USSR," in particular an article on legislative trends in Eastern Europe by K. Grzybowski and J. L. Alder.

and more strictly subordinated to government and party. Public Security was usually separated from the Ministry of the Interior, and placed under a committee, the chairman of which was not normally a member of the top party organs. There were large scale releases of unjustly condemned persons from labor camps and prisons, and victims were publicly rehabilitated in varying degrees. This was, however, a delicate operation as it threatened to undermine the position of the regime and especially the leaders mainly responsible for past terror. For instance, Nagy, in Hungary, found it extremely difficult to implement such a policy in the face of Rakosi's opposition. The later macabre rehabilitation of Rajk, and his reinterment, was a potentially explosive event that had serious political repercussions.[21] In Czechoslovakia, official resistance to a redress of past legal injustice continued long after the Twenty-second Congress of the CPSU, and yielded only to intense public pressure in 1963. Late in that year, the trials of the 1950's were almost without exception declared miscarriages of justice, based on complete fabrications, and the victims were exonerated, sometimes posthumously.[22]

MILITARY INFLUENCE

The position of the armed forces has remained much the same, although changes have occurred in the manner of their functioning. The national armies have ceased to imitate openly all Red Army practices and have in some cases been freed from direct Russian interference. In Hungary, however, Soviet military controls have hardly lessened since the days before 1956. The dismissal of Rokossovsky from the command of the Polish forces in 1956 was a high point in the liberation of Poland from domination. Yugoslavia and Albania are entirely independent of outside military restraints. All the other communist states, as members of the Warsaw Pact and its armed defense system, are still subject to the substantial influence of the USSR as the dominant power in the alliance.[23]

Russian troops were withdrawn from Rumania in 1958, but have remained in Poland, Hungary, and East Germany. Agreements concluded by the USSR with Poland and Hungary after the events of 1956 forbade interference by the Soviet forces in

[21] Váli, *op. cit.*, pp. 143–51, 246–49.

[22] *Rudé právo*, August 22, 1963. See H. Gordon Skilling, *Communism National and International* (Toronto, 1964), esp. chaps. 6 and 7.

[23] See Chapter 18 below.

internal affairs, and required special agreements between the governments concerning their disposition and movements.[24] In Hungary, however, they are still almost equivalent to an army of occupation, but are confined to certain areas and kept as much as possible out of sight. In East Germany, where 20 Soviet divisions—as many as all the other Soviet forces in Eastern Europe—are stationed, their presence is more obtrusive, and the treaty relating to them places fewer limitations on their freedom of action. Even where there are no Soviet forces, their proximity in the neighboring USSR remains a kind of instrument of "remote control" and "psychological deterrence."[25]

LEGAL REFORM

Changes in the legal system proper have reflected the reforms made in the USSR, although as in other spheres, the differences have been great from country to country. The structure and general status of the courts, the prosecutor, judges, and lawyers were not fundamentally altered, but an effort was made to modify their procedures and to extend the rights available to the individual. New criminal and other codes were enacted, and were usually characterized by a lessening of penalties and a more precise definition of crimes. The determination of the outcome of court proceedings by prior investigations, including forced confessions, was reduced and in some cases largely eliminated. The burden of proof tended to shift to the prosecutor, although the presumption of innocence was not everywhere accepted. The right of defense for the accused was made more real in the courtroom and sometimes extended to the pretrial examination. The powers of the prosecutor were in some respects enhanced, especially by his added responsibility to protect the individual against arbitrary arrest or unwarranted police interrogation.

The outcome of the tumultous decade since Stalin's death is difficult to assess with any accuracy. As in the Soviet Union, the general system of coercion has retained its main features, and still includes elements both of legality and of violent repression. Some degree of terror undoubtedly remains, greater in some states than in others, and always present as a potential force in case of need.[26]

[24] Richard Hiscocks, *Poland: Bridge for the Abyss?* (London, 1963), pp. 229–30; Váli, *op. cit.*, pp. 431–32.

[25] See Andrew Gyorgy, in Stephen Fischer-Galati (ed.), *Eastern Europe in the Sixties* (New York and London, 1963), pp. 189–90. See also Chapter 18, pp. 222–23, below.

[26] Gyorgy in *ibid.*, p. 188.

The downgrading of the security organs has not meant their complete elimination, nor served as a guarantee against their future resurgence. The safeguards against a return to Stalinism are to be found, not in legal or institutional forms, but in the climate of opinion and in the dangers of a resort to outright repression. Similarly, the possibility of military action by Soviet troops is not excluded, although the disadvantages of a repetition of Budapest is no doubt recognized and hence likely to be consciously avoided.

SOCIAL COMPULSIONS

The decline of terror does not, of course, mean the end of compulsion in its less violent or repressive forms. There has been no ending of the administrative obligations of the bureaucratic system, or of the coercive pressures of propaganda and agitation noted in the preceding chapter. Nor has the legal system itself changed in its essentials. A rule of law can hardly be said to have been established. Law is still regarded largely as something to be enforced and obeyed, and as an instrument of the regime and a buttress of the state and the social order. In most countries of Eastern Europe, in imitation of the Soviet Union, new forms of "social coercion" have been introduced, such as the volunteer brigades, for aiding the police in maintaining order and apprehending offenders against social mores, and the "comrades' courts." Although the latter are mainly for minor offenses and are not intended to replace the courts in their spheres, they are agencies for enforcing conformity of behavior in a manner that lacks the safeguards of a legal system. Although they have an important purpose of moral suasion and education, they are also supplementary instruments of coercion, not as dangerous or all-pervasive as the earlier brutal terror, but less fair and impartial than an ordered system of courts. The organs of people's control, set up also on the Soviet model, fulfill similar functions. As in the Soviet Union, there has thus emerged, as Berman terms it, a new dualism of law and social pressure.[27]

[27] Berman, *op. cit.*, p. 88.

PART SIX

TOTALITARIANISM IN TRANSITION

Introduction

Communist states have traditionally been called "totalitarian" and classified together with other systems of this kind such as Fascist Italy or Nazi Germany. Nonetheless, there has been considerable difference of viewpoint as to the exact meaning of totalitarianism, and more recently doubts have been expressed as to the appropriateness of this concept for the analysis of communism.[1] For some, the term connoted "extreme etatism" or the "unlimited extension of state functions," with the state interfering in almost all spheres of life, public and private.[2] For others, it involved a syndrome of indispensable components, including an official ideology, a single party led by one man, terroristic police control, a near-complete monopoly of the means both of mass communications and of armed combat, and central direction of the entire economy.[3] Brzezinski stressed what he regarded as the crucial element, namely, the commitment of the leadership to "a total social revolution," seeking to destroy the old society, to build a new one, and in the process to mold a new type of man.[4] In his view, the dynamic drive toward social change conditioned and explained all other aspects of the totalitarian system, giving it an inescapable inner compulsion toward permanent revolution, and the subordination of all other social groups to the single party.

Most of these views minimized, but did not entirely exclude, the possibility that totalitarianism could be present in differing

[1] See the symposium edited by Carl J. Friedrich, *Totalitarianism* (New York, 1954). Cf. Robert C. Tucker's comment on Z. K. Brzezinski, "The Nature of the Soviet System," in *Slavic Review*, XX, 3 (October, 1961), 379–82.

[2] Hans Kelsen, as quoted by Tucker, *op. cit.*, p. 379, and N. S. Timasheff in Friedrich, *op. cit.*, p. 39.

[3] Carl J. Friedrich and Zbigniew K. Brzezinski, *Totalitarian Dictatorship and Autocracy* (Cambridge, 1956), pp. 9–10.

[4] See Z. K. Brzezinski, "The Nature of the Soviet System," *Slavic Review*, XX, 3 (October, 1961), 351–68, and his "Totalitarianism and Rationality," *The American Political Science Review*, L, 3 (September, 1956), 751–63. Cf. also Martin Drath in his introduction to Ernst Richert, *Macht ohne Mandat* (2d ed.; Köln and Opladen, 1963), pp. xi, xxvii, xxxiii.

degrees in successive stages of development, and that it might in the future experience substantial modification of some of its components. Some, however, expressed the idea of a "continuum" running from liberalism to totalitarianism, and others envisaged a future erosion of totalitarianism in the Soviet Union.[5] Eastern European communist societies, it was also argued, were not fully totalitarian during their first decade, but at the best, "partialitarian" or "semi-totalitarian," with terror and ideology not fully developed.[6] Later, the diminution of terror in the USSR, the decline of ideology, the growing importance of rational methods, the introduction of new forms of social control, and other changes since Stalin's death were noted.[7] This process of "mellowing" has gone further in some communist countries than in the USSR. Although the single-party system remains, administrative and social groups have more and more influence in politics; outright terror and military domination have given way to other forms of compulsion and to persuasion; even the control of communications has been counterbalanced in some degree by the influence of public opinion. In other words, some communist states have become *less* and not, as predicted by some, *more* totalitarian.[8]

Two aspects of communism yet to be discussed are the command economy and the official ideology, both normally regarded as essential elements of a totalitarian system. The communist dictatorship, it has been said, has had as its outstanding characteristic "the active indoctrination of the society in the party's ideology" and "the shaping of all social relations according to that ideology." The doctrine has comprised "a total critique of the antecedent form of societal organization and a prescription for a complete reconstruction of society and man."[9] Marxism-Leninism proclaimed that the goal of socialism would be achieved by the draconic mobilization of resources, human and material, for the sake of economic development, and by the creation of a command economy, relying on centralized planning and a vast bureaucratic apparatus. More than that, the theory has been the legitimizer of complete control of society, embodying, as it does, not only a theory of politics and economics, but a general framework of thought in all realms.

[5] Timasheff in Friedrich, *op. cit.*, p. 43; George Kennan in *ibid.*, pp. 31–32, 34, 83; Paul Kecskemeti in *ibid.*, p. 379.

[6] Gyorgy in *ibid.*, pp. 381, 383n.

[7] Brzezinski, "Totalitarianism and Rationality," pp. 760–63; Brzezinski, "The Nature of the Soviet System," pp. 355–61.

[8] Friedrich and Brzezinski, *op. cit.*, p. 300.

[9] Brzezinski, "The Nature of the Soviet System," pp. 365, 353 respectively.

In the two chapters that follow, the economy and ideology of Eastern Europe will be examined in greater detail. As in other respects, the development has differed in the various countries, and has followed a zigzag course. In neither sphere has totalitarianism in fact been complete; in some cases it has declined. The introduction of market elements, improvements in the methods of planning, and the beginning of production for the consumer, rather than for its own sake, have somewhat weakened the centralized control of economic life. Changes in education, religion, and literature have affected the position of ideology and its content, and led to a decline in communist faith. In both cases, the impulse towards social change and permanent revolution seems to have weakened. The effort to indoctrinate has been placed second to the desire to produce, and the desire to produce has been directed more to meeting social demands than economic transformation. The ideology has begun to reflect, rather than actively shape, the economy and society, and the human mind.[10]

Another aspect of the traditional view of communism also requires modification. It was assumed during the heyday of Stalinism that communism was uniform and unchanging through the communist world. Differences were minimized by outside observers as well as by communist leaders themselves. The rebirth of nationalism has had a profound effect on this totalitarian feature, eroding its monolithic character and creating "national communism." This has led to a relativization of the ideology, as varying interpretations of the doctrine have been espoused, notably in Yugoslavia and China.[11] It has also led, for instance, in the case of Rumania, to a direction of the economy in the pursuit of national interests, and has thus further diminished the unity and harmony of the communist states.[12]

[10] Cf. Tucker, *op. cit.*, p. 381.
[11] Brzezinski, "The Nature of the Soviet System," pp. 367–68.
[12] See Chapter 18 below.

16: Planned Revolution and a Free Market

Communist doctrine and the experience of the USSR offered Eastern Europe a blueprint for drastic economic and social change and a totally controlled economy. Although the Soviet model was not at once introduced full-blown everywhere, it seems likely that from the first it constituted the ultimate goal. This model was totalitarian in several senses. It envisaged the complete transformation of the existing economic and social system, following the pattern of the permanent revolution that had been completed in the Soviet Union in the space of three decades. It involved the intervention by the state power in all spheres of life, particularly in the economic, with the establishment of central direction of the economy through a system of planning, the nationalization of industry and trade, the collectivization of agriculture, and the subordination of labor and the peasantry to the command economy thus created. The converse of this far-reaching statism was the elimination of almost all areas of freedom of choice and autonomy of action, such as the free market or collective bargaining. The dynamic of the new system required it to exert constant pressure on the population for the greatest possible fulfillment of the production targets established by the plans.

FROM A MIXED ECONOMY TO SOCIALISM

The approach to this ultimate goal was gradual, although in some respects faster than the corresponding process had been in the USSR. There was a natural variation among the Eastern European countries, resulting from the differing degree of economic development, ranging from the mature industrial countries, East Germany and Czechoslovakia; through the agricultural and raw-material producing countries, with substantial processing facilities, Poland and Hungary; to the agricultural and raw-material producers with only small processing facilities, Rumania, Yugoslavia, Bulgaria, and Albania. The countries were also differentiated politically as to whether they had participated in the war on the side of the Western Allies or the Axis powers.[1] East Germany and

[1] These distinctions, and much of what follows, are based on Nicolas Spulber, *The Economics of Communist Eastern Europe* (New York, 1957), a comparative study of six countries, excluding Albania and East Germany. See also chapters on agriculture (L.A.D. Dellin), industry (S. J. Zyzniew-

Albania, dependent on the Soviet Union and Yugoslavia respectively, had a specific evolution of their own, somewhat different from the other six. As time went on, it became clear that other important factors, such as the nature of the communist leadership or past political experience, would produce even sharper contrasts.

During the first period of communist rule, lasting roughly down to 1948, the economies and the social structure of Eastern Europe were by no means fully remodeled on the Soviet pattern, although substantial reforms were introduced. Some countries proceeded further and faster than others, but none did more than lay the foundations for the attainment of a total economy. There were many respects in which their economies differed from each other, and departed from a perfect totalitarian model. Whatever the ultimate intentions of the regimes, many persons, including some communists, no doubt assumed, or hoped, that the "mixed" economy would be maintained indefinitely, or in any case for a considerable length of time. By 1948, however, a new phase began, characterized by radical steps towards the totalitarianization of the economy, and the mobilization of society for the attainment of maximum economic objectives. If the communist leaders had earlier spoken of a gradual transition to socialism, they now urged "the completion of socialism" as the target of the near future, and openly espoused the approximation of their systems to the Soviet prototype. Although the total society was not fully completed even by 1953, the areas of individual initiative or spontaneous action had been by that time severely limited.

NATIONALIZATION OF INDUSTRY

In successive stages, each country moved toward the nationalization of industry, banking, wholesale and retail trade, and foreign commerce. The tempo of nationalization differed, however, proceeding somewhat more rapidly in the former allied countries than in the ex-enemy states, due in part to the expropriation by the Soviet Union of some parts of industry and trade in the latter as "German assets." In Hungary and Rumania, a substantial private sector continued until 1947 and 1948. In Czechoslovakia, although the first wave of socialization was far-reaching, there

---

ski), and trade (J. Wszelaki) in Stephen Fischer-Galati (ed.), *Eastern Europe in the Sixties* (New York and London, 1963), and Irwin T. Sanders (ed.), *Collectivization of Agriculture in Eastern Europe* (Lexington, Ky., 1958).

was greater resistance to its continuation than in any other allied country, as a result of the existence until 1948 of a strong entrepreneurial class and powerful noncommunist parties. In Poland and Yugoslavia, in Bulgaria and Albania, nationalization was begun almost immediately after the war, and advanced more rapidly. In Eastern Germany, most large firms were confiscated at once as the property of Nazis and war criminals, but full nationalization of industry and trade came only after 1948. With this exception, government ownership of industry and trade had to all intents and purposes been completed by that date in Eastern Europe. Although there were variations in the organization of industrial management in the several countries, the units of production and distribution were usually grouped together in national enterprises or corporations, and placed under the direction of central ministries.

COLLECTIVIZATION OF AGRICULTURE

Agriculture presented a very different picture, even after 1948. Prior to that year, official policy had sought to break up large estates where they existed, and to distribute the land to the peasants, thus increasing rather than diminishing private ownership. This had been particularly true of Hungary, Poland, Czechoslovakia, and, to a lesser extent, Albania and Rumania. In Czechoslovakia and Poland, land reform had a strong nationalist tinge, involving the expropriation of former German properties (and of Hungarian in the Czech case), and was supplemented by a mass colonization of formerly German-occupied territories by Czech and Polish peasants. Collectivization was attempted on a modest scale from 1945 only in Bulgaria and Yugoslavia, and state farms were important only in Poland. The initial reforms were the reverse of "socialist" and did not contribute toward the totalitarian transformation of agriculture.

From 1948 on, however, and especially after 1950, the governments adopted new policies discriminating against capitalist elements in the countryside, and encouraging the socialization of agriculture. This included an increase in the number of state farms; the creation, on the Soviet model, of machine tractor stations; and above all, the beginning of the drive for the collectivization of agriculture. The pace of the latter was much slower than in the Soviet Union in the thirties, and more cautious, with the use of four different types of "agricultural cooperative," varying according to the extent of joint operations and the proportion of income based on ownership or work.[2] The approach to collectivization was to be gradual, attained by a series of transitions from one type to another. In fact, the pace differed greatly between the countries and was nowhere complete by 1953. In that year in Bulgaria, the producers' cooperatives of all types held 60 per cent of the total arable land. Elsewhere the figures were much lower: Poland, 7 per cent; Rumania, 11 per cent; Hungary, 26 per cent; Czechoslovakia, 33 per cent; East Germany, in 1954, 12 per cent; Albania, in 1955, 11 per cent; Yugoslavia, 21 per cent. Even with the inclusion of state farms, the socialist sector in agriculture reached a maximum of only 63 per cent in Bulgaria, and was as low as 18 per cent in Poland.[3] Needless to say, the private sector was also subjected to increasingly strict governmental controls and regulations, but continued to supply an important proportion of grain and other products.

A PLANNED ECONOMY

The initial phase of planning, launched in 1947 or 1948, was on a modest scale, taking the form of short-term reconstruction plans designed to restore the economy after wartime dislocation and damage. Only Yugoslavia embarked on a plan of reconstruction and development, for a longer period, from 1947 to 1951. In most countries, a mixed economy continued to exist, a free market was maintained, and trade unions played a significant part. In the next phase, after 1948, one government after another launched long-term plans consciously modeled on the Soviet five-year plans, with emphasis placed on rapid industrial expansion, and in particular, on the development of the metal-working industry, especially the production of machinery.[4] As industry and trade were almost completely nationalized by this time, and as the trade unions were totally subordinated to the party, this phase represented the inauguration of a command economy designed to direct in considerable detail the productive efforts of the nation.

The targets of production, and of the national income as a whole, were set very high, and due to mounting international tension in the early fifties, were increased still more. The plans

[2] Spulber, *op. cit.*, pp. 255–57.

[3] *Ibid.*, pp. 259–61; S. Skendi (ed.), *Albania* (New York, 1958), p. 162; Stephen D. Kertesz (ed.), *The Fate of East Central Europe* (Notre Dame, 1956), p. 174; Fischer-Galati, *op. cit.*, p. 61.

[4] Spulber, *op. cit.*, pp. 286–89, 303–5.

thus constituted a kind of forced march for maximum output and swift expansion. They also involved fundamental changes in the structure and the location of the industrial sector, including a conscious effort to stimulate the development of backward areas (such as Slovakia). The results were impressive in some fields, but discouraging in others. In all the countries concerned, the growth of industrial production was astounding, and little short of spectacular in the output of capital goods, especially in favored categories such as engineering.[5] The development of agriculture, however, and the improvement of living standards were both sacrificed to the attainment of the industrial targets. Agriculture suffered a noticeable lag, and remained far less productive than in Western Europe. Since the provision of capital for industrial expansion was financed largely from each country's domestic resources, and at a very high rate of capital accumulation, the share of income reserved for consumption remained low. The collective farms were under constant pressure to deliver a large share of their produce to the state and to the machine-tractor stations, and the private farmers were hampered by continuing restrictions and discriminations. Workers in industry were under similar constraint, through the system of norms and the necessity of their fulfillment, to meet the extraordinarily high goals set by the regime. The economy underwent great stress, and resources, both material and human, were constantly overstrained. Even if quantity was achieved, quality of production often suffered. Somewhat paradoxically, the national plan in each country had similar objectives, and involved, in each case, the creation of a largely self-sufficient or autarkic economy. Dependence on trade with the Soviet Union and the bloc increased substantially, reaching proportions of 70 to 90 per cent, and trade with the nonbloc world declined, but there was no real effort to establish an integrated economy, based on an international division of labor, within the Soviet bloc.

THE NEW COURSE

In 1953, as a result partly of these economic imbalances, and partly of political factors, such as the effect of the death of Stalin and the uprisings in East Germany and Czechoslovakia, all the countries of Eastern Europe followed the Soviet Union in

[5] See George Kemény, "Eastern Europe: Developments in Social and Economic Structure," *World Politics*, VI, 1, (October, 1953), 67–83.

launching a so-called "new course."[6] The changes of policy introduced did not involve a basic alteration of the economic structure, and indeed were relatively short lived, but, as long as they lasted, they represented an effort to correct some of the more glaring defects. There was a revision of the current long-term plans, including a slowing down of the tempo of industrial development; a reduction in the rate of investment; an increase in the production of light industry and agriculture; and an effort to improve living standards and to increase the availability of consumers' goods. In agriculture, the drive to collectivize was stopped for the time being, and in some cases, notably in Hungary, but to some extent in Czechoslovakia and East Germany, also, a considerable number of existing collective farms were liquidated. Other measures were taken to provide incentives for greater agricultural production. There was also a tendency to turn to the West for trade, and at the same time to seek a more rational integration of the bloc economies through the revival of the dormant Comecon. This set of measures constituted a partial retreat from the strenuous efforts of 1949–53. Although the latter were in some degree resumed in the second five-year plans drafted in mid-1956, the grains of the new course were not completely abandoned, and after 1956, there was a renewed effort to grapple with the problems of reforming the economy.

THE YUGOSLAV MODEL

Meanwhile, Yugoslavia had already begun to move toward economic reforms in the early fifties. She had patterned her earlier institutions and practices on the Soviet Union, and had in some respects moved more fully and rapidly in this direction than the other communist countries. Her first five-year plan, launched in 1947, broke down in failure, partly under the weight of its own defects, and partly as a result of the break with the communist bloc and the subsequent economic blockade.[7] Fundamental changes were not introduced at once, but serious reforms ante-

[6] Fischer-Galati, *op. cit.*, pp. 87–90; Spulber, *op. cit.*, pp. 265–68, 354–62; G. Ionescu, *Communism in Rumania, 1944–62* (London, 1964), pp. 219–22.

[7] G. W. Hoffman and F. W. Neal, *Yugoslavia and the New Communism* (New York, 1962), p. 99. For discussions of the Yugoslav economy, see *ibid.*, chap. 15; Robert F. Byrnes (ed.), *Yugoslavia*, pp. 235ff. in the series *East-Central Europe under the Communists*, under the general editorship of Robert F. Byrnes (New York, 1956–57); R. V. Burks, "Yugoslavia: Has Tito Gone Bourgeois?" *East Europe*, XIV, 8 (August, 1965), 2–14.

dated the "new course" elsewhere and eventually cumulated in a thoroughly transformed system.

In agriculture, paradoxically, there was a renewed drive for collectivization right after the split with Moscow, bringing the share of the agricultural area held by collective farms (Peasant Work Cooperatives) to a high point of 18.5 per cent in 1952. The machine-tractor stations were, however, abolished in 1950, and compulsory deliveries of agricultural products ended in 1951–52; and there was a slackening of the compaign for collectivization in 1951. In 1953, a major innovation was introduced by legislation which made collectivization voluntary, and permitted peasants to leave existing cooperatives of the *kolkhoz* type. The result was a mass exodus and the virtual liquidation of collectivized agriculture. Another law of the same year confiscated all peasant land above 10 hectares and distributed it to collectives and state farms. Yugoslavia remained, however, a country of small owners. By 1959, only 1.2 per cent of the land was held by the work cooperatives, 4.6 per cent by state farms, and the overwhelming share—90 per cent of the area and 98 per cent of holdings—was in private hands. Although the socialist transformation of the countryside remained the goal, this was to be attained by gradual and voluntary means, in particular through close cooperation between the private and the socialist sectors.[8] More emphasis was placed on the General Agricultural Cooperatives, which had been the main agency for purchasing grain from the peasants and providing them with loans and the use of machinery, and which were henceforth to assist the private farmers in the conduct of joint operations on a voluntary basis. After 1957, private farmers were encouraged to collaborate with the Peasant Work Cooperatives, too, although retaining the private ownership of their land and operating in a largely free and competitive market. These measures, as well as a more equitable treatment of both private farmers and cooperatives in investment, prices, and taxation, had positive results in stimulating agricultural production.

Changes in industrial management and in the planned economy as a whole began to be made in Yugoslavia as early as 1950, with the establishment of the worker's councils. Although there have been frequent modifications since that time, and some oscillation between centralizing and decentralizing tendencies, the new economy established in the early fifties has not changed

[8] Hoffman and Neal, *op. cit.*, p. 298.

markedly, and was quite distinct from that which continued to prevail elsewhere in communist East Europe. It has been called by outside observers "laissez-faire socialism," or "a blending of free enterprise and collective ownership," and by one of its own protagonists, a synthesis of planning and a market economy.[9] Another foreign analyst called it "a most interesting laboratory experiment"—"an attempt by a government with definite goals regarding the organizational framework and the type and rate of growth of the economy, to achieve these goals by means of a mixed system combining various degrees of government planning with increased reliance on market forces and local initiative. The system is an attempt to benefit from both planned supervision by the central government and the free working of economic incentives."[10]

The Yugoslav model is too complex to be adequately described in a few sentences,[11] but a crucial feature has been the decentralization of planning and industrial management by the transfer of authority over industry and investments from the now defunct central ministries to advisory bodies, and to the republics and the communes. The chief responsibility for running industry has been assigned to elected workers' councils in each enterprise, and to management boards and directors appointed by them. Each firm has become a self-governing unit, functioning in a competitive and comparatively free market and subject only to indirect federal and republican supervision and some regulation by local government. Other controls are exercised by chambers and associations in a given industry and by the party and the union in the plants, but not so as to negate the wide sovereignty of the workers' councils.

On a national scale, there has been an attempt to combine planning and a market system, as mentioned above. Although five-year plans were introduced again after 1957, and annual "social plans" are formulated at every level, they represent merely general sets of targets, not binding in detail on the enterprises. Neither wages nor prices are centrally determined, and business is carried on, even in foreign trade, as much as possible within

[9] *Ibid.*, pp. 264 and 240 respectively, and Janez Stanovnik, "Planning Through the Market: The Jugoslav Experience," *Foreign Affairs*, XL, 2 (January, 1962), 252–63.

[10] Egon Neuberger in Byrnes, *op. cit.*, chap. 10.

[11] Apart from Hoffman and Neal, *op. cit.*, chap. 14, and Byrnes, *op. cit.*, chap. 10, see Fischer-Galati, *op. cit.*, pp. 111–17, and J. M. Montias, "Economic Reform and Retreat in Jugoslavia," *Foreign Affairs*, XXXVII, 2 (January, 1959), 293–305.

a free market in which supply and demand operate. Since 1957, the general priorities have been shifted so as to moderate the one-sided concentration on industry, particularly heavy industry, which had continued even after the abandonment of the first five-year plan in 1952 and the launching of the annual social plans. Later five-year plans have sought a more balanced development of the economy and have achieved notable successes in improving the standard of living and supplying more and better consumers' goods.[12]

CRISIS AND REFORM

In the years since 1953, changes in the economic scene in the rest of communist East Europe have been much less striking than in Yugoslavia.[13] The decade has in fact been characterized by a somewhat zigzag course and without a basic shift in direction or in institutions. As we have noted, the new course was short-lived. The events of 1956 produced another spell of moderation, especially in Poland and Hungary, where the most shattering events had occurred in agriculture, resulting in the almost complete dissolution of the collective farms. By 1957–58, however, the regimes had recovered from the shock of 1956, and had in most cases resumed their march towards the completion of socialism. There was a general tightening of economic controls and an increase in targets of industrial production. Although the scale of priorities of the new course was not resumed, somewhat greater attention was paid to the needs of agriculture and to living standards than prior to 1953. Production in industry, however, continued to surpass that in agriculture, which still lagged behind. There was a greater effort to achieve a more rational division of labor within the communist bloc, which would have resulted in a growing dependency on the Soviet Union.[14]

The evolution since 1948 has not changed the comparative industrial ranking of the countries of Eastern Europe, but simply advanced them all on the ladder of economic development. The changes after 1953 did not by any means eliminate the imbalances

[12] Hoffman and Neal, *op. cit.*, chaps. 16 and 18.

[13] See Jan Wszelaki, "Economic Development in East Central Europe, 1954–1961," in Stephen D. Kertesz (ed.), *East Central Europe and the World: Developments in the Post-Stalin Era* (Notre Dame, 1962), chap. 10; L. A. D. Dellin and S. J. Zyzniewski in Fischer-Galati, *op. cit.*, chaps. 3 and 4; E. Taborsky, *Communism in Czechoslovakia, 1948–1960* (Princeton, 1961), chaps. 15, 16, and 17.

[14] See Chapter 18 for fuller discussion of this development.

and strains of earlier periods, and indeed in some cases, such as Czechoslovakia, did not avert a catastrophic crisis in 1961 and 1962. The basic pattern of economic organization was retained throughout the bloc, although there was a noticeable effort to find new methods of greater efficacy and rationality in agriculture and industry. The spate of reforms in the Soviet Union under Khrushchev encouraged a similar tendency in Eastern Europe, but there were many variations. The Soviet pattern had been brought into serious question, and in Poland a radically altered "model," relaxing the central planning system and providing for a freer market, was devised by Polish economists.[15] Although this was not fully applied in Poland, nor imitated elsewhere, there was an effort in all countries to improve the procedures of planning, and in some cases, a tendency towards decentralization of industrial administration. However, the Yugoslav model was condemned as heretical. Where workers' councils had emerged, in Poland and Hungary in 1956, they were soon transformed into ineffective forms of workers' participation, far removed from the Yugoslav prototype. Backward steps towards recentralization were taken in Poland and Czechoslovakia. In agriculture, there was a renewed drive in 1958 towards collectivization, led by Bulgaria, and followed, one after the other, by Albania, Czechoslovakia, East Germany, Hungary, and Rumania, all of whom proclaimed its completion by 1960 or 1961. Czechoslovakia and Bulgaria imitated the abolition of the machine-tractor stations in the USSR; Bulgaria and East Germany undertook the formation of gigantic collectives on the Soviet model. Except for Albania, East Germany, and Poland, compulsory deliveries to the state were replaced by contractual arrangements at higher prices. In Poland, agriculture remained overwhelmingly private, but this was combined with a unique form of cooperative, the "agricultural circle," which served as a purchasing organization for the peasants, and received a share of the state's profits from sale of compulsory deliveries toward the purchase of commonly-owned farm machinery.

ECONOMIC REVISIONISM

What may be a new phase of great importance began in the early sixties with an outburst of economic controversy in most Eastern European countries and significant changes in policy,

[15] J. M. Montias, "The Polish 'Economic Model'," *Problems of Communism,* IX, 1 (January–February, 1960), 16–24.

varying considerably from one to another.[16] The ferment of what has been called "economic revisionism" was the product of crises at home, particularly in Czechoslovakia, coupled with the freer atmosphere that prevailed in certain states. It reflected the serious discussions among economists and administrators in the Soviet Union, typified by the reforms proposed by the Kharkov professor, Liberman, during the closing years of the Khrushchev period. No doubt, too, the knowledge of Western economics and management methods resulting from cultural exchange and less rigid control of communications, and the example of Western European prosperity, contributed to the debate. Yugoslav experience was no longer taboo, and indeed was studied by other countries, including the Soviet Union. Another factor was the social transformation in Eastern Europe, and the rise of a new class of technocrats—intellectuals and specialists, who were keen to play a greater role in a more rationally organized society.[17]

The common feature of these debates was an exceedingly critical evaluation, indeed condemnation, of the previous system of command planning based on directives from above, and a generally expressed desire to reform the methods of planning and combine them with some elements of a market economy. The reformers spoke of such things as the restoration of material incentives for farmers, workers, and managers; the payment of interest on capital; a profit index for measuring productivity; the freer formation of prices, according to supply and demand; more attention to consumers' needs and demands; greater autonomy for plant directors, and, in some cases, greater participation of workers in management. In general, the underlying theme was the transfer of decision-making from the party leaders and the central planners to the new managerial classes in the factories, and to a lesser degree, through the market, to the population as a whole.

[16] For an account of these discussions and reforms, see Michael Gamarnikow, "The Growth of Economic Revisionism," *East Europe,* XIII, 5 (May, 1964), 16–21, and XIII, 7 (July, 1964), 16–21; H. G. Shaffer, "New Tasks for the Enterprise Director?" *East Europe,* XIII, 8 (August, 1964), 10–20; V. Holesovsky, "Czechoslovakia's Economic Quandry," *East Europe,* XIII, 11 (November, 1964), 7–13, and his, "Czechoslovakia's Economic Debate," *East Europe,* XIII, 12 (December, 1964), 13–19; V. Meier, "Czechoslovakia: The Struggle for Reform," *East Europe,* XIV, 8 (August, 1965), 26–28; H. G. Shaffer, "Out of Stalinism," and V. Holesovsky, "Problems and Prospects," both in "Czechoslovakia's New Economic Model," *Problems of Communism,* XIV, 5 (September–October, 1965), 31–40, 41–45 respectively.

[17] Ionescu, *op. cit.,* pp. 346–48.

Apart from Albania and Rumania, the regimes themselves, conscious of the defects of previous patterns and aware of crises, either actual or impending, permitted and encouraged this discussion and adopted piecemeal some of the proposed reforms. In 1963, Hungary introduced an interest payment on capital in industry, and incentive payments, based on sharecropping, in the collective farms. In 1964, Bulgaria experimented with more extensive authority and material incentives for individual enterprises. In 1963 and 1964, East Germany and Poland promulgated "theses" concerning a revision of planning, and began step by step to introduce some of the proposed improvements. Bulgaria and Hungary also indicated their intention to prepare gradually for the eventual introduction of a new planning system. Most dramatically, in Czechoslovakia, after its economists had boldly advocated experimentation and fundamental changes during the whole of 1963, the regime committed itself to a far-reaching modification of the economy to begin in February, 1965, in certain enterprises, and to be more widely applied in future years. Although not going as far as the earlier Polish model or the Yugoslav practice, Czechoslovakia became the trailblazer for what may be a general revision of planning and management in the entire bloc, with the possible exception of Rumania and, of course, Albania.

The present economic system in communist East Europe has therefore lost some of the essential features of a totalitarian economy. True, the central plan is still the dominant factor everywhere, and central controls over the economy remain extensive. Industry and trade have continued to be nationalized, and agriculture, apart from Yugoslavia and Poland, collectivized. Yet pockets of autonomy remain—the private ownership of farming in Poland and Yugoslavia; the individual plots of the collective farmers elsewhere; the restoration of some private retail trade and crafts in certain countries; the broadening authority of managers, and even of unions; more influence for consumers' demands; and in Yugoslavia, a decentralized system and a more competitive market. Exaggerated faith in the effectiveness of planning—the "cult of the Plan" as a Czech economist called it—has waned; more hope is placed in incentives, competition, and the free play of natural forces. It is true that the reforms have just begun, in some countries have been minimal in scope, and are strongly resisted by more conservative elements, so that it is difficult to predict whether the present trends will continue or be reversed. What can be said is that there has been a general inclination, not to adopt a system of free enterprise, but to relax seriously the central directives of a command economy.

Moreover, the momentum of total social change has been lost for the time being. The prediction that the totalitarian economies would continue to be oriented exclusively to the final goal of communism and would not permit people to make important choices at variance with that goal has not been fully borne out.[18] The regimes are no longer seeking to implement a totally planned order, as envisaged by communist ideology, but are pragmatically seeking, through reforms, to eliminate the weaknesses of a system once thought of as a panacea. The goal is not the blueprint of a perfect order, nor production for its own sake, but an efficient and profitable working economy, capable of meeting consumers' needs as well as fulfilling planned targets of industrial development, and of competing with the West in world markets.

[18] Z. K. Brzezinski, "Totalitarianism and Rationality," *The American Political Science Review,* L, 3 (September, 1956), 760–61.

: Ideology and the Minds of Men

It is widely recognized that a political community cannot exist without a "system of beliefs," expressing the ideas of the citizens concerning their relationship to one another and to their rulers, and holding them together in "a community well knit and purposively organized."[1] No matter how much "belief-systems" differ in content, each provides the indispensable cement of a society, inspiring the members with a faith in their leaders, winning the obedience of the former by willing consent, and legitimizing the coercion exercised by the latter. There may be wide diversity in belief and significant differences in the interpretation of the prevailing faith, but without some degree of consensus on fundamental political ideas, a community can be held together solely by coercion and is likely to disintegrate as a result of its inner contradictions. In addition to these domestic functions, a belief-system serves the useful purpose of creating a favorable image of the state abroad, and winning support among foreign peoples.

IDEOLOGY AND POLITICAL CULTURE

A belief-system may include, as in the communist states, a set of ideas, such as Marxism-Leninism, explicitly formulated in a body of doctrine, and proclaimed by the rulers as the established creed. Such an "ideology" serves some of the same functions as the political ideas of noncommunist states, but differs from them, not only in its actual content, but also in its role in society and politics.[2] For one thing, the ideology is official, and its content, interpretation, and application are determined not by the creative thought of individual minds but by the fiat of powerful leaders, aided by party theoreticians, and in Eastern Europe, often of foreign rulers and their ideologists in the Soviet Union.[3] The doctrine has usually been highly dogmatic and intolerant, claiming to embody the sole correct view of politics and history, and rejecting any conflicting theories, or even unacceptable interpretations of the orthodox faith. The notion of a pluralism of

[1] Sebastian de Grazia, *The Political Community: A Study of Anomie* (Chicago, 1948), pp. ix, xiv–xvi, 188.

[2] See Z. K. Brzezinski and Samuel P. Huntington, *Political Power: USA/USSR* (New York, 1964), chap. 1, esp. pp. 19–21.

[3] For the role of ideologists and the transmission of the ideology, see Chapter 14 above.

competing theories is anathema, although rival schools may in fact emerge within the body of the faithful and challenge the official interpretation. Moreover, Marxism-Leninism is an all-embracing world-view, defining the correct form and content, not only in politics and economics, but also in education, scholarship, philosophy, literature, and the arts, and leading, in Djilas' words, to "tyranny in all areas of intellectual activity."[4] Although all societies, even the freest, have their "conventional wisdom" and their established orthodoxies, the totalitarian society, in its purest form, institutionalizes and dogmatizes its doctrine, and allows hardly a crevice for independent thought, heretical ideas, or even autonomous associations capable of being the bearers of rival creeds.

A country's belief-system is not, however, to be found only in its official ideology, if it has one. Intermingled with the doctrine are other elements, derived from tradition, and not necessarily formulated in words, namely the ideas and attitudes held by rulers and citizens and affecting their political behavior. A "political culture," as it is sometimes called,[5] embraces both systematic doctrine and traditional attitudes, and thus includes the implicit as well as the explicit, the emotional as well as the rational, practice as well as theory, all of these disparate elements existing in tension and conflict with each other. In the Soviet Union, for instance, it is an amalgam of the theory of communism, derived from Marx and Lenin, but modified by Russian conditions, with traditional opinions and current practices, all merged in an unsystematic (and often self-contradictory) set of values that exert influence on political behavior.

The role of ideology in communist states has been hotly debated for years, exaggerated by some, minimized by others. In fact, there are two aspects of communist ideology, neither of which can be ignored. On the one hand, the doctrine is a powerful driving force, believed in, wholly or in part, by some or all of the leaders and the people, and influencing their thinking and their actions in the political realm. On the other hand, ideology is also an instrumental creed, used by the ruling party (or sometimes an opposition) to defend their own interests and often cynically manipulated for their own purposes. In this respect, the ideology is not a matter of belief but a weapon of political struggle, employed by communists to justify their actions and to control or eliminate their opponents.

[4] Milovan Djilas, *The New Class* (New York, 1957), p. 129.

[5] Samuel H. Beer and Adam B. Ulam, *Patterns of Government* (New York, 1958), p. 12.

In Eastern Europe, the role of ideology and its relation with traditional attitudes is more complicated than in the Soviet Union. The doctrine of communism, which in Russia had some indigenous roots and was molded to meet Russian conditions and the shifting needs of Soviet society, was imposed on Eastern Europe by the USSR and its local communist supporters, and was therefore much more alien, less related to national needs and circumstances. Even its changing content was in large part the result of Russian interpretation and only recently has reflected native ideas. From the beginning the doctrine was in intense conflict with the traditional political culture of each nation in the area, in particular with religious beliefs and nationalist attitudes.[6] Although all societies suffer from a similar tension between official and unofficial views, this phenomenon had a much more explosive character in Eastern Europe. The need for coercion was all the greater, and coercion itself was much less willingly endured, in the absence of a freely accepted and rationally adapted faith capable of enlisting the loyalties of the population. This was particularly the case in the Stalinist period when an imposed conformity trampled on national traditions, religious convictions, and literary freedom.

WAR FOR THE MINDS OF MEN

The official attitude towards ideology is well expressed in the present Czechoslovak constitution, which proclaims that "the entire cultural policy . . . shall be directed in the spirit of the scientific world outlook, Marxism-Leninism." Although there was no parallel for this in the other constitutions, including the Soviet, the same idea has been openly asserted by all communist parties from the beginning of their rule. This has meant that education and scholarship in all its branches, including even the natural sciences, were to be based on Marxism-Leninism as the only correct viewpoint for teacher, scholar, and student alike, at every level of study. It has also involved the rejection and the ultimate elimination of religion as an opium for the mind, and the substitution of an atheistic world outlook based on the allegedly scientific laws of dialectical and historical materialism. It has included an effort to replace traditional nationalism with a new "socialist patriotism" involving loyalty to the Soviet Union and solidarity with the other communist states. Finally, it has signified that literature and the creative arts should be permeated with

[6] See F. A. Váli, *Rift and Revolt in Hungary* (Cambridge, 1961), pp. 497–501, on the conflict of communism and nationalism.

"socialist realism" and the "party-spirit," and should inculcate positive views about communist society. In sum, what was envisaged was a revolution in the minds of men as incisive and complete as the transformation of society, that is, the molding of a new type of "socialist" man, who would voluntarily accept communism and reject nationalism, religion, and bourgeois ideas generally, and who would be loyal to the existing regime and obedient to its commands, and faithful also to the Soviet Union and world communism.

As in other spheres, there have been differences in the speed and direction of the intellectual revolution among the various countries of Eastern Europe, and substantial shifts in the content of the official doctrine and in its relationship to traditional political beliefs. In most states, a more moderate period in the early years was followed by a radical phase after 1948. With Stalin's death, the official ideology met with serious challenge. In recent years, the regimes have been more and more forced to admit their failure to eliminate competing ideas in the form of nationalism or religion and have been compelled to retreat somewhat from their goal of total transformation in the name of the doctrine.

During the first stage of communist rule, the new states were regarded as "people's democracies," a political form distinct from bourgeois democracy, but different also from Soviet "democracy."[7] This original concept was developed by leading Soviet scholars and by Eastern European leaders to interpret the postwar course of events and to fit the new systems into Marxist-Leninist theory. It was assumed that the regimes had been established as a result of national and democratic revolutions, which had liberated the peoples from foreign rule, had eliminated feudal elements where they existed, and had begun to reform society in a democratic direction. They were not considered to be "proletarian dictatorships," but rather, multiclass systems, with the working class leading a coalition of socialist and nonsocialist parties representing the workers, peasants, and petty bourgeoisie. They were embarked on a "national path" to socialism, distinctive to each country, and markedly different from that followed by the Soviet Union.

In certain states, notably Yugoslavia, even in the early years, the full totalitarian model of the Soviet Union was copied, and

[7] For fuller discussion, see H. Gordon Skilling, "People's Democracy, The Proletarian Dictatorship and the Czechoslovak Path to Socialism," *The American Slavic and East European Review*, X, 2 (April, 1951), 100–16; and H. Gordon Skilling, " 'People's Democracy' in Soviet Theory," *Soviet Studies*, III, 1 (April, 1951), 16–33, and III, 2 (July, 1951), 131–49.

was reflected in a theory of the people's democracy as equivalent to a proletarian dictatorship. In Albania, and soon afterward, in Bulgaria and Rumania, the practice, although not the theory, was closer to Yugoslavia's. In Czechoslovakia, Hungary, and Poland, however, there was at first no open campaign against the church and religion, educational reforms were moderate, and cultural expression was not seriously restricted. To this degree, the political culture was a symbiosis of various elements, including a temperate variant of Marxism-Leninism and certain traditional national and religious views, and permitting the participation of other parties in power and the existence of nonsocialist elements in a mixed economy. A strongly nationalist mood expressed itself in the expulsion of Germans from Poland and Czechoslovakia, and the transfer of Turks from Bulgaria and Magyars from Czechoslovakia, but did not prevent equitable treatment of other national minorities, especially by providing schools using their own languages. In Czechoslovakia and Yugoslavia, an effort was made to guarantee educational and other rights and a favorable position for the minority partners, the Slovaks, and the Croats and other national groups, respectively.

TOTAL REVOLUTION BEGINS

From 1948 to 1953, a more extreme course was adopted in the intellectual realm and was reflected in the prevailing ideology. As a result of a statement by the Bulgarian leader Dimitrov, at the end of 1948, supported at once by Soviet and Eastern European scholars, the doctrine of people's democracy underwent a complete transformation. It was identified with the dictatorship of the proletariat, said to be firmly established everywhere in Eastern Europe except in Yugoslavia. All of the states had passed from the first stage of democratic and national revolution to the second stage of socialist revolution. The concept of a national path to socialism was branded as heresy, and replaced by the dogma that all must proceed on a Leninist course as traced by the USSR. Indeed, this pattern was to be the model for all communist countries, and Soviet practices were to be introduced in all spheres of life. Some national differences were still to be permitted, but only within the so-called "*zakonomernosti*" (common patterns) of the transition to socialism. The divergencies would progressively decline and ultimately disappear as the countries fully approximated the Russian prototype.

Within this changed ideological framework, the campaign for a total revolution in the mental outlook of the population was launched. A massive indoctrination in Marxism-Leninism was designed to produce what one Polish émigré writer called "the captive mind."[8] A complete reorganization of education at all levels was begun, with the purpose of creating a new intelligentsia, politically loyal to the state and to socialism and technically skilled. Scholarship was coordinated in freshly formed or reorganized academies of sciences, enjoying a monopoly on research. A full-scale assault on the churches was initiated to subordinate them to the state and to eliminate religion as a competing force. Although educational and cultural rights were maintained for national minorities, there was a much more ruthless effort to subordinate them ideologically and politically to the ruling nation. Strict party control of literature and the arts was established under the banner of "socialist realism." Writers, like teachers and priests, were called upon to follow the dictates of state and party and severely punished if unwilling to toe the line. National traditions, unless they were deemed "progressive," were replaced by communist or "proletarian" and Soviet ideas. Russification of the intellectual world proceeded apace, with compulsory instruction in Russian and the adoption of Soviet techniques in all fields. At the same time, the communist countries were more and more isolated intellectually from the West, as contacts were severely restricted.

Radical reforms in education, affecting both schools and universities, were introduced.[9] A unified system from kindergarten to university was established, with all schools subjected to public control under the Ministry of Education. Ultimate authority, of course, rested with the party and its Agitprop department. The curricula were revised so as to stress specialized technical and professional training, at the expense of the humanities and social sciences. Teaching personnel were purged, and an accelerated effort was made to train instructors of the requisite political trustworthiness. Teaching in all subjects was permeated with the communist world-view, and special courses in Marxism-Leninism were compulsory in higher institutions. Admission to the universities discriminated in favor of children of workers and peasants with the necessary political reliability. Youth movements played an important role in the political education of students

[8] Czeslaw Milosz, *The Captive Mind* (New York, 1955).

[9] See John S. Reshetar, "The Educational Weapon," in Joseph S. Roucek (ed.), *Moscow's European Satellites* (*The Annals of the American Academy of Political and Social Science*, CCLXXI [September, 1950]), pp. 135–44, and George Bereday, "Education and Youth," in Henry L. Roberts (ed.), *The Satellites in Eastern Europe* (*The Annals*, CCCXVII [May, 1958]), pp. 63–70.

and in the regulation of their academic and extracurricular lives. Although the schools and the universities suffered from the debilitating effects of these measures, educational opportunities were greatly expanded, and the general level of education was on the whole maintained. In some countries, an effective campaign was waged against illiteracy.

CAMPAIGN AGAINST RELIGION

In regard to religion, the aim was to achieve a "controlled religious life," with normal worship allowed, but to prepare for its ultimate elimination.[10] All churches—Moslem, Protestant, Orthodox, Catholic, and Jewish—were placed under an Office of Religious Affairs, and obliged to conclude agreements with the government outlining mutual rights and responsibilities. Although State and Church were "separated," the former in fact retained far-reaching authority over the latter, providing the bulk of their funds and regulating all appointments, and the churches were in turn obliged publicly to profess loyalty to the state and to support its policies. Their position was further weakened by the confiscation of their landed properties and charitable organizations, such as *Caritas* in Poland, and by trial and imprisonment of priests and leading figures. Although mastery was effected with relative ease in the case of the Orthodox and Protestant churches, the regimes became involved in more or less continuing war with the Roman Catholics. Leading personalities such as Archbishops Stepinac and Beran in Yugoslavia and Czechoslovakia, and Cardinals Mindszenty and Wyszynski in Hungary and Poland, were imprisoned at various times. In these countries in fact, and in Rumania, the state regimes sought nothing less than the formation of schismatic Catholic churches, led by loyal priests and bishops, and with no Vatican ties.

The constitutions proclaimed "freedom of religion," but this did not prevent the conduct of vigorous campaigns against religious beliefs. Atheism and a scientific interpretation of life and society were propagated by the party, the communist youth movement, and ancillary organizations. The compulsory teaching of religion in the schools was abolished, although in countries such as Poland, it remained widespread on an optional basis. Civil marriages were required by law. The presentation of the religious viewpoint in the press or in literature was rendered almost impossible, except in limited degrees in church publications.

[10] See Clarence A. Manning, "Religion Within the Iron Curtain," in Roucek, *op. cit.*, pp. 112–21.

THE YUGOSLAV CASE

Yugoslavia, which had been out of step with the other communist states during their moderate period, again broke the ranks in the extremist phase. The schism with the USSR did not lead at once to the rejection of the current version of Marxism-Leninism, but gradually a distinctive ideology emerged and was given full expression in the party program of 1958.[11] The new creed represented an attempt to evolve a version of Marxism and Leninism adapted to the special conditions of Yugoslavia, and reflecting the reforms in her institutional life. Although it was officially promulgated, the program was a less dogmatic version of theory. The Yugoslavs denied that their communism was "national," but argued that there were many roads to socialism. Their state was conceived of as a dictatorship of the proletariat, but one that had begun to shake off bureaucratic vestiges and to "wither" away through radical decentralization and social self-government. Theirs was a new form of "socialist democracy"—"direct democracy based upon the self-government of men in all spheres of social life," as Kardelj expressed it in a speech in Oslo in 1954.

Changes in the intellectual realm were less pronounced than in the economic and social fields. Yugoslavia remained communist, and continued to seek to embody this point of view in education and literature, and to combat religion. In general, ideological controls were less rigid than in the rest of the communist world, and the effort to mold the minds of men was less intense. In education, Russification was abandoned and the Russian language put on an equal basis with English, French, and German. Reorganization of administration restored university autonomy and placed schools under social management. Doctrine played a much less important role in education, and in literature and the arts, and "socialist realism" virtually disappeared. The campaign against religion was not continuous, and the regime and the churches lived in uneasy toleration. Above all, in blending elements of nationalism with Marxism, and creating a common Yugoslav patriotism among the several nations of the country, the belief-system became more effective in winning the loyalty of the masses and reconciling them to communism.[12]

[11] See S. Pribechevich (trans.), *Yugoslavia's Way: The Program of the League of the Communists of Yugoslavia* (New York, 1958).

[12] G. W. Hoffman and F. W. Neal, *Yugoslavia and the New Communism* (New York, 1962), pp. 234–36, 373–77, 400–7.

REVOLT OF THE INTELLECTUALS

The death of Stalin produced throughout most of the communist world what has been graphically called "the revolt of the mind."[13] Frustrated and embittered by Stalinism and most particularly by its stifling impact on creative thought, the intellectuals rose against the system. The participants were mainly writers and journalists, scholars and students, and included distinguished elder Marxists, such as György Lukacs and Ernst Bloch; young philosophers, such as Leszek Kolakowski and Wolfgang Harich; noted writers, such as Tibor Déry and Adam Wazyk; and even political leaders, such as Nagy and Djilas. The resistance was expressed largely in their writings, but often, ironically enough, occurred at the congresses of the very Union of Writers that had been designed to harness literary activities. The storm was not confined to one or other country, but at various times spread throughout the bloc, beginning as early as 1953 in East Germany and Hungary, gathering force in Hungary and Poland during 1954 and 1955, and reaching a climax in these two countries during the October events of 1956. Even the more orthodox Bulgaria, Czechoslovakia, and Rumania were seriously affected during 1956 and 1957. Although churchmen and religious spokesmen did not play a prominent part, they had long resisted the efforts of the regime to curb religion.

The intellectual revolt was in the main a debate within a communist framework of thought, but unlike the Yugoslav case, was a soul-searching discussion by individuals and not an official reformulation of theory. Ostensibly at least, these persons were seeking to cleanse the doctrine of its evil excrescences and restore it as a rational approach to society and politics. Their discussions, however, often overstepped the bounds of Marxism-Leninism and called into question fundamental aspects of the accepted creed. Kolakowski, for instance, in attacking what he called "institutional Marxism," that is, Marxism as defined by "the Office" (the Soviet party), went beyond this to a penetrating re-examination

[13] The title of the book by T. Aczel and T. Meray (New York, 1959), describing the intellectual resistance in Hungary. See also Heinz Kersten, *Aufstand der Intellektuellen* (Stuttgart, 1957), which deals with the whole bloc. A brief summary of events is given by D. Gömöri, "Cultural and Literary Developments: Poland and Hungary," in Roberts, *op. cit.*, pp. 71–78. Excerpts from revisionist writers are given in E. Stillman (ed.), *Bitter Harvest: The Intellectual Revolt Behind the Iron Curtain* (New York, 1959).

of the entire philosophy, especially criticizing its neglect of the moral considerations of human action.[14] The party's repression of freedom was the main target of attack. Wazyk, in his poems, wrote of "empty words," "rags of dogma," and "the lie" which had become "their daily bread." More directly, the Hungarian writer Déry declared: "The main source of our troubles is the lack of freedom." The neglect, indeed the suppression, of nationalism was another cause of bitter discontent; the students demanded the end of compulsory study of Russian and Marxism-Leninism and of the Russification of education and of literature.

REGIME COUNTERATTACK

Wherever and whenever it was challenged, the party fought back, defending the official theory and its own right to control intellectual life, and resorting to "administrative measures," that is, repression, to silence the dissidents, usually successfully. In Czechoslovakia and Bulgaria, for instance, writers' revolts were brought under control easily, and the supremacy of the party and its doctrine vindicated. In Hungary, however, the rebellion of the intellectuals reached a climax in national revolution, the complete disintegration of the Communist party, and the collapse of the official ideology. After the insurrection had been crushed, the counterattack was resumed even more fiercely, with the execution of Nagy, the reorganization of the Writers Union, bitter attacks on nationalism, liberalism, and revisionism, and renewed persecution of the churches. In Poland, the compromise solution that was reached permitted a continuance of the intellectual thaw for a year or more, with a remarkable degree of intellectual freedom. Other marks of the change were the end of Marxist-Leninist instruction in Polish universities, and of the compulsory study of Russian in the schools, and the conclusion of a far-reaching agreement with the Catholic Church. By 1957 and 1958, however, revisionism came under increasingly severe attack, both by the Polish regime and from other parts of the bloc. There were restrictions on freedom of expression and sharp conflicts between regime and church, especially over religious instruction in the schools.

Although these events suggested a resurgence of ideology, reforms in education, which were adopted almost everywhere in

[14] For his essay, "Permanent and Transitory Aspects of Marxism," see P. Mayevski, *The Broken Mirror: A Collection of Writings from Contemporary Poland* (New York, 1958), pp. 157–74.

Eastern Europe from 1959 on, and placed great emphasis on practice rather than theory, implied the contrary. On the Soviet model, there was a widespread adoption of polytechnical forms, involving a close interrelationship between practical labor and study in high schools, and periods of work in production as a condition for university admission. The changes, however, varied considerably, with Rumania and Bulgaria following the Soviet pattern closely, Czechoslovakia and East Germany less strictly, and Hungary and Poland moving at a much slower pace. In general, the regimes seemed to be relinquishing the idea of molding a new man and to be adapting education to concrete economic needs and social pressures.[15] At the same time, educational policy for minority groups was modified in order to diminish national separatism, and to promote closer mutual relations and perhaps ultimate assimilation, for example, by the fusion of the Rumanian and Magyar universities in Cluj and the establishment of mixed elementary and high schools in other countries.

Nevertheless, from 1957 to 1961, the campaign against revisionism continued and was directed against both the official Yugoslav program and unofficial deviations in other countries. According to a Soviet philosopher, for instance, Kolakowski was said to be doing in theory what Nagy had done in political practice. An even more extreme and dogmatic school of Marxism began to develop in China and Albania, and the regimes there sought to maintain or restore Stalinist methods of control. There was therefore no longer one single doctrine, authoritatively interpreted by Moscow, but instead, "an active communist debate on the nature of communist ideology," threatening to result in the disintegration of the bloc's political unity.[16] Moscow stood between conflicting versions of Marxism-Leninism, each suffused with the mounting nationalism of its proponents. Although at first the Soviet Union seemed closer to the new dogmatism and bitterly opposed revisionism, its position gradually shifted, as the challenge of dogmatism became more vigorous and threatening.[17]

[15] See M. V. Pundeff, "Education for Communism," in Stephen Fischer-Galati (ed.), *Eastern Europe in the Sixties* (New York, 1963), pp. 26–51, and Bereday, *op. cit.*

[16] See Z. K. Brzezinski, "Communist Ideology and Power: From Unity to Diversity," *The Journal of Politics*, XIX, 4 (November, 1957), 550, 590.

[17] The interpretation of people's democracy was modified somewhat during these years. Even under Stalin, a novel variant, expounded by A. I. Sobolev, condemned both the earlier versions of people's democracy, equated the revolutions in Eastern Europe with the "uninterrupted revolution" first formulated by Lenin, and laid greater stress on national differ-

Khrushchev's renewal of the assault on Stalinism in late 1961, and his condemnation of Albania and later China, touched off fresh controversy in Eastern Europe. In 1963, in Czechoslovakia, the abuses of Stalinism were censured and demands for greater freedom boldly raised, and the Slovaks lifted their voices in favor of a fuller recognition of their national interests.[18]

THE DECLINE OF IDEOLOGY

The belief-system of communism has everywhere come into sharp conflict with traditional ideas, and has produced a situation close to what has been called "acute anomie," involving the disintegration of an ideology and a loss of faith in the rulers.[19] Although efforts have been made to revitalize belief through various forms of official and unofficial revisionism, there can be little doubt that its position has been seriously undermined both by the abuse of Marxism-Leninism under Stalin and by the post-Stalin trend toward greater freedom and national independence. The failure of the doctrine to capture the minds of the younger generation was manifested by the events after Stalin's death. The "ideology" of the Hungarian revolution, it has been noted, was largely an expression of traditional ideas of freedom and nationalism, and was almost entirely devoid of Marxist-Leninist content or terminology.[20] In Poland, polls of student opinion in 1958 revealed that only 13 per cent answered affirmatively to the question, "Are you a Marxist?"[21] People have ceased to believe in Marxism, wrote a Polish journalist, and no one will ever restore this belief.[22] Recent party statements in Czechoslovakia and Hungary have indicated

---

ences. This was a flexible formula, however, which was used later to justify greater uniformity within the communist camp, and, still later, greater diversity. It was the basis of Khrushchev's theoretical statements in 1956 and of the manifestoes of the Moscow conferences in both 1957 and 1960. See H. Gordon Skilling, "People's Democracy and the Socialist Revolution: A Case Study in Communist Scholarship," *Soviet Studies*, XII, 3 (January, 1961), 241–262, and XII, 4 (April, 1961), 420–35.

[18] This development is fully discussed in H. Gordon Skilling, *Communism National and International* (Toronto, 1964), esp. chap. 7. See also Chapter 11, pp. 128–29, above.

[19] The term used by De Grazia, *op. cit.*, pp. 73–74.

[20] F. A. Váli, *Rift and Revolt in Hungary* (Cambridge, 1961), pp. 332–33.

[21] Results of the polls are reported in full in *Polish Perspectives*, No. 7–8 (November–December, 1958), pp. 31–43.

[22] Harold Laeuen, "Polens Verhältnis zur Ideologie," *Osteuropa*, XI, 7–8 (July–August, 1961), 517–26.

the tenacity of "bourgeois" ideas such as nationalism, democracy, democratic socialism, and religion.[23] This is not to say that ideology is dead, or that it does not continue to exert an influence on thought and action. There has, however, been a diminution of faith in the official theory despite persistent efforts to impose it on the minds of men.

Totalitarianism in the intellectual world has therefore been sapped and undermined. There have always been limits to the capacity of party and state to achieve total control of the mind,[24] and these have been extended as a result of the resistance of intellectuals and religious spokesmen to such coercion. True, Marxism-Leninism is still the official creed in Eastern Europe, imposing strict limits on the freedom of writers, scholars, and students. The idea of peaceful co-existence in the ideological sphere is rejected. The struggle against bourgeois ideas is continued, and indeed has recently been intensified in Poland and Hungary.[25] The effort to transform the thinking of men, however, although not abandoned, has become less intense, and the measures to inculcate the doctrine less coercive. The ideology has itself been modified by official interpretation and has become more pragmatic and flexible, reflecting to some extent contemporary social forces. In fact, if not in theory, the regimes have had to relax some of their restraints, to grant more freedom to writers and scholars, and to make some concessions to the churches. In education, as we have seen, the drive toward uniformity has lessened, and the emphasis is placed on technical training. The dynamism of totalitarian indoctrination has been checked by the tenacity of the human mind in its striving for freedom.

[23] See, for example, the Czech party statement on cultural periodicals (*Rudé právo*, April 3, 1964), and the Hungarian party's ideological guidelines (*Társadalmi Szemle*, April, 1965).

[24] See David Riesman, "Some Observations on the Limits of Totalitarian Power," *Antioch Review*, XXII, 2 (June, 1952), 155–68.

[25] See the report by I. Szirmai, *Társadalmi Szemle*, April, 1965, and his article in *World Marxist Review*, No. 7, 1965.

18: Empire or Commonwealth?

Since the death of Stalin, a great transformation has taken place in the relations of the communist states with each other and with the USSR, and as a corollary, in the nature of political rule in each state. Prior to 1953, the Eastern European countries, apart from Yugoslavia, belonged to what might be called a "national empire," and were strictly subordinated to control from the imperial capital, Moscow, and its "emperor," Stalin.[1] They were truly "satellites," as their policies were largely laid down by the controlling power, and even the most intimate aspects of their domestic rule were strongly influenced, if not determined, from outside. The facade of constitutional sovereignty scarcely concealed the fact of "political satellitism."[2] Since 1953, there has emerged, however, a system called by its supporters "the socialist commonwealth of nations," welded together by the links of "proletarian" or "socialist" internationalism, but recognizing the equality, independence, and sovereignty of the individual members.[3] Although this official designation does not fully reflect the realities of bloc relationships, it is sufficiently accurate to underline the change that has occurred in Eastern Europe. As we shall see below, the conduct of domestic politics is no longer a mere reflection of foreign dictation, and has in some cases become exclusively a matter of national decision.

[1] See Z. K. Brzezinski, "The Organization of the Communist Camp," *World Politics*, XIII, 2 (January, 1961), 208–9. This article is a detailed analysis of the mechanism and processes of bloc relations. See also the same author's *The Soviet Bloc: Unity and Conflict* (Cambridge, 1960).

[2] See F. A. Váli, *Rift and Revolt in Hungary* (Cambridge, 1961), pp. 13–17. Váli defines this as "a method whereby another country may be controlled or made dependent on another state without incorporation or any other legal or official admission of the *de facto* reality of dependency" (p. 15). This subordination, he points out, may be voluntary or involuntary, in the interest of the dependent country, or against it. Cf. O. Lattimore, "Satellite Politics: The Mongolian Prototype," *Western Political Quarterly*, IX, 1 (March, 1956), 36–43.

[3] For a comprehensive legal analysis, see Kazimierz Grzybowski, *The Socialist Commonwealth of Nations: Organizations and Institutions* (New Haven and London, 1964); for citation, pp. 252–53. See also Kurt L. London, "The 'Socialist Commonwealth of Nations': Pattern for Communist World Organization," *Orbis*, III, 4 (Winter, 1960), 424–42. For a review of the changing political relations of the communist countries, see Paul Shoup, "Communism, Nationalism and the Growth of the Communist Community of Nations After World War II," *American Political Science Review*, LVI, 4 (December, 1962), 886–98. See also Ghita Ionescu, *The Break-up of the Soviet Empire in Eastern Europe* (London, 1965).

During the early postwar years, the full-fledged monolithic design of the Stalinist bloc was not at once established. In countries where communist rule was not complete, the basis for future Russian hegemony was laid through the growing power of the communist parties, themselves under strong Soviet influence. Where communist rule *was* complete, the pattern of the future of the entire bloc was already adumbrated in the control of these countries by Moscow through the intermediary of the communist parties, who usually subordinated themselves willingly to the mother party and its directives. In the absence of an effective "directing center," such as the Comintern, which had been dissolved in 1943, Soviet mastery was not, however, always assured, as the case of Yugoslavia was soon to demonstrate. Even elsewhere, there were indications of what has been called "domesticism," a certain orientation of local communists toward internal considerations and national interests, without, however, a rejection of their loyalty to Moscow and to the bloc.[4]

In the ex-enemy states, direct influence was exerted by Soviet armed forces, which enjoyed the rights established by virtue of military occupation, and extended them *de facto* by their relations with the local communist parties. Other means of domination were available in the form of reparation payments, Soviet ownership of certain properties, and, in particular, the joint companies. The latter were organized in most cases by using expropriated German assets as the capital for Soviet participation, and were run by the General Manager, a Soviet citizen. It was thus possible, particularly in Hungary, Rumania, and East Germany, for the Soviet Union to exploit vital sectors of the local economy in its own interests.[5] Albania was, until 1948, a special case, as it was tightly bound to Yugoslavia through a similar system of joint enterprises and other economic and political links. Elsewhere, trade had not yet emerged as a powerful instrument of Soviet control. Bilateral treaties, normally of a year's duration, were concluded, and trade increased substantially between the USSR and Eastern Europe, and within the bloc. A considerable commercial exchange continued with noncommunist countries, especially in the case of Poland, Hungary, and Czechoslovakia. By 1948, only Bulgaria and Rumania depended on the communist bloc for more than 50 per cent of their foreign trade.

[4] Brzezinski, *The Soviet Bloc*, pp. 52–58.

[5] Fully described in N. Spulber, *The Economics of Communist East Europe* (New York, 1957), pp. 35–41, 182–202. See also Grzybowski, *op. cit.*, pp. 42–47, 52–53.

THE MONOLITHIC BLOC

With the consolidation of communist rule in the whole of Eastern Europe, the foundations were laid for a unified bloc ruled directly from Moscow. Organizational forms were created—the Communist Information Bureau (Cominform) in 1947, and two years later, the Council of Mutual Economic Assistance (CEMA or Comecon), both designed to integrate the member states and bind them more tightly to the USSR. Nonetheless, these multilateral institutions remained, as we shall see, largely "empty forms," mere symbols of a unity which was in fact imposed from Moscow.[6] Much more important were the bilateral relationships, including military alliances, trade treaties, and not least, the direct relations between the CPSU and each of the respective parties.

The Cominform was ostensibly formed as an agency of communication and information, but appeared at first to be a reincarnation of the Comintern as an instrument of direct Soviet control. Its members included, apart from the French and Italians, the ruling parties of Eastern Europe, with the exception of the East German and Albanian. The new organization was designed to correct the damage done to bloc interests by the lack of unity of action, as illustrated by the Czech and Polish initial willingness to accept Marshall Plan aid, and to make sure that similar deviations did not occur. It was also considered to be a means of coordinating the domestic policies of the member parties. For these reasons its creation was opposed by Gomulka, the Polish leader. In fact, it soon turned out to be no more than a propaganda office, and held only four conferences, the last in Budapest in 1949. When its original chief protagonist, Yugoslavia, was expelled, the action was taken by the USSR alone, through direct correspondence, and was only subsequently endorsed at a general meeting. The newspaper, *For a Lasting Peace, For a People's Democracy!* was a useful channel for communicating major lines of policy to the member parties, but was only one of many available devices of this kind.

A much more important link was the direct contact of the parties with each other, especially with the CPSU, through the visits of their top leaders to Moscow and other capitals, the attendance of fraternal delegates at party congresses, and standing

[6] Grzybowski, *op. cit.*, p. 4.

representation at each other's headquarters. Indeed, the most binding element was the general psychology of most communist cadres, which produced an almost automatic submission to Soviet instructions or imitation of her decisions. As we have seen earlier (chapters 6 and 7), the leaders had been chosen by Moscow in most cases, and could usually be removed in the same way, if necessary. The Soviet exposition of ideology was also an important instrument of control, as it indicated the direction of policy and compelled the subordinate parties to adapt to it. Josef Stalin himself contributed to unity as a symbol and object of devotion, but there were other more secret ties welding the parties together. The Soviet ambassadors were an important source of information for local leaders and, if necessary, issued direct instructions. Soviet advisers in government ministries, in the army, and in the security police, as well as highly-placed native communists with long time residence in the USSR and Soviet citizenship, were useful in keeping the satellites in line.[7] None of these provided an absolute guarantee of unity, as the Yugoslav case showed, but all were usually effective in the climate of outright terror that prevailed in the last five years of Stalin's rule. Significant also was the fact that the bloc members, although closely bound to Moscow, were largely isolated from one another, and thus individually weakened *vis-à-vis* the USSR.

In the military sphere, the communist states possessed at this time no multilateral organization, but were linked together by bilateral treaties of friendship and mutual assistance. Although some were concluded earlier, most of these treaties dated from 1948, and numbered 26 in all by 1950. The USSR had such pacts with its five main allies, Czechoslovakia, Bulgaria, Hungary, Poland, and Rumania, and each of them had similar treaties with the others. Yugoslavia's treaties with the USSR and its other partners were rendered void by her exclusion from the Cominform. Albania was not fully included in the alliance system, and after the lapse of her pact with Yugoslavia, had only one, with Bulgaria. East Germany had only friendship agreements with her fellow communist states until 1964, when full-fledged pacts of mutual aid were concluded.[8] The content of the treaties was almost identical, committing the signatories to close cooperation and

[7] See Brzezinski, *The Soviet Bloc*, pp. 111ff. and B. Bruegel, "Methods of Soviet Domination in Satellite States," *International Affairs*, XXVII, 1 (January, 1951), 32–37.

[8] See Brzezinski, *The Soviet Bloc*, p. 109, for table.

consultation, and collaboration against West German or other aggression, and prohibiting alliances against a treaty partner.[9] They did not provide for the stationing of Soviet forces on the territories of the countries, but by virtue of the peace settlement, such troops were present in all except Bulgaria, Czechoslovakia, and Albania. As indicated in Chapter 15, the presence of the Red Army and the inclusion of many Soviet and Soviet-trained officers in the national armies provided an extremely efficacious means of subordinating the smaller states to their powerful military partner.

In the economic field, the Council for Mutual Economic Assistance (Comecon), formed in early 1949, soon showed itself to be no more meaningful an instrument of multilateral integration than was the Cominform in the political sphere. Its original membership of six (USSR, Czechoslovakia, Bulgaria, Hungary, Poland, and Rumania) was broadened to include Albania (1949) and East Germany (1950). Comecon was established in part as a response to the Marshall Plan to which the Eastern European states were forbidden by the USSR to adhere, and as a substitute for this Western scheme of economic unity. Its proclaimed purposes included the coordination of foreign trade, planning, and industrial production, as well as the exchange of information and consultation. It was also a response to the Yugoslav break, and was presumably intended as a mechanism for preventing future defections. In fact, however, Comecon did not become an organ of real economic integration during the first five years of its existence. Its council met only a few times, and its secretariat, in Moscow, was limited mainly to technical matters. The individual states retained their sovereignty in formulating their plans and in conducting their foreign trade. Furthermore, all the satellites launched a five-year plan of development at this time, each devoted to building an identical type of economy featuring heavy industry. Economic autarky, with almost no specialization of production, was the order of the day. A series of long-term bilateral agreements for exchanges of goods were concluded by the members of the bloc with Moscow and with each other. The web of trade treaties was supplemented, in the case of Hungary, Rumania, and East Germany, by the continuation of reparations and the joint companies. As a result of this deliberate policy of

[9] See Richard F. Staar, "The East European Alliance System," *United States Naval Institute, Proceedings*, #739, XC, 9 (September, 1964), 26–39. See also P. S. Wandycz, "The Soviet System of Alliances in East Central Europe," *Journal of Central European Affairs*, XVI, 2 (July, 1956), 177–84.

bloc trading, as well as of the embargo launched by the West, trade with nonbloc nations declined. By 1952, most of the communist countries conducted from 67 per cent to 100 per cent of their foreign trade within the bloc, and from 29 per cent to 58 per cent with the USSR.[10]

YUGOSLAV DEFIANCE

Yugoslavia alone proved unwilling to accept integration into a Soviet-dominated bloc and was capable of escaping from it. She had never been a satellite in the usual sense, as she had established her communist system largely by her own efforts, in the course of an armed struggle during which leaders and people alike had been strongly impregnated with nationalist feelings. She had been a model communist country and a close partner of the USSR after 1944, but by her own choice, largely out of ideological convictions of the rightness of this line. The ensuing conflict with the USSR was partly related to differences concerning the policies to be followed at home and abroad, but also to growing resentment of Soviet domination of Yugoslav life through diplomatic representatives, military and civilian advisers, joint companies, and so on. The central issue was that of Yugoslav independence, in other words, whether Yugoslavia was to be controlled by Belgrade or Moscow. Having taken her stand in 1948, Yugoslavia was able to survive economic blockade, military threat, and political pressure, and, gradually, develop her own distinctive foreign policy, her own institutions, and her own ideology. Supported from 1950 by substantial American military and economic aid, she was successful in re-orienting her trade away from the bloc, and evolved a more pro-Western official attitude. From that point on, she offered an alternative to the enforced conformity of the bloc and a standing demonstration of the possibility, and the advantages, of "national communism."[11]

The death of Stalin brought significant changes in intrabloc relations which at first sight seemed somewhat contradictory, but which were eventually seen to be directed toward the creation

[10] N. Spulber, in S. Kertesz (ed.), *The Fate of East Central Europe* (Notre Dame, 1956), chap. 17, esp. p. 411. On the early years of Comecon, see "Integrating the Satellites," *East Europe*, VIII, 11 (November, 1959), 3–6.

[11] See G. W. Hoffman and F. W. Neal, *Yugoslavia and the New Communism* (New York, 1962), chaps. 8, 9, 10, and 17, and H. Gordon Skilling, *Communism National and International* (Toronto, 1964), chaps. 1 and 5.

of a more viable form of East European organization. On the one hand, from 1954 on, there was a gradual abandonment of some of the direct Soviet controls, including notably the termination of the joint companies and the sale of their assets to the individual countries,[12] and also the lessening of interference in internal affairs through military and civilian advisers, and agents of the security system. On the other hand, there was an effort to multiply the multilateral ties between the governments, with the signing of the Warsaw military pact, and the measures taken to rejuvenate Comecon.

THE WARSAW ALLIANCE AND COMECON

The Warsaw Treaty was signed in May, 1955, as a direct response to the North Atlantic Treaty Organization, and in form resembled the Western alliance. Its original signatories were Albania, Bulgaria, Czechoslovakia, East Germany, Hungary, Poland, Rumania, and the USSR. Like NATO, the pact was an agreement for mutual military assistance in the event of an attack on one of its signatories, and established an organ of consultation, the Political Consultative Committee, and a unified military command under a commander-in-chief. Like NATO, too, it was a vehicle for associating a former enemy state, in this case East Germany, with the other partners. In fact, the committee seldom met and the international command was not formally constituted, so that WTO was primarily a symbolic expression of unity, a legal formulation of the military alliance already established by the bilateral agreements, and extended to include East Germany. The appointment as commander-in-chief of a Soviet officer, Marshal Ivan Konev, who was also Soviet First Deputy Minister of Defense, and of his colleague, General Aleksei Antonov, as chief of staff, documented the predominance of Soviet armed forces, and the association of the satellite defense ministers as deputy commanding officers of WTO subordinated them openly to the Moscow ministry.[13] The Warsaw pact was also significant in legitimizing the presence of Soviet troops in certain countries, in particular in East Germany, which in theory ceased to be under occupation.

[12] Spulber, *The Economics of Communist East Europe*, pp. 202–5. Reparations had already terminated by 1953.

[13] See Staar, *op. cit.*, pp. 28–29; Grzybowski, *op. cit.*, pp. 174 *et seq.* Konev was replaced in 1960 by another Soviet marshal, A. A. Grechko.

The attempt to revive Comecon did not at first involve fundamental changes in the factual relations between the Soviet Union and its partners. The primary aim, like that of WTO, was defensive, that is, to counteract the growing success of the European Economic Community in Western Europe and to prepare the ground for a similar effort at integration in the east. Meetings of the council in 1954, 1955, and 1956 professed the need for making a greater reality of what had for so long been merely a pious ideal, especially the coordination of long-term plans, and laid the basis for this by establishing a number of technical commissions in various economic sectors. Yugoslavia was invited to attend as an observer in 1956 and 1957. The meetings of the council were infrequent, however, and the secretariat was not very active. Planning continued to be the prerogative of each national government, and coordination was achieved through negotiation conducted *inside* and *outside* Comecon.[14] Dependence on trade within the bloc, although lessened, continued to be heavy.

THE SOCIALIST COMMONWEALTH AND NATIONAL COMMUNISM

These were but the initial steps, somewhat limited and largely negative in inspiration, in search for a more effective and stable system—a "socialist commonwealth"—to replace Stalin's policy of direct domination through bilateral arrangements. As first expounded in an editorial in *Kommunist* in October, 1955, the relations of the members of the commonwealth would be based on "fully equal rights, genuine friendship, fraternal cooperation in the sphere of politics, economics and culture, and mutual assistance in the construction of a new life." No doubt what Khrushchev sought to achieve was a firmer bloc unity, under Soviet leadership, by the admission of a certain amount of diversity and the establishment of joint institutions, embodying, at least on paper, the equality and sovereignty of the members. This purpose was made more manifest in his effort to reach a reconciliation with Yugoslavia, by means of his visit to Belgrade in 1955 and the subsequent issuance of a Soviet-Yugoslav communiqué and the normalization of trade between the two countries, and by the abolition of the Cominform in April, 1956. Khrushchev's hope of winning Yugoslavia over was frustrated by the contradiction

[14] Spulber, *The Economics of Communist East Europe*, p. 431; see also "Integrating the Satellites," pp. 7 *et seq.*

between his design and Tito's own conception of a remodeled pluralist structure based on the principle of complete independence which Yugoslavia had been able to vindicate for herself.[15] Convinced that his country's course offered a pattern for the entire bloc, Tito intervened more actively in Eastern European affairs, interesting himself particularly in Hungary. At the same time, he was anxious that improved relations with the Soviet Union should not be at the expense of friendship with the West, and sought, through a policy of "active co-existence," to preserve a position of neutralism between East and West.

The crisis of 1956 brought into jeopardy the entire system of emerging relationships among the communist states. "National communism" expressed itself in both Hungary and Poland, although in various forms and degrees. In Hungary, Imre Nagy, strongly influenced by the Yugoslav example, evolved, during his earlier period of rule from 1953 to 1955, a belief in the necessity of national independence and sovereignty for the bloc countries. In his brief tenure as the head of the revolutionary regime in October, 1956, he carried this belief to the extreme of attempted withdrawal from the Warsaw alliance and a policy of neutralism. The USSR, which had been directly interfering in Hungarian affairs by dictating changes of leaders, responded by intervening militarily to destroy the revolution and to impose the Kádár regime on the country. The Soviet declaration of October 30, in favor of a "commonwealth of socialist nations" based on independence and sovereignty and nonintervention in domestic affairs, lost much of its force in the light of these events. In Poland, another form of "national communism," involving a more limited autonomy within a united communist camp under Soviet leadership, was sought by Gomulka and ultimately accepted by Khrushchev. Although Tito finally brought himself reluctantly to endorse Soviet intervention in Budapest, the gap between the viewpoints of Belgrade and Moscow was clearly revealed. The latter soon resumed its ideological condemnation of a Yugoslavia that remained independent and outside the bloc.

SEARCH FOR NEW FORMS OF COORDINATION

The search for a more satisfactory system of intercommunist relations continued after the disaster of 1956. Although there was some support, especially in Moscow, for the creation of a political

[15] For the above, see Brzezinski, *The Soviet Bloc,* esp. pp. 165–81, and Hoffman and Neal, *op. cit.*, chap. 20.

organization to unify the entire communist world, its realization was prevented by strong resistance, especially by Poland (and outside the bloc, by Yugoslavia), to any thing that smacked of a restoration of the Comintern or the Cominform. Politically, therefore, the communist states of Eastern Europe continued to lack a permanent institution capable of making collective decisions and settling interparty disputes, and had to rely instead on multilateral conferences, such as those convened on a world basis in Moscow in 1957 and 1960, and others restricted to East European countries, and on direct contacts between the parties, mainly bilateral in form.[16] The importance of such meetings can hardly be minimized, as they provided forums for frank debate and negotiations, *in camera*, and the occasions for pronouncements on fundamental ideological matters and on high policy, binding on the states concerned. In the last analysis, however, they assumed more and more the character of diplomatic assemblages of states and parties that were becoming "sovereign" in relation to each other, and possessed no effective means of enforcing decisions on dissidents.

The leading role of the CPSU and the USSR in the communist camp was formally recognized in the manifesto of the 1957 conference. Although this formulation was later dropped, most parties in Eastern Europe continued to acknowledge Soviet paramountcy and to support policies propounded by the USSR. Declarations of world conferences, as well as bilateral communiqués, usually endorsed the positions taken by the Soviet Union. Even decisions of the CPSU at its own meetings, such as, for instance, the Twentieth Congress, were widely accepted as binding on the other parties and used as the basis of their actions. Nonetheless, a momentous change became discernible in the relationship of the Soviet Union and its hitherto client states, a change that became more than ever obvious with the rising Sino-Soviet dispute and the dissidence of Albania. Endorsement of the Soviet position was no longer automatic, and even smaller states, such as Albania, were ready to express their disagreements openly at successive conferences. The Soviet Union had therefore to an increasing extent to take into consideration the viewpoints of its partners and, in some cases, to seek to satisfy them by concessions and compromise. Albania was, however, excommunicated as a result of the major speech by Khrushchev at the Twenty-second Congress of the CPSU in 1961. This unilateral action made clear

[16] The various methods of communication are fully analyzed by Brzezinski, "The Organization of the Communist Camp," pp. 190ff. Brzezinski counts 10 conferences between 1957 and 1960.

that the Soviet Union no longer had the means of enforcing its will even on the weakest of the so-called satellites. Moreover, Yugoslavia still remained outside the camp, unwilling to accept even the limited discipline of membership, and insistent on its own complete independence.

There were other means for consultation and coordination of action in the political field, especially through the CPSU's Central Committee department for liason with bloc parties, which was as effective as any more formal organizational link might have been. The Soviet Union often appointed experienced party cadres as Soviet ambassadors to the East European capitals. Top-level party-government delegations became major channels of communication and discussion. Khrushchev himself visited the Eastern European countries repeatedly, and his opposite numbers in these lands visited Moscow even more frequently. At a lower level, "exchange of experiences" was effected by visits of leading party functionaries, as well as top administrators, scientists, and trade union and youth leaders. Another important medium was the organ of world communism, *Problems of Peace and Socialism*, the successor to the Cominform newspaper, published in Prague in fifteen languages. Soviet publications such as *Fundamentals of Marxism-Leninism*, as well as, of course, *Pravda*, *Kommunist*, and others, set forth the current orthodoxies in ideology and policy for the benefit of other parties.

The Warsaw Treaty Organization continued to function as a symbol of military integration, but did not greatly advance the actual coordination of the Eastern European states.[17] Albania was dropped from membership, over its protest, at a meeting in 1962. Yugoslavia showed no desire to become affiliated. The Political Consultative Committee met only six times between 1956 and 1963, usually for the ceremonial endorsement of a key Soviet foreign policy, such as the proposed abolition of NATO and WTO and their replacement by a general system of European security. Neither this organ, nor the WTO Committee for Foreign Policy, developed into agencies of real consultation on foreign and defense matters, still less, of control over common bloc policy. It is doubtful if even the joint command contributed much to military integration, as Soviet hegemony was already assured, especially through the presence of Soviet forces in certain countries. After the crisis of 1956, this was legitimized, as a requirement of WTO strategy, through bilateral treaties with Poland, East Germany, Rumania, and Hungary. On paper, the

[17] For the following discussion, see Staar, *op. cit.*, esp. p. 30, and Grzybowski, *op. cit.*, chap. 5, esp. pp. 182, 189.

forces in Poland and Hungary were subjected somewhat more to limits imposed by the local governments than in East Germany, where they could circulate without prior approval and could act to meet "a threat to their security."[18] Their withdrawal from Rumania in 1958 no doubt relieved that country of one form of pressure from the USSR.

MULTILATERALISM VERSUS BILATERALISM IN COMECON

The most serious step toward greater integration was taken in the economic field. The crisis of 1956 had emphasized the serious deficiencies in intrabloc economic relations and had led to the first measures to strengthen Comecon as an instrument of consultation and planning. Meetings of its council became more frequent, usually taking place twice a year from 1958. The secretariat and the Conference of Representatives, permanently residing in Moscow, were more active in supervising joint activities. Twelve standing commissions of experts were set up in 1956, with others added later, and became centers of growing influence. In 1960, Comecon was finally equipped with a charter that described its purposes and its organizational structure. It was still not a supranational body, with power to impose decisions on its members; the latter retained the ultimate authority to decide on whether to implement recommendations, and relied largely on bilateral arrangements to do so. The really authoritative body lay outside the Comecon structure—the occasional conference of the first secretaries of the communist parties, convened *ad hoc* to lay down a major economic policy. In 1962, an important change occurred with the formation of an Executive Committee, with each government represented by a deputy prime minister who was to devote his time exclusively to Comecon affairs. Each state continued, however, to possess what amounted to a veto, as it was not bound by Executive Committee decisions in which it had not concurred.[19]

[18] Grzybowski, *op. cit.*, pp. 203–10.

[19] For Comecon in its later phases, see, in particular, Andrzej Korbonski, "Comecon," *International Conciliation*, No. 549 (September, 1964); Grzybowski, *op. cit.*, chaps, 3 and 4; R. S. Jaster, "CEMA's Influence on Soviet Policies in Eastern Europe," *World Politics*, XIV, 3 (April, 1962), 505–18; M. Gamarnikow, "The Work of Comecon," *East Europe*, IX, 4 (April, 1960), 3–9; M. Gamarnikow, "Comecon Today," *East Europe*, XIII, 3 (March, 1964), 2–9. See also Philip E. Uren, "Economic Relations Among the Communist States," in A. Bromke (ed.), *The Communist States at the Crossroads: Between Moscow and Peking* (New York, 1965), chap. 11.

The meeting of the council which announced the creation of the Executive Committee also endorsed the "Basic Principles of the International Socialist Division of Labor." These were aimed at planned specialization of production, so that each state would concentrate on those branches for which it was economically best suited, and the effort to achieve "universalized production" in each country would be abandoned. This would, it was hoped, stimulate trade within the bloc, an objective that had not been satisfactorily fulfilled, in spite of years of effort. As a corollary, Comecon might also achieve another goal that had been sought, largely in vain, since 1958, namely the coordination of the long-term plans of the individual countries. The aim, as Khrushchev himself put it in a major article published in *Problems of Peace and Socialism*, was "to construct a world socialist economy as a unified complex," involving common plans for each individual branch of production, coordination of investment plans, joint investment projects, specialization of production, and international planning and regulation of foreign trade.[20] This "grand design," if implemented, would have subjected the individual members of Comecon to the common organs, and would have subordinated their special national interests to a common interest collectively determined. Although its motivation was in part economic, seeking a more efficient bloc economy, the plan had also a political rationale, as it would have resulted in a much more effective unification of Eastern Europe than had so far been achieved.

The major objectives of this plan have not in fact been reached. Bloc trade continues to depend on bilateral agreements, and has grown but slowly. Although an International Bank was created in 1964, it was still greatly hampered by the absence of a multilateral clearing system. The coordination of national plans has also been minimal, and the idea of a common bloc plan has been more or less shelved. Nor has much progress been made in effecting specialization of production, although some steps have been taken in certain industries. Increasing importance has been assigned to bilateral intergovernmental commissions between the USSR and individual countries, namely, Bulgaria, Czechoslovakia, Hungary, and Poland.[21]

Much of the failure to achieve economic integration has been due to intractable economic problems, but it is also related to the

[20] No. 9, September, 1962; also published in *Kommunist*, No. 12, 1962.

[21] Brezhnev later announced that similar organs would be created with East Germany, Rumania, and Yugoslavia (*Pravda*, September 30, 1965).

desire of the states to preserve their freedom of action. The most extreme expression of this view was given by the Rumanian party, in April, 1964, when it referred to "the planned management of the national economy" as "one of the fundamental, essential, and inalienable attributes of the sovereignty of the socialist state," and rejected the transfer of this power to "superstate or extra-state bodies."[22] The more developed countries, such as East Germany and Czechoslovakia, and even Bulgaria, Hungary, and Poland, perhaps more for political reasons, have been willing to support some of the Soviet efforts to achieve an integrated economy. The less-developed countries have not been so willing to accept the implications of the international division of labor as proposed by Khrushchev. In particular, Rumania has refused to abandon its plans, Stalinist in conception, for the full and rounded development of its economy (with heavy industry as the core), for the sake of concentrating on production in those branches for which she had comparative advantage. Largely due to her resistance, which can be traced back to 1956,[23] Khrushchev's proposals became more or less a dead letter by 1963. At the same time, his idea of "a simultaneous transition to communism," which implied the rapid advance of the underdeveloped bloc countries and seemed to contradict the idea of specialization, has also been frustrated, mainly because the developed countries, such as Germany and Czechoslovakia, have been reluctant to provide the requisite investment aid.

This does not mean that nothing has been accomplished. Comecon has emerged as an organization no longer unilaterally controlled by the Soviet Union, and is capable of exerting influence on its members. It has made some progress in the economic realm, and might eventually become more effective as its commissions gain in authority.[24] Most notable have been the joint bodies created in specialized areas, such as the power grid linking Poland, Czechoslovakia, Hungary, East Germany, and the USSR (and later Rumania and Bulgaria); the Friendship oil pipeline between the USSR, Hungary, East Germany, Poland, and Czechoslovakia; a common freight-car pool; and a number of joint pro-

[22] Partial text in *East Europe,* XIII, 6 (June, 1964), 25–30.

[23] See John Michael Montias, "Background and Origins of the Rumanian Dispute with Comecon," *Soviet Studies,* XVI, 2 (October, 1964), 125–51. For later developments, see G. Ionescu, "Communist Rumania and Nonalignment (April 1964–March 1965)," *Slavic Review,* XXIV, 2 (June, 1965), 241–57.

[24] See the views of Jaster, *op. cit.,* pp. 513–18, and Grzybowski, *op. cit.,* pp. 88–89, 119–20.

duction arrangements, on a bilateral or multilateral basis, such as *Intermetall*, coordinating the Czech, Polish, and Hungarian metallurgical industries. Moreover, the agencies of Comecon provide a forum for open debate, and thus afford the individual states some participation in decision-making. Perhaps its most significant feature is that it provides a way by which smaller countries, such as Rumania, may prevent resolutions regarded as deleterious. If the Soviet Union is willing to accept such limitations on its unilateral action, and to assume also the responsibilities placed upon it by Comecon decisions that express a collective interest perhaps opposed to its own, the organization may become an increasingly effective instrument of coordination.[25]

INTEGRATION OR INDEPENDENCE?

The final picture that emerges in Eastern Europe is a composite one, including elements of both integration and separateness. Certainly the old system of complete domination by Moscow has been replaced, but by something that cannot be defined or classified easily. It is not, as its proponents argue, a commonwealth of totally independent states, because national action can take place only within the limits set by the control and influence emanating from the Soviet Union in the political, military, and economic realms. Nor is it an "international empire," as suggested by Brzezinski,[26] because the central power can no longer rule by command, as in the past. Eastern Europe might better be considered a bloc or alliance of states, held together, it has been said, by "a more or less loosely woven web of ideological, economic and political [and, one might add, military] threads."[27] The institutional forms, whether multilateral or bilateral, are far less important in maintaining unity than the reality of the diplomatic might of the USSR, its military presence in Eastern Europe, the economic dependence of the smaller states upon her, and their acceptance of her leadership of the communist camp.

As in other alliances, centrifugal and centripetal forces operate, and the interests of the dominant power may conflict with those of the subordinate associates. Some states have even ceased

[25] In 1964, Yugoslavia was given a special status in Comecon, receiving the right to participate, with an advisory vote, in the council and Executive Committee, and in individual commissions as desired.

[26] "The Organization of the Communist Camp," pp. 208–9.

[27] John Michael Montias, "Communist Rule in Eastern Europe," *Foreign Affairs*, XLIII, 2 (January, 1965), 335.

to belong to the alliance and have severed most of the binding threads. Those that remain enjoy varying degrees of autonomy, semi-independence, and dependence.[28] The absence of Yugoslavia and Albania, the defiance of Rumania from within, the loyal but voluntary cooperation of Bulgaria, Czechoslovakia, Poland, and Hungary, the enforced subordinacy of East Germany—all testify to the looser and polyform system that exists.

Complete integration of the communist states with each other and with the Soviet Union has not been achieved, either in the sense of effective subordination of all of them to Soviet power, or in the sense of complete coordination based on voluntary cooperative action for the attainment of a common goal.[29] What the system lacks is a set of organs for systematic rule-making and coercive enforcement of decisions.[30] Only the conferences of the party first secretaries can be regarded as capable of authoritative policy formation, and then only on the basis of unanimity.[31] Implementation of decisions rests with the national states and parties, through the medium of their own institutions described in this book, and not with the Soviet Union or any of the international organizations of the bloc. Nonetheless, the system has become a more sophisticated one, based on "mutual concessions, conference and discussion."[32] Institutions, multilateral and bilateral, serve as links to bind the communist states together, but also as means by which the smaller members may exert pressure on Moscow. In some respects this system may, as Brzezinski suggests, be better able to meet the stresses and strains of intrabloc frictions and conflicts than the Stalinist one, which almost disintegrated under the impact of events in Hungary and Poland and failed to contain Yugoslavia. Yet it is not assured of continuing unity, as the examples of Albania and Rumania clearly indicate, and under the influence of increasing diversity may experience further disintegration in the years to come.

[28] See Skilling, *Communism National and International*, chaps. 2 and 8.

[29] Jan Triska, *The Rift in the Communist World* (Stanford, 1964, mimeographed), p. 11.

[30] See Jan Triska *et. al.*, *The World Communist System* (Stanford, no date, mimeographed), p. 18.

[31] Ernst Richert, *Macht Ohne Mandat* (2d ed.; Köln and Opladen, 1963), pp. 6–9.

[32] Grzybowski, *op. cit.*, p. 2.

Future Perspectives

Predictions in politics are always hazardous, whatever the type of system concerned. Forecasts about the communist future are often little more than guesses—sometimes strongly influenced by wishful thinking. There is a dynamic and zigzag quality in the development of communism, which is not characteristic of more settled or less revolutionary societies, and which renders generalizations and prophecies particularly risky. In the past, it has been impossible to predict such crucial events as the Soviet-Yugoslav breach, the Hungarian revolt, or Rumania's independent stance. The sudden removal of Khrushchev, although it did not lead to significant changes in Eastern Europe, was a reminder that the future may hold other surprises. One thing seems certain, however: that communism in Eastern Europe, having passed through several distinct, and even contradictory, phases in the past twenty years, is likely to continue to shift and change. The purpose of scholarly study should be to acquire knowledge about the relatively clear tendencies of the past and the much less discernible trends of the present, and to indicate a range of possible alternatives for the near future. It cannot, however, forecast which of these prospects will in fact materialize, nor foresee entirely new ones, which will, no doubt, make themselves evident in the long run.

One of the most striking features of contemporary Eastern Europe is the differentiation taking place among the communist states. Communism established itself in a region of remarkable heterogeneity, and sought at first to stamp out differences and to mold the entire area and its peoples into a more or less uniform identity. The attempt failed, at least in its Stalinist form of total conformity, and variations have more and more appeared. This has in part reflected the deep divergencies of national tradition, but has also represented varying adaptations of communism to unique conditions. In a sense, communism has been "nationalized" in each country, just as Marxism was once Russified in Russia.

This is not to deny that communism was partly successful in rooting out national traditions and establishing a framework of common institutions and practices. The differences have represented variations on a common theme, especially in the realm of politics and economics. Nor can a reversion to conformity be excluded as a future possibility. In view of the present fragmentation of the communist world, and the depth of national feelings, the likelier perspective is an ever-increasing distinctiveness in the forms and substance of Eastern European communism, and a broadening ability of each state to shape its future in its own way.

The aim of the Soviet Union to establish a greater unity of political allegiance in an area noted for its lack of this commodity has not been fully attained. The historic counterpoint of aspirations for national freedom and subjection to foreign rule has repeated itself within a communist framework. In the short period of two decades, five of the East European regimes, weak as they were in contrast to their mighty Soviet leader, have claimed greater independence, twice with complete victory (Yugoslavia and Albania), twice with at least partial vindication of their efforts (Rumania and Poland), and only once with total failure (Hungary). The continuing Sino-Soviet rift is likely to encourage the centrifugal forces and facilitate independent action by other states still subservient.[1]

At the same time, although the more vigorous assertion of national interests may in some cases lead to complete independence, it need not necessarily prevent a continuing association with the Soviet Union and the bloc, on a more or less voluntary basis. Like all small states, the former satellites must adapt themselves to living in the neighborhood of a great power capable of snuffing out their independence and, as communist states, have to work out an adjustment between their national aspirations and the requirements of bloc solidarity. The sources of Soviet influence are still considerable, and diverse means of control are available. Even a return to a system of coercive domination by Moscow might result from changing political ideas in the Soviet Union, and from shifts in the constellation of forces within the communist bloc and in the world at large; its success would depend on the intensity of the desire of the communist regimes and their peoples for independence, and their readiness to defend these aspirations against renewed encroachments.

Within the bloc itself, communism has sought to submerge historical national conflicts under a veneer of international solidarity, so far with considerable success, but with no real guarantee of a permanent solution. As each state more vigorously defends its own national interest, traditional territorial frictions and nationality antagonisms are likely to reappear. For instance, Rumania's territorial aspirations in regard to Bessarabia, or Hungary's with reference to Transylvania, are a vivid reality in the

[1] See R. V. Burks, "Die Auswirkungen des Sowjetisch-Chinesischen Konflikts auf die Kommunistischen Parteien in Südosteuropa," *Osteuropa*, XV, 6 (June, 1965), 393–408.

consciousness of the people concerned, and may be more openly expressed in future. Similarly, the conflict of Bulgaria and Yugoslavia over Macedonia, at present quiescent, may revive in the bitter forms of an earlier period. Within each state, deep national feelings may reassert themselves. Frictions between Czech and Slovak, and Serb and Croat, have made themselves felt in recent years, and are not likely to disappear.

The crystal ball becomes more opaque as one considers the future of communist domestic politics. Decision-making will presumably continue to rest, as always, in the hands of a few persons occupying the pinnacles of the party and state hierarchies, with the former still in supreme command. The personal authority of a single leader seems to be lessening, as leaders of "heroic" proportions such as Dimitrov, Gottwald, Gheorghiu-Dej, and eventually Gomulka and Tito, are replaced by less colorful *apparatchiki.* Collective leadership has come to the fore, but may not prevent internecine struggles and the ultimate gravitation of power into the hands of strong personalities.

There is at present no visible trend towards a genuinely constitutional system, nor any sign of a diminution of the powerful position of the ruling party. A certain regularity of political processes, and even a greater regard for legality, may be developing, but both will remain subject to the arbitrary fiat of the party. The rise of interest groups and an enhancement of the role of experts and administrators, however, have changed the function of the party, probably permanently, and assigned to it the task of articulating or mediating competing interests and viewpoints.

Some have detected and predicted for the future a mounting rationality in decision-making and a corresponding decline in ideology. Certainly the complexity of a modern society augments the need for the well-trained expert capable of applying his knowledge to social problems, and may well lead to a "functionalization of society toward the plan," as has been said of East Germany. "The highly qualified technical specialist" will advance in importance in comparison with "the revolutionary inspired with revolutionary élan."[2] State administration may more and

[2] Ernst Richert, *Macht ohne Mandat* (2d ed.; Köln and Opladen, 1963), pp. 281–85. Cf. the article by the Hungarian economist Istvan Friss, who wrote that there was "no unerring measure for the establishment of truth. There is, however, an infallible device, with the help of which we can establish or approach truth, and this is science. Thus far, we have not utilized this device in our social life to the desired extent." ("The Party and Some Important Topical Tasks of Economic Science," *Társadalmi Szemle*, August/September, 1965). See Michael Gamarnikow, "The End of the Party Hack," *East Europe*, XIV, 11 (November, 1965), 3–8.

more rival the party apparatus. Yet seldom in history has a regime of administrators or experts guaranteed the rational conduct of public affairs, and least of all is it likely to do so in communist states, where the evils of bureaucracy are particularly acute. Moreover, despite a decline in ideology as a faith, the party and its functionaries remain ardent exponents of ideological and partisan considerations, and may still counteract the claims of rationality. The party will also persist as a powerful instrument of indoctrination, impeding the free flow of information and the exchange of views necessary to assure a more reasoned approach to policy-making. As in East Germany, two elements, the *Party-State* and the *Economic combine* (Wirtschafts-kombinat) will likely continue to affect society and to struggle with each other for complete control.[3] A reassertion of the preeminence of the party-man and the rule of doctrine is not excluded, nor is a victory of the technical intelligentsia assured. An uneasy compromise between both elements may well be the shape of the future, with the regimes caught up in a dilemma between their theoretical aims and the practical goals of increased production and greater welfare.

In all states, rational decision-making may be counteracted, not only by doctrinal imperatives, but also by the pressure of special group interests, or of an ill-informed and emotional citizenry. A representative or democratic system, which gives play to such forces, may discourage rationality, although it will also strengthen the latter by preserving the freedom of debate. In the communist states, there is little or no evidence of a great enlargement of the authority of elected assemblies and autonomous associations, still less, of unrestricted discussion of national issues. The representative institutions may indeed seek increasingly to embody, not the "public will," but the specialized and expert views of various segments of society.[4] Special interests may make them-

[3] Richert, *op. cit.*, p. 289. Cf. Karl C. Thalheim, "Ideology and Economic Policy in the Soviet Sphere," *Modern World,* III (1963–64), (Köln-Berlin, 1965), 93–103.

[4] In Czechoslovakia, doubts have recently been expressed as to the qualifications of the representative bodies, as presently constituted, for dealing with technical questions of public policy. A greater role for experts and specialists in the committees of the assembly and of local government was urged, and a study of the Yugoslav system of specialized representation was recommended. It was necessary "to adapt the principle of democracy of management to that of managerial and technical proficiency." See Z. Mlynář, "The State, Democracy, Law and Man," *Věda a Život,* No. 1 (1965), pp. 1–7.

The necessity of linking "the interests of the working collectives" as expressed by the trade unions with the need for "skilled management"

selves more forcefully heard, diverse views may be expressed more freely, and a kind of public opinion may impinge on policy-makers. It is unlikely, however, that a system deserving the title "democratic" will emerge, although it may become less totalitarian, and its authoritarianism may be diluted by greater regard for the people's needs and technical requirements, and even by some responsiveness to popular demands.

The decline in the use of force and terror as modes of enforcement has been a striking feature of the past few years. The regimes have resorted to less severe methods of administrative compulsion and to more reasonable forms of persuasion. No doubt the instruments of force are still available and would be employed in a time of crisis or panic. Such a step would, however, generate wide unrest and perhaps even rebellion, and hence undermine the capacity of the party to enforce its will. Barring a serious crisis, the rulers will more likely continue to rely on other procedures for securing obedience, including an administrative hierarchy that will remain highly centralized, a system of propaganda that will be largely one-directional and partisan, a judicial system of somewhat limited legality, new forms of social control, and in reserve as a last resort, the armed forces and police terror. Courts and local government, even if granted somewhat greater leeway, will remain subordinate. No real freedom to dissent, let alone disobey, will be permitted. The individual's rights will be secondary to the security of the regime and the achievement of its goals.

To what extent, under these circumstances, will the communist rulers elicit from their peoples a willing consent that will safeguard the permanence of their regimes? In the early years, the revolutionary changes in all spheres of life collided with national traditions and with deeply-rooted attitudes, and evoked discontent and sometimes outright resistance. Only terror could enforce such an uninterrupted revolution, especially since it was in large measure imposed from outside and reflected few indigenous aspirations. Even then, stability was not attained, although the entire structure of society was greatly transformed. As time passes, economic and social transformations such as nationalization, planning, and even collectivization become more deeply rooted and easier therefore to maintain in the foreseeable future.

---

was also discussed by M. Lakatoš, "The Societal Organization and the Interests of the Workers," *Hospodářské noviny*, No. 12, March 26, 1965. "The authority of skilled management is indispensable," he wrote.

Radical measures affecting intellectual activity and religious faith, however, have been more sharply resisted, and may not be permanently defensible. Moreover, the pace of change has slowed down in all spheres, and targets have been more and more adapted to realities. In turn, the population, while not imbued with faith and fervor, has tended pragmatically to adjust to the existing fact of communism. The system may not reflect the specific wishes and demands of many people, but it has won a kind of grudging acquiescence, and even, among the crucially important technical intelligentsia, a more positive loyalty. This is especially true in countries where the regimes have successfully resisted the Soviet Union and thereby tapped deep nationalist feelings, but is not excluded even under the more subservient regimes.[5]

The outlook is therefore not unpromising for a greater stabilization of communism, buttressed, not by crude coercion, but by more voluntary concurrence. There are seeds of trouble, however, in the fact that many people in Eastern Europe aspire to greater freedom and more genuine participation, and for a more far-reaching revision, and in some cases, the end, of communism. Freedom of expression, religious faith, and nationalist beliefs have proved much less malleable than assumed, and have become obstacles to the planned transformation of society and of human beings. In a refrain constantly repeated in all countries and most recently in Rumania, the writers and intellectuals demand an opportunity to think for themselves, and to carry on their creative work free of ideological controls. Similarly, the churches seek a wider realm of freedom for worship and other religious practices. In almost every country, a tug of war is in progress between those who wish to project the trend away from totalitarianism still further, and those, especially the leaders and the *apparatchiki*, who wish to move more slowly in making concessions and to retain control of the situation. It is hard to predict whether the retreat by most of the regimes wil continue or be reversed; whether the pressure from below will lead to more concessions or to an abrupt end of relaxation. The outcome of struggles over such momentous issues cannot be forecast in any society. One alternative in Eastern

[5] In East Germany, for instance, it has been argued that there has been a process of "consolidation," involving a kind of "arrangement" between the political leadership and the "social-economic core," with a notable degree of "loyalty" expressed towards the state as the "provider" and "orderer" (Richert, *op. cit.*, pp. 286–87). See also Richert's latest book, *Das zweite Deutschland: Ein Staat der nicht sein darf* (Gütersloh, 1964). The conspiracy in Bulgaria, in April, 1965, involving a Central Committee member and several high ranking military officers, suggests an alternative possibility.

Europe is a less extreme authoritarianism, more widely accepted by the people; another alternative is an erosion of the power of the rulers, and frantic efforts to re-establish authority by repression. Even the possibility of the total elimination of communism by a tidal wave of opposition in one or other country cannot be entirely discounted. The most likely prospect in the foreseeable future, however, is the continuing metamorphosis of communism in a more liberal and national direction, and the multiplication of the distinctive features of the individual systems.[6]

The comparative approach employed in this volume does not necessarily imply that the communist systems are converging with the noncommunist. States will always exhibit distinctive features, reflecting the infinite diversity of national conditions and history, and complete identity can never be expected. The differentiation among communist states may bring some of them closer to the noncommunist, and separate others more sharply; there may be tendencies toward divergence in some features, convergence in others.[7] The comparative approach starts with the assumption, however, that communist states are not unique as political systems, and that by examining objectively the features common to all, students may more clearly comprehend the distinctive nature of these states and better appreciate the differences among them. Communism will be seen not as an unchangeable and monolithic identity but as variegated and fluctuating as other systems, and as unpredictable.

[6] Cf. the prognosis of R. V. Burks, "The Thaw and the Future of Eastern Europe," *Encounter*, August, 1964, pp. 24–32. The prospect, he writes, "if the development is not interrupted or diverted, is a shift from totalitarian to a form of more traditional dictatorship; from a system which rules everything by terror to one which abjures the use of terror except in unusual circumstances; from a one-party structure in which all important decisions are taken by a few men at the top to a one-party structure in which substantial areas of autonomy are vouchsafed to nonparty elite groups; from an atmosphere of continuous crisis and struggle to one in which results seem more important than doctrine, and life proceeds at a more or less normal pace; finally, from close coordination of foreign policy with the Muscovite 'centre of world revolution' to the practice of some diplomatic independence" (p. 24).

[7] See H. Gordon Skilling, "Soviet and American Politics: The Dialectic of Opposites," *The Canadian Journal of Economics and Political Science*, XXXI, 2 (May, 1965), 273–80, a review of Z. K. Brzezinski and Samuel P. Huntington, *Political Power: USA/USSR* (New York, 1964). For the present Soviet attitude, see A. Khromushin, "The Anti-Soviet Essence of the Theory of 'Increasing Convergence'," *Kommunist*, No. 11 (July, 1965), pp. 99–107.

Selected Bibliography

The following is a brief guide to the major scholarly works, mainly in the English language, relating to Eastern Europe as a whole or to individual countries. Further references, especially to journal articles, are given in footnotes throughout the text.

EASTERN EUROPE

Geographic, Demographic, and Economic

Agrarian Problems from the Baltic to the Aegean (London: Royal Institute of International Affairs, 1944).

Economic Development in S.E. Europe (New York: Political and Economic Planning, 1945).

FITZGERALD, WALTER, *The New Europe: An Introduction to its Political Geography* (London, 1945).

KIRK, DUDLEY, *Europe's Population in the Interwar Years* (Geneva: League of Nations, 1946).

MOORE, WILBERT E., *Economic Demography of Eastern and Southern Europe* (Geneva: League of Nations, 1945).

ROBERTSON, C. G., AND J. G. BARTHOLOMEW, *An Historical Atlas of Modern Europe: From 1789 to 1922* (2d ed.; London, 1924).

SHEPHARD, WILLIAM R., *Historical Atlas* (8th ed.; New York, 1956).

Historical

BAYNES, N. H., *The Byzantine Empire* (New York, 1926).

BURKS, RICHARD, *The Dynamics of Communism in Eastern Europe* (Princeton, 1961).

GRAHAM, M. W., JR., *New Governments of Eastern Europe* (New York, 1927).

———, *New Governments of Central Europe* (New York, 1924).

HALECKI, OSCAR, *Borderlands of Western Civilization: A History of East Central Europe* (New York, 1952).

JÁSZI, OSCAR, *The Dissolution of the Habsburg Monarchy* (Chicago, 1929).

KANN, ROBERT A., *The Multinational Empire: Nationalism and National Reform in the Habsburg Monarchy, 1848–1918* (2 vols.; New York, 1950), esp. vol. 1.

KOLARZ, WALTER, *Myths and Realities in Eastern Europe* (London, 1946).

LUKACS, JOHN A., *The Great Powers and Eastern Europe* (New York, 1953).

MACARTNEY, C. A., *Hungary and Her Successors* (London, New York, and Toronto, 1937).

———, *National States and National Minorities* (London, 1934).

———, AND A. W. PALMER, *Independent Eastern Europe: A History* (London, 1962).*

RUNCIMAN, STEVEN, *Byzantine Civilization* (London, 1933; new ed., New York, 1956).

SETON-WATSON, HUGH, *Eastern Europe between the Wars, 1918–1941* (London, 1945).

TAYLOR, A. J. P., *The Habsburg Monarchy, 1809–1918* (London, 1941; 2d ed., 1948).

WHEELER-BENNETT, J. W., *Munich: Prologue to Tragedy* (London, 1948).

WOLFF, ROBERT L., *The Balkans in Our Time* (Cambridge, 1956).

After World War II: The Early Years

BETTS, R. R. (ed.), *Central and South East Europe, 1945–1948* (London and New York, 1950).

FARBEROV, N. P., *Gosudarstvennoe pravo stran narodnoi demokratii* (Moscow, 1949).

GSOVSKI, VLADIMIR, AND KAZIMIERZ GRZYBOWSKI, *Government, Law and Courts in the Soviet Union and Eastern Europe* (2 vols., New York, 1959).

GYORGY, ANDREW, *Governments of Danubian Europe* (New York, 1949).

KERTESZ, STEPHEN D. (ed.), *The Fate of East-Central Europe: Hopes and Failures of American Foreign Policy* (Notre Dame, 1956).

ROUCEK, JOSEPH S. (ed.), *Moscow's European Satellites* (*The Annals of the American Academy of Political and Social Science*, Vol. CCLXXI, September, 1950).

SETON-WATSON, HUGH, *The East European Revolution* (3d ed.; New York, 1956).

SHARP, SAMUEL L., *New Constitutions in the Soviet Sphere* (Washington, 1950).

SPULBER, N., *The Economics of Communist Eastern Europe* (New York, 1957).

ULAM, ADAM B., *Titoism and the Cominform* (Cambridge, 1952).

WARRINER, D., *Revolution in Eastern Europe* (London, 1950).

* Contains an excellent bibliography.

After Stalin

FISCHER-GALATI, STEPHEN (ed.), *Eastern Europe in the Sixties* (New York, 1963).
HALLOWELL, JOHN H. (ed.), *Soviet Satellite Nations: A Study of the New Imperialism* (Gainesville, Fla., 1958).
KERTESZ, STEPHEN D. (ed.), *East-Central Europe and the World: Developments in the Post-Stalin Era* (Notre Dame, 1962).
KOTOK, V. F. (ed.), *Gosudarstvennoe pravo stran narodnoi demokratii* (Moscow, 1961).
ROBERTS, HENRY L. (ed.), *The Satellites in Eastern Europe* (*The Annals of the American Academy of Political and Social Science*, Vol. CCCXVII, May, 1958).
ROTHSCHILD, J., *Communist East Europe* (New York, 1964).
SKILLING, H. GORDON, *Communism, National and International: Eastern Europe after Stalin* (Toronto, 1964).
ZINNER, PAUL E. (ed.), *National Communism and Popular Revolt in Eastern Europe: A Selection of Documents on Events in Poland and Hungary, February–November, 1956* (New York, 1956).

The Communist Bloc

BASS, ROBERT, AND ELIZABETH MARBURY (eds.), *The Soviet-Yugoslav Controversy, 1948–1958: A Documentary Record* (New York, 1959).
BROMKE, ADAM (ed.), *The Communist States at the Crossroads: Between Moscow and Peking* (New York, 1965).
BRZEZINSKI, Z. K., *The Soviet Bloc: Unity and Conflict* (Cambridge, 1961).
DALLIN, A., AND J. HARRIS (eds.), *Diversity in International Communism: A Documentary Record, 1961–1963* (New York, 1963).
FARRELL, R. BARRY (ed.), *Yugoslavia and the Soviet Union, 1948–1956* (Hamden, Conn., 1956).
Fundamentals of Marxism-Leninism (2d ed.; Moscow, 1963); English version of *Osnovy marksizma-leninizma* (Moscow, 1959).
GRIFFITH, WILLIAM E., *Albania and the Sino-Soviet Rift* (Cambridge, 1963).
——— (ed.), *Communism in Europe: Continuity, Change, and the Sino-Soviet Dispute* (2 vols., Cambridge, vol. 1, 1964; vol. 2 to appear).

———, *The Sino-Soviet Rift* (Cambridge, 1964).
GRZYBOWSKI, K., *The Socialist Commonwealth of Nations: Organizations and Institutions* (New Haven, 1964).
IONESCU, GHITA, *The Break-up of the Soviet Empire in Eastern Europe* (London, 1965).
PRYOR, F. L., *The Communist Foreign Trade System* (Cambridge, 1963).
SOBOLEV, A., *People's Democracy* (Moscow, 1954).
Soviet-Yugoslav Correspondence (London: Royal Institute of International Affairs, 1949).

INDIVIDUAL COUNTRIES

Historical

BLACK, C. E., *The Establishment of Constitutional Government in Bulgaria* (Princeton, 1944).
BUELL, RAYMOND L., *Poland: Key to Europe* (New York and London, 1939).
KERNER, ROBERT J. (ed.), *Czechoslovakia* (United Nations Series, Berkeley, 1940).
——— (ed.), *Yugoslavia* (United Nations Series, Berkeley, 1949).
MACARTNEY, C. A., *Hungary* (London, 1934).
ROBERTS, HENRY L., *Rumania: Political Problems of an Agrarian State* (New Haven, 1951).
ROSE, WILLIAM J., *Poland: Old and New* (London, 1948).
SCHMITT, BERNADOTTE E. (ed.), *Poland* (United Nations Series, Berkeley, 1945).
SETON-WATSON, R. W., *A History of the Czechs and Slovaks* (London, 1943).
———, *A History of the Rumanians* (Cambridge, 1934).
TAYLOR, A. J. P., *The Course of German History: A Survey of the Development of Germany since 1815* (New York, 1946).
THOMSON, S. HARRISON, *Czechoslovakia in European History* (Princeton, 1943).
WISKEMANN, ELIZABETH, *Czechs and Germans: A Study of the Struggle in the Historic Provinces of Bohemia and Moravia* (London, New York, and Toronto, 1938).

Communism

BYRNES, ROBERT F. (gen. ed.), *East-Central Europe under the Communists* (New York, 1955–57). The seven volumes in the series are V. Busek and N. Spulber (eds.), *Czechoslovakia*

(1956); R. F. Byrnes (ed.), *Yugoslavia* (1957); L. A. D. Dellin (ed.), *Bulgaria* (1957); S. Fischer-Galati (ed.), *Rumania* (1956); O. Halecki (ed.), *Poland* (1957); E. C. Helmreich (ed.), *Hungary* (1956); and S. Skendi (ed.), *Albania* (1956).

DRAGNICH, ALEX N., *Tito's Promised Land—Yugoslavia* (New Brunswick, N.J., 1954).

DZIEWANOWSKI, M. K., *The Communist Party of Poland: An Outline of History* (Cambridge, 1959).

HISCOCKS, RICHARD, *Poland: Bridge for the Abyss?* (New York and Toronto, 1963).

HOFFMAN, GEORGE W., AND FRED W. NEAL, *Yugoslavia and the New Communism* (New York, 1962).

IONESCU, GHITA, *Communism in Rumania, 1944–1962* (London, New York, and Toronto, 1964).

KECSKEMETI, PAUL, *The Unexpected Revolution: Social Forces in the Hungarian Uprising* (Stanford, 1961).

MCVICKER, C. P., *Titoism: Pattern for International Communism* (New York, 1957).

NAGY, IMRE, *On Communism: In Defense of the New Course* (New York, 1957).

RICHERT, ERNST, *Macht ohne Mandat: Der Staatsapparat in der Sowjetischen Besatzsungszone Deutschlands* (2d ed.; Köln and Opladen, 1963).

ROTHSCHILD, JOSEPH, *The Communist Party of Bulgaria: Origins and Development, 1883–1936* (New York, 1959).

STAAR, RICHARD F., *Poland, 1944–1962: The Sovietization of a Captive People* (New Orleans, 1962).

TABORSKY, EDWARD, *Communism in Czechoslovakia, 1948–1960* (Princeton, 1961).

VÁLI, FERENC A., *Rift and Revolt in Hungary* (Cambridge, 1961).

ZINNER, PAUL E., *Communist Strategy and Tactics in Czechoslovakia, 1918–48* (New York and London, 1963).

———, *Revolution in Hungary* (New York and London, 1962).

THE USSR

BRZEZINSKI, Z. K., AND SAMUEL P. HUNTINGTON, *Political Power: USA/USSR* (New York, 1964).

CURTIS, JOHN S., *The Russian Revolution of 1917* (Princeton, 1957).

FAINSOD, MERLE, *How Russia Is Ruled* (2d ed.; Cambridge, 1963).

HAZARD, JOHN N., *The Soviet System of Government* (Chicago, 1957; 3d ed., 1964).

MOORE, BARRINGTON, JR., *Terror and Progress: Some Sources of Change and Stability in the Soviet Dictatorship* (Cambridge, 1954).

SCHUMAN, FREDERICK L., *Government in the Soviet Union* (New York, 1961).

JOURNALS DEVOTED TO EASTERN EUROPE

East Europe (New York, Free Europe Committee)

Journal of Central European Affairs (Boulder, Colo.). Ceased publication.

Osteuropa (Stuttgart)

Problems of Communism (Washington, United States Information Agency)

Slavic Review (formerly Seattle, Wash.; now New York)

Survey: A Journal of Soviet and East European Studies (London)

World Marxist Review (Prague). Translation of *Problemy mira i sotsializma.*

INDEX